New Directions in Latino American Cultures

Series Editors

Licia Fiol-Matta
Latin American and Puerto Rican Studies
Lehman College
Bronx, New York, USA

José Quiroga
Emory University
Atlanta, Georgia, USA

The series will publish book-length studies, essay collections, and readers on sexualities and power, queer studies and class, feminisms and race, post-coloniality and nationalism, music, media, and literature. Traditional, transcultural, theoretically savvy, and politically sharp, this series will set the stage for new directions in the changing field. We will accept well-conceived, coherent book proposals, essay collections, and readers.

More information about this series at
http://www.springer.com/series/14745

Lamonte Aidoo • Daniel F. Silva

Editors

Emerging Dialogues on Machado de Assis

Editors
Lamonte Aidoo
Duke University
Durham, North Carolina, USA

Daniel F. Silva
Middlebury College
Middlebury, Vermont, USA

New Directions in Latino American Cultures
ISBN 978-1-137-54343-1   ISBN 978-1-137-54174-1   (eBook)
DOI 10.1057/978-1-137-54174-1

Library of Congress Control Number: 2016942078

Cover illustration © The Print Collector / Alamy Stock Photo

Printed on acid-free paper

This Palgrave Macmillan imprint is published by Springer Nature
The registered company is Nature America Inc. New York

Foreword: Machado de Assis: The Brazilian Master Then and Now[1]

> *"Life is an opera and a grand opera.... God is the poet. The music is by Satan, a young maestro with a great future, who studied in the conservatory of heaven."*
>
> —*Machado de Assis,* Dom Casmurro *(1899)*

Machado de Assis's prestige as a world-class writer stands primarily upon his contribution to the novel and the short story, where his mordant sociopolitical criticism of Brazilian society and his deft perception of the human condition prevail. In addition, his *crônicas* and correspondence furnish vivid insights into the daily social and political life of his time. Moreover, despite the pervasive popularity of his work, adapted in Brazil for stage, cinema, television, and other venues of art and performance, Machado's prose is, above all, recognized for its uncanny invocation of the Brazilian ethos as well as its insidious and duplicitous play of psychological relationships dramatized in the universal comedies of men and women. The above epigraph evokes another of the major themes reverberating in most of Machado's works, one orchestrating the opera of good and evil within the human condition but complicating and populating this drama with ambiguous situations and enigmatic characters. The epigraph also serves as a good example of Machado's use of irony, paradox, and inter-textuality when he identifies Satan as having studied in the conservatory of heaven.

With all-too-human, flawed Brazilian tenors, baritones, sopranos, divas, and choruses, acting out the social maladies of nineteenth-century Brazil,

Machado set his novels and stories against the backdrop of the former Portuguese colony, declared grandiloquently as empire after independence in 1822. This Empire of Brazil, a monarchy lasting approximately 70 years of nearly status-quo sociopolitical structures until abolition in 1888 and its republic in 1889, reflected the continuing practices of patrons or power elites, notable vestiges of colonialism, but within a postcolonial frame of ongoing slavery, while simultaneously projecting political independence and professed liberalism. In short, with its ancient regime dictating the social and political realms, and its intellectuals and writers contributing to the romantic, nation-building, foundational literary project going beyond the first half of the nineteenth century, Brazil clearly posed a challenge for later antiromantic novelists with realist aspirations. According to contemporary Brazilian scholar Roberto Schwarz (2014), Brazil's social maladies were stimulated by the dissonance between paternalistic, patriarchal authorities as well as a growing bourgeoisie with pseudoliberal, modernizing ideas from Europe on the one hand and an unjust master-slave structure riddled with dependent souls living at the whims of elite indifference on the other. While projecting liberalism and modern progress, this scenario attempted to camouflage the nation's delayed sociopolitical development, what João Cezar de Castro Rocha (2005, xxiii) calls "belated modernity"[2]—an imbalance characterized by the asymmetrical behavior of a callous patriarchy toward its slaves and other subalterns, which for Machado became a richly aesthetic resource for his literary project. However, alongside Schwarz's perceptive thesis with its Marxist ideological underpinnings, there are many interpretations or approaches up for option in deciphering Machado's prose, particularly when one considers that Machado's universal appeal also transcends Brazil's national sociohistorical borders and performs very successfully on the level of universal human behavior.

To achieve this goal, Machado raised his literary opera to the level of grand opera, not romantic melodrama but a unique version of realist expression—evoking quotidian scenarios, verisimilitude narration, but with antirealist aesthetics, such as having one of his aggravating bourgeois protagonists, the fickle and presumptuous Brás Cubas, narrate his own life story after he has died. In this vein, Machado created literary grand opera by focusing most astutely on the divided self and challenging, with deft psychological, social, and philosophical insights, the very idea of a unified identity. God may have written the libretto of life but its music and rhythm certainly belong to the satanic impulse within human beings. In this sense, it is understandable why Machado is frequently referred to as a modernist avant la lettre and, in some critical views, even a postmodernist. The intimate treatment of the self grappling with multiple points of view, including all its contradictions and ambiguities, takes center stage in Machado's operatic human theater, evident in his sly, devilish creation of unreliable narrators, complex characterizations, and ironic discourse—techniques he gleaned from reading eighteenth-century French and British literatures.

First-person narrative techniques that comprise the majority of Machado's prose served, then as well as now, as the seductive trap for nineteenth-century readers. Repeatedly called upon by engaging yet untrustworthy and complex narrators, developed sometimes over weekly newspaper installments, those readers were forced to become intimate witnesses or narratees to the protagonist/narrator's privileged and cultured self who nonetheless still manifested what some postcolonial scholars such as Walter Mignolo refer to as the "coloniality of power" (2001, 426). Machado's construction of intricate and persuasive subjective voices did occasionally show these as admitting to being subjective; however, they also insistently professed to being primarily objective. Despite their authoritarian roles as paternalist fictional autobiographers, these voices cleverly and persuasively guided different readers to relate intermittently to psychologically splintered selves who invariably still struggled with the inconsistencies of existence. In so doing, these narrator/protagonists operate between questionable memory and misguided self-analysis. In a word, Machado's readers had to be self-reliant in order to stay afloat in the Machadian psychological sea of inner turbulence and exterior complacency.

For purposes of focusing on Machado's central contributions, I have thus far emphasized the writer's so-called second period of five major novels whose narrative approaches are primarily subjective due to his masterful technical exploitation of first-person narration in four of these volumes. Calling special attention to this narrative technique is warranted here because each of these novels appears to be written by three first-person minds—the fictional narrator who tells the story, the real or implied author who constructs the novel with a proposition or plan within and beyond the narrative voice, and the self-reliant or duped reader. Readers' input is elicited by the many direct invocations of themselves as narratees whose mental rewriting of the story stems in part from their own gestalt or human experience. This incisive, intimate, ironic but ambiguous narrative treatment is what makes Machado so universal and enduring. Notwithstanding Schwarz's Marxist interpretation underscoring nineteenth-century Brazil's imbalanced and unjust socioeconomic structure, above all, Machado's narrative pull is drawn principally from his play of the demonic musical tones of the grand opera in our fickle, vulnerable, and self-delusional heart and soul.

Born in 1839, poor, mulatto, a stutterer, later epileptic, Machado was sensitive to the callous daily practices embedded in ruthless behavior during the nineteenth-century period of nation building, when personal and social gains among the bourgeoisie took precedent. As a nation yearning for a nationalist and liberal image of progress, Brazil was critically read by Machado in light of the mad drive to be a civilized society during a period of sociopolitical and financial ambition, yet still dependent on slaves. As a political and outspoken journalist in his twenties and thirties, very active in the Liberal Party, Machado witnessed the contradictions and masked insincerities within individuals. During his thirties, he also became more and more critical of the reigning romantic movement and the younger generation of aspiring writers. He challenged the latter vociferously in his famous essay "Nationalist Instinct" (1873) by calling for a literature that expressed Brazil's ethos instead of stressing descriptive scenarios of local color. In that seminal essay, Machado recommended that writers look outside Brazilian culture in order to engage in intertextual dialogue. For Brazil, the spirit of literary romanticism, inspired primarily by the French masters, stressed the local and the native, which fueled the nineteenth-century foundational narratives of a new nation with exotic and colorful images, captured best by the great literary legacy of José de Alencar. Perceiving that the literary approach of fusing local color with nationalist themes did not contribute to delving into the cultural impulse inherent in the Brazilian ethos, Machado, as literary critic, spoke not only against literary romanticism, but also vehemently opposed the mere realist documentation as well as the emerging naturalist movement with its commitment to scientific formulae above human sentiment and psychology.

Although Machado's novels, short stories, chronicles, poetry, theater, and correspondence repeatedly cast potent depth charges into the capricious actions of upper-crust Brazilian society, Machado's overall target was the intimate self, a vast and fathomless psycho-social realm where his insights into the insidious blindness of the powerful pointed to their weaknesses as vain, volatile, and despotic individuals living the social mores of a misplaced national ideology. Throughout Machado's narratives, the reader repeatedly comes across inured patriarchs who are also portrayed as persons fraught with existential uncertainties and fears. In fact, it is the critique of human folly performed within a quotidian Brazilian bourgeoisie scenario that explains Machado's special brand of mordant irony, justified skepticism, and surreptitious humor. Machado's critique of the Brazilian power structure served as his thematic basis for creating a context to evoke the human drama and as an incisive mode for analyzing sociopolitical and historical Brazil from a humanist point of view—a sort of reciprocal discursive strategy involving the universal and the local. The major difference between Machado's early novels and his later major works rests principally with his decision to reconstruct the points of view of the bourgeoisie instead of siding with the downtrodden, since the latter approach would only replay the one-note theme of oppression at the expense of unmasking the multilayered shenanigans of the powerful, who alternate between their capricious paternalism and destructive class prejudices across all layers of society.

Critics tend to agree that the emergence of Machado's new narrative strategy, gradually but firmly developed during the 1870s, reached a level of sophisticated insight in the late 1870s, for him a period of serious physical illness marked by a restful stay away from Rio, thereby affording Machado the critical distance needed to forge ahead and finish his first major work after having published theater, poetry, chronicles, numerous stories, and his first four short novels. However, Machado's wry use of narrative point of view to unearth his dissatisfaction with the abuses of the upper echelons of society regarding class, race, and status can also be discovered as subtle intimations permeating his early work. His first major work, *The Posthumous Memoirs of Brás Cubas* (1881), a substantive novel sparked by the dramatic conceit of a wealthy and privileged narrator telling his story from the grave, definitely challenged the imitation-of-life approach found in realist novels or sordid and scabrous naturalist tales. Furthermore, this groundbreaking novel was not a mere imitation of a deathlike existence, but rather a display of death as a trope or ploy for exploiting a supposedly nothing-to-gain stance in order to reveal instead the individual's all-consuming and never-ending self-interest and desire for life that resonate beyond the grave, thereby leaving vestiges of their pervasive destruction. This narrative position enabled Machado to uncover, despite their higher station, how the privileged and, by extension, all individuals strategically nurture, inflate, and deceive themselves as sincere beings. Although individuals adhere to the implacably fierce and incommensurable demands of making ethical and moral choices, Machado dramatizes how these choices are frequently inhibited by social norms, appearances, finances, prestige, responsibilities, courtships, and pressures that inevitably smother any healthy form of self-knowledge. It is safe to state that the intimate portrayal of the unconscious in Machado via troubled identities that modernism was to develop regarding the self—and here Machado prefigures Freud—not only applies to Brazil, but also to the rest of Western civilization because, despite the different social constructs and political ideologies, all nations in the West, and particularly in Central and South America, were deeply tainted in one way or another by the insidious vestiges of colonizing power structures. Furthermore, these power structures prevailed amid the advent of modernizing practices, ultimately resulting in erratic and imbalanced societal relations and intricate psychological configurations.

Machado was born in a Rio de Janeiro of about 300,000 inhabitants, half slaves, to a humble, free black father from Rio and a Portuguese mother from the Azores who were workers and "attached" dependents or *agregados* of the household of a wealthy widow. Here Machado was tutored early on but gradually paved his way as an autodidact with little formal education from cashier to typographer, copyeditor, poet, popular playwright, journalist, writer, and public servant, reaching the pinnacle of national intellectual and literary prestige, reserved only for the very few— even to the point of being one of the founders of the Brazilian Academy of Letters (1896) and serving as its first president. How do we explain this rise? And more than 100 years after his death in 1908, how do we read him and his vibrant heritage today within and beyond the framework of the nineteenth century? How can we consider him to be a world-class writer and perhaps the greatest Brazilian writer, if in world literature he is often bypassed and not acclaimed as equal to a Henry James or Flaubert or Balzac, as a few world-class critics and scholars such as Harold Bloom have registered—despite Bloom's reference to Machado as "the supreme black literary artist to date" (2002, 674)? How do we understand his ascendance in a slave-holding society if, for example, as a young mulatto male, his correspondence reveals that he supposedly rarely encountered overt racial prejudice, and moreover, his literature never placed the iniquities of slavery on the center stage of his fiction, but rather in his journalistic production? As alluded to earlier, the strategic choice of focusing socially and psychologically on a flawed elite was indeed a deliberate move to show how power mongers and other ruthless individuals often treat dependents as well as each other as throwaway pawns on the chessboard of life. Owing to the many social-class positions occupied by Machado during his lifetime, the modern reader can easily apply to him Jean Starobinski's (1975) term, the "outsider within."[3] Thus, the modern reader can also marvel at how the playful, witty, amorous, bohemian, and music-loving young artist in the late 1870s gradually transformed himself into the mature, wise, political, and acclaimed novelist of devastating irony. Moreover, after the death, in 1904, of his beloved wife, Carolina—his critical eyes and ears—how Machado, though slipping into the role of a melancholy and despondent soul, nevertheless became loved and hailed as a great Brazilian writer. As a great, if not the greatest, Brazilian writer, should Machado be considered a satirist, realist, antirealist, pre-modernist, modernist, or a profoundly skeptical author? Even though some critics who labeled him a pessimist have been debunked, how does the reader interpret the ubiquitous tragedies, ambiguities, and skepticism rampant in his fiction?

Prior to addressing some of these issues, it is paramount for the modern reader to recognize Machado's intense ongoing popularity in today's Brazil. Thus, in the spirit of reception, the "Now" of our title will be treated followed by the "Then," concluding with a return to the "Now." Beyond the usual attention afforded to the critical celebration of any author, Machado's oeuvre has indeed passed the test of time because, over the years, he has become the guiding light or virtual mentor for most twentieth-century Brazilian writers as well as required reading for Brazilian school children since he is regarded as the major voice of the Brazilian ethos and promoted as the iconic figure of Brazilian wit, grace, and intelligence.

All of Machado's major works have been translated into English and numerous other languages, such as Arabic, Catalan, Dutch, Danish, German, French, Spanish, Italian, Polish, Romanian, Russian, Serbo-Croatian, Swedish, Czech, and Turkish. Many of his works have also been adapted for the theater, radio, television, cinema, opera, children's literature, and comic books. Film festivals have been dedicated to adaptations of his works; they are available on DVD, and there have been thousands of reeditions and hundreds of bookstore launchings. Interestingly, the Nós do Morro theatrical group from the favela of Vidigal in Rio, founded in the mid-1980s, had already performed Shakespeare in Portuguese in 2006 at Stratford-on-Avon in England, and then in 2008 decided, for the celebration of the Machado centennial, to read the author again, this time over a three-month period of intense discussion, study, research, and rehearsal, in order to adapt and perform his novella/short story *O alienista* (The Psychiatrist, 1881), a witty and biting tale challenging the thin line between madness and reason as well as pretentious but naive all-consuming beliefs in scientific progress. The result was an acclaimed performance—Machado on a prestigious Rio stage—a resounding musical of corrosive irony and social satire.

In addition to the countless scholarly volumes and thousands of critical articles on Machado since his death, including the proliferation of studies in anticipation of the 2008 centennial year, there is the venerable issue of *Cadernos de Literatura Brasileira* (nos. 23–4, July 2008) dedicated to Machado and published by the Moreira Salles Institute, a volume providing one of the most lucid bio-bibliographic critical publications to date after José Galante de Sousa's (1969) bibliographic resources. Also of note is ambassador and critic Sérgio Paulo Rouanet's (2008–2015) comprehensive publication of Machado's correspondence in five volumes, with volume 1 of 200 letters from his youth (20 unpublished), revealing a bohemian, lively, outgoing fellow in contrast to earlier portrayals of Machado as a timid soul. In this correspondence, Machado also emerges as a bold defender of abolition in his journalistic writings and even in the forgotten short stories published prior to abolition—"Virginius (narrativa de um advogado)" ("Virginius, Narrative of a Lawyer") in the *Jornal das famílias* in 1864 and in the same publication, "Mariana" in 1871, both portraying how low social position and race lead to devastating consequences. For many decades, critics had taken Machado to task because his only well-known stories about slavery—"O caso da vara" ("The Rod of Justice") (1891) and "Pai contra mãe" ("Father versus Mother") (1906)—were published after abolition, suggesting that Machado was extremely cautious in protecting himself and even masking his racial background or abolitionist advocacy. These earlier stories, in addition to his sociopolitical activism in newspapers, disprove that misguided reading. Machado was an avowed abolitionist, and Eduardo de Assis Duarte's 2007 study addresses the misconception and documents Machado's social activism and literary contributions to racial issues.

In later volumes edited by Rouanet, the correspondence conveys a very political Machado as well as a patron-client Brazil full of pleas for employment, social favors, and attempts at all sorts of political pull. The correspondence also names a considerable number of intellectuals of Machado's circle who had Afro-Brazilian backgrounds. For example, Machado became apprentice to and was mentored to be a journalist by the well-known mulatto typographer Paula Brito. Many of the letters in the second volume of Rouanet's compilation had never before been published. In short, this correspondence depicts the pluralist or multiple faces of Machado and thus will fill in some of the biographical gaps, but above all will provide more psychological and literary dimensions to the man and his work. In addition to the ongoing flurry of publications and studies, there are innumerable critical online sites dedicated to Machado with bio-bibliographical references, including critical studies by scholars that can also be accessed online via the Brazilian Academy of Letters. Moreover, in view of the ever-growing online highway, my own research in 2008 revealed more than 1000 items in English and Portuguese by or about Machado at Amazon.com.

Regarding Machado's reception, there is a long, intermittent and at times intense history of studies, interpretations, opinions, and myths about the writer and his literary production. During his thirties Machado was already recognized as a productive poet, playwright, translator, chronicler, and author of four novels. However, even after his major novels received critical praise as well as some mordant criticism, especially from the Brazilian critic, Silvio Romero (1897, xii), his high reputation as a genius and a stylist became the critical focus but was curiously always accompanied by some voiced aesthetic discomfort—that it was insufficiently nationalist because it did not describe the Brazilian landscape or local customs, or that it did not deal openly with political questions of the period such as slavery or the decadence of the Empire—all of which he actually did dramatize in his prose but always obliquely or in a subtle manner as alluded to above. Criticized for having been too influenced by French or English writers, Machado was way ahead of his time for Brazil, since in today's climate of reevaluating what constitutes world literature, Machado was actively reading international authors like Shakespeare and consciously rereading aspects of their texts and inventively applying them to his own fiction, that is, intertextually, which Rocha (2005), in high praise, considers to be "creative" plagiarism. On the other hand, his reputation as a gifted stylist was to be the critical hallmark that his countrymen bestowed on Machado during his lifetime, and for several decades after his death, he was enshrined primarily as a great stylist. On the international scene, six months after his death, on April 3, 1909, the Académie Française held an event at the Sorbonne to honor Machado and later that year published the volume, *Machado de Assis et son oeuvre littéraire* (Machado de Assis and His Literary Work) with a preface by Anatole France.

It was only decades after his death that Machado's reception led to new pathways of exciting, innovative readings. According to Hélio de Seixas Guimarães (2008), Machado's critical reception can be divided into several periods that disclose a myriad of diverse readings, a characteristic that prestigious Brazilian literary scholar Antônio Cândido (1977) believes to represent the mark of a great writer whose work invokes a treasure trove of meanings, inviting critics and readers of different periods to offer their insights, whether they be in the form of divergences, polemics, dissensions, or new discoveries. During the 1850s, Machado received critical praise for his plays and since then the body of critical studies has increased exponentially to reflect his prodigious output in poetry, drama, journalism (chronicles), and prose. These critical treatments are cast within social, political, cultural, psychological, philosophical, ideological, and literary contexts. Following Hélio de Seixas Guimarães's (2008) idea of a chronological format[4] and paraphrasing some of his observations, my presentation will divide the critical work into four periods.

The first of these periods points to how Machado was recognized and consecrated during his lifetime, beginning especially during the 1860s and 1870s, when he was known as a celebrated writer but was often misunderstood. Several of the so-called flaws alluded to earlier, such as the omission of nationalist and local themes in his writings, were fodder for negative commentary, which became more pronounced during the 1870s and 1880s, when he was referred to as cold, unsentimental, and unimaginative. However, in 1882, the most negative and vicious criticism came from the then well-known Brazilian critic and historian Sílvio Romero, who read *As memórias póstumas de Brás Cubas* as musty and sluggish. Romero also labeled Machado an opportunist in view of his growing prestige and went so far as to call him a "tapeworm" (1882, 341–367). Romero excluded Machado from his *History of Brazilian Literature* (1888) and reserved much of his anti-Machado bile for his book, *Machado de Assis: Estudo Comparativo da Literatura* Brasileira (A *Comparative Study of Brazilian Literature*, 1897), which, regrettably, was the only book dedicated entirely to Machado during his lifetime.

Fortunately other critics, such as José Veríssimo, responded to Romero's unjust attacks, which went so far as to employ deterministic and evolutionary elements to explain why a poor, humble, unschooled, and supposedly unpatriotic writer, overly influenced by foreign literary traditions, was a supreme failure. According to Hélio de Seixas Guimarães (2008, 278), these unjust attacks were actually an indication of Machado's importance as an original writer because they reflected how his fictional work was out of step with the limited expectations of the time when in fact he was a visionary, ahead of his time.

In defense of Machado, during his lifetime, José Veríssimo (1903, 33–45) was the first critic to single out the novelist's special use of the first person as a filter for understanding the narrative's central drama, a very significant observation that will only be developed in depth in the second half of the twentieth century. Frustrated by not being able to classify Machado in a specific literary school, Veríssimo labeled him a humorist and set him apart from the rest of Brazilian writers (1892, 1–2). This critical view of him as humorist was to be repeated and developed in the first posthumous study on Machado, by Alcides Maya (1912). Other biographical and literary studies were published in 1917, 1930, 1936, and 1938.

The second critical period presented new views by other national critics as well as a delicate topic revisited by the French sociologist Roger Bastide, whose 1940 study, "Machado de Assis, paisagista" (landscape artist), revealed how Machado's work did indeed include dimensions of Brazil's nature and locale. This period is, above all, dominated by national critics, especially Astrojildo Pereira, Lúcia Miguel Pereira, and Augusto Meyer, who emerged with major studies in the late 1940s and 1950s, but Lúcia Miguel Pereira (1936) had already put forth the concept that Machado's novels as a whole followed his social and cultural ascension, underlying the theme of social ambition so prevalent in his work. Her biographical and somewhat pathological study was inspired by psychological theories prevalent at the time and, although her publication reflects a traditional type of literary study—The Man and His Work—devoid of theoretical and critical literary mediation, her perceptive insights are nevertheless valid today. However, it is due to the advent of the centennial of Machado's birth in 1939 as well as the larger political and cultural context of dictator Getúlio Vargas and his Estado Novo (New State) constructing new national myths that another flurry of publications surged from 1939 onward, projecting the official image of Machado being the poor mulatto man of the people and the exemplary public servant who ascended to the top of Brazil's cultural scene. Interestingly, it is the celebration of centennials and half-century commemorations that will inspire critics and academics, primarily Brazilians, to produce an increasing number of studies, resulting in a relatively steady critical output after this period. In terms of accessibility to Machado's works on an international scale via foreign translations, to date there have been approximately 150 translations, the earliest being the first Spanish translation of the *Posthumous Memoirs* in 1902, followed by a French translation in 1911 and an Italian version in 1929. In 1924, one of Machado's short story collections (*Contos fluminenses*) was translated into German. Besides English, Spanish is the only other foreign language in which all of Machado's major titles have been published over the course of the twentieth century. The only translation into Russian is a collection of selected stories published in 2007. During the first half of the twentieth century, the production of translations appears to have exceeded the production of foreign criticism, which in turn increased dramatically after the 1960s.

Lúcia Miguel Pereira (1950) dedicated a chapter to Machado and omitted the pathological and psychological interpretations of her earlier study but at the same time focused on how Machado the man was indeed representative of Brazilian culture and how his writings denoted an aesthetic model for Brazilian literature. Augusto Meyer, in a series of essays begun in 1935 and later published in the volume *Ensaios escolhidos* (*Selected Essays*) in 1958, stressed Machado as author, excluding his origins and psychological profile and comparing him to Pirandello, Nietzsche, and Dostoevsky. Later, Astrojildo Pereira became the critic who contextualized Machado within a historical frame by referring to him as "the writer of the Second Kingdom" (1944). Although there are other biocritical studies between this second critical period and the beginning of the third in the late 1970s—such as that of the French scholar Jean-Michel Massa (1971) and Raimundo Magalhães Júnior's four-volume *Vida e obra de Machado de Assis* (1981), which followed earlier studies in the mid-1950s by Magalhães Júnior—another Brazilian critic, Eugênio Gomes, received attention for drawing philosophical parallels between Machado and Schopenhauer as well as addressing the enigmatic elements in his prose. An insightful bio-literary essay by Antônio Cândido (1977), the prominent literary critic at the time and today Brazil's venerable scholar, became a benchmark in Machado criticism. Other volumes appeared at this time, affording special attention to Machado's foreign sources, a line of research that continues today and is relevant in light of the attention given to world literature and Machado as author of Brazilian and world literatures. Moreover, in 1951, Machado's reception by the international market was given an added boost with the first translation into English of a Machadian novel, *The Posthumous Memoirs of Brás Cubas*, titled in some editions as *Epitaph of a Small Winner*, by William L. Grossman. (A new translation of *Brás Cubas* by Gregory Rabassa was published in 1997 as *The Posthumous Memoirs of Bras Cubas*). In 1963, Grossman and Helen Caldwell translated *The Psychiatrist and Other Stories*, a notable publication in hardcover and paperback for presenting Machado de Assis to an English-speaking audience as a gifted short story writer.

Interestingly, eight years after the first English translation, it was the work of another American, Helen Caldwell, also a prodigious translator of Machado's novels into English, who contributed substantially to Machado criticism with her pioneer work, *The Brazilian Othello of Machado de Assis: A study of Dom Casmurro* (1960). This study rocked Machado criticism because it not only focused on Machado's intertextual reading of Shakespeare, but offered a completely new reading of the famous 1899 novel's primary dramatic crisis or dilemma—the supposed adultery of the heroine Capitu. In this novel, the first-person narrator, Bento Santiago, condemns his wife out of suspicion of her adultery with his best friend. Deconstructing the narrator as symbolic Iago/Othello, Caldwell read *Dom Casmurro* as a tour-de-force narrative of ambiguity since the supposed adultery never takes place in the novel. Superstition and insecurity within the demonic mind of the narrator-husband motivate him to condemn his wife. Thus, Caldwell shifted the guilt from the heroine to the male narrator, in contrast to earlier readings, inspiring many later gender interpretations about women in Machado's nineteenth-century Brazil. Another line of thinking suggests that Machado, as the Wizard of Cosme Velho, as he was called, had duped, trapped, or allowed earlier patriarchal or male readers to believe without question in the enigmatic Capitu's guilt. It is as if Machado had been accurately reading the flawed patriarchal elite of his country while awaiting an alternative or outside view to add another interpretive dimension. This reversal of the then-dominant misreadings of *Dom Casmurro*—considered later to be the perfect Brazilian novel, similar to the status of F. Scott Fitzgerald's *The Great Gatsby*, for its deft use of narrative technique—opened the floodgates for a multitude of studies acknowledging Machado's sophisticated narrative artistry and technical mastery. Most importantly, Caldwell's reading convinced Brazilian and foreign readers not to trust Machado's narrators, for they were deceptively unreliable. From this point onward, Brazilian and foreign criticism of Machado's works increased markedly.

Caldwell's work may serve as the precursor to the third period of criticism, led in the late 1970s by the pioneering work of Roberto Schwarz as mentioned above, noted for his Marxist reading of the dissonance between patriarchal authority, slavery, and professed liberalism, which he referred to as "misplaced ideas." His *Ao vencedor às batatas* (*To the Winner Go the Potatoes*, 1977) and later *Um mestre na periferia do capi-*

talismo: Machado de Assis (*A Master on the Periphery of Capitalism*, 1990), very much influenced by the work of critic Antônio Cândido, also stand as notable hallmarks of Machado criticism. The other recognized scholars of Schwarz's generation are the Brazilian Alfredo Bósi (1999, 130), who focused on Machado's philosophical, psychological, and existential leanings without dismissing the sociohistorical context, which the British scholar John Gledson (1984; 1986) systematically develops in accordance with Brazilian history and class conflicts and also via studies of Machado's chronicles. Gledson continues this work with more emphasis on characterizing Machado's narrators in *Por um novo Machado de Assis* (*Toward a New Machado de Assis*, 2006). Another recognized scholar of this generation is Sérgio Paulo Rouanet (2007), who zeroes in on the influence of Laurence Sterne's "Shandian form" on Machado.

This third period includes other respected contemporary Brazilian scholars like Raymundo Farao and North Americans such as Earl Fitz, Paul Dixon, and Maria Luiza Nunes and occasional journalistic essays by such luminaries as Susan Sontag's (1990) article about Brás Cubas and Machado's skillful narrative aesthetics. Also, José Raimundo Maia Neto (1994) provides the first in-depth study in English of Machado as a skeptic by comparing him to Pyrrho of Elis and his brand of skepticism of suspending judgment and achieving tranquility.

Given the significant productivity of the third period, although the dates of some of their publications will overlap, it is reasonable to suggest a fourth period of writers and scholars who manifest more recent critical dedication to Machado's oeuvre: the Portuguese Abel Barros Baptista (2003a, 2003b); Sidney Chaloub (2003), a very discerning reading of Machado as a source for writing history; João Luiz Passos (2007), focusing on Machado's main protagonists as dramatic personae; Hélio de Seixas Guimarães (2004); João Cezar de Castro Rocha's voluminous critical edition (2005), with Rocha's original introduction speaking positively of Machado's intertextual plagiarism and underscoring the critical value in understanding his use of Brazil's "belated modernity." (xxiii). In addition to these publications, there is journalist Daniel Piza's very accessible bio-bibliographical volume (2006) with its epigraph by Machado: "Ninguém sabe o que sou quando rumino" (Nobody knows what I am when I ruminate); Marta de Senna's lucid comparative study (2008), and most recently, K. David Jackson's (2015) text that contextualizes Machado as a world author via diverse readings.

Indeed, after more than a century of ever growing Machado criticism, new editions, and a mounting number of translations, while the author himself may remain a mystery considering the famous epithet "O bruxo" (the wizard), recognition and study of his work are expanding at a steady pace. The 2008 centennial inspired the lush scholarly and bibliographical issue published by the Instituto Moreira Salles (2008), as well as Luiz Antonio Aguiar's (2008) celebratory centennial volume, written for a very broad audience and chock-full of information, curiosities, and literary sorceries, hexes, and witchcrafts, the latter suggesting Machado's skill at literary abracadabra. For Machado scholars and specialists, the invaluable *Dicionário de Machado de Assis: Língua, estilo, temas* (2010) by Castelar de Carvalho is a significant reference work of high caliber.

The image of Machado as sorcerer weaving and manipulating his wizardry relates to his skillfulness as a writer but above all to how this skill affects the reader—how he wields his magic upon us. Appropriating Hélio de Seixas Guimarães's view, it is as though while trying to read Machado, we have simultaneously been read by him (2008, 291). Recalling the above reference to those readers who were duped by Machado's *Dom Casmurro*, believing for decades that the heroine was the guilty party, what does not remain a mystery is Machado's sharp analysis of his own society, especially of human behavior in general, but above all his readers, then and now. If in Machado's grand opera of human comedy, human beings manifest uneven and unbalanced behaviors of good and evil, who can say that we as readers are not part of his narrative aim? The insidious and deceptive intimacy he ironically recreates between characters, narrators, and readers still affects us profoundly, even today, implying that while, after more than one hundred years, we may still not be able to read or fully grasp his personal life and his provocatively ambiguous narratives, he, on the other hand, has insidiously been reading us for more than a century.

Nelson H. Vieira

NOTES

1. This foreword is drawn from excerpts of a keynote I delivered for "The Languages of Machado de Assis: A Symposium" (co-coordinated by Lídia Santos) at New York University (September 17, 2008) on the occasion of the centennial of Machado de Assis's death. In addition, during that centennial year, the original inspiration for presenting Machado de Assis to a wider

public had begun with an exhibit on Machado at the John Hay Library, Brown University (April 15–June 5), curated by Ana Catarina Teixeira and Patricia Figueroa in collaboration with myself.

2. Here, Castro Rocha's term is an allusion to Brazil's status as a periphery nation, not dissimilar to the periphery developed in Schwarz's significant study (1990). The term nevertheless stresses the importance of reading "belatedness as a critical project" (Castro Rocha 2005: xxiii), thereby freeing the nation from hierarchical traditions and categories.

3. Starobinski (1975) develops this concept of the "outsider within" as it applies to individuals victimized or marginalized by racial, ethnic, and economic prejudices.

4. I am deeply indebted to Hélio de Seixas Guimarães for his informative article, "O escritor que nos lê" (2008) in terms of its scope for my preparation of the sequence of critical periods on Machado. Although Guimarães divides his sequence into three critical periods, I have opted for four in light of the increasing scholarship since 2008. Furthermore, since my early readings of Machado, the concept of Machado "reading" his readers has been very central to my own teaching and scholarship.

REFERENCES

Aguiar, Luiz Antonio. 2008. *Almanaque Machado de Assis: Vida, obra, curiosidades e bruxarias literárias*. Rio de Janeiro: Record.

Assis, Machado de. 1909. *Machado de Assis et son oeuvre littéraire*. Paris: Louis-Michaud.

Baptista, Abel Barros. 2003a. *A formação do nome: Duas interrogações sobre Machado de Assis*. São Paulo: Editora da Unicamp.

Baptista, Abel Barros. 2003b. *Autobibliografias: Solicitação do livro na ficção de Machado de Assis*. Campinas: Editora da Unicamp.

Bastide, Roger. 1940. Machado de Assis, paisagista. *Revista do Brasil* 3(29):1–14.

Bloom, Harold. 2002. *Genius: A mosaic on one hundred exemplary creative minds*. New York: Warner Books.

Bósi, Alfredo. 1999. *Machado de Assis: O enigma do olhar*. São Paulo: Editora Ática.

Helen Caldwell. 1960. *The Brazilian Othello of Machado de Assis: A study of Dom Casmurro*. Berkeley: University of California Press.

Cândido, Antônio. 1977. Esquema de Machado de Assis. In *Vários escritos*, 2nd ed. São Paulo: Duas Cidades.

Carvalho, Castelar de. 2010. *Dicionário de Machado de Assis: Língua, estilo, temas*. Rio deJaneiro: Lexikon.

Chaloub, Sidney. 2013. *Machado de Assis Historiador*. São Paulo: Companhia das Letras.

Duarte, Eduardo de Assis. 2007. *Machado de Assis afro-descendente: Escritos de caramujo*. Belo Horizonte: Crisálida.

Galante de Sousa, José. 1969. *Fontes para o estudo de Machado de Assis*. 2nd ed. Rio de Janeiro: Instituto da Educação e Cultura.

Gledson, John. 1984. *Deceptive realism of Machado de Assis*. Liverpool: Francis Cairns.

Gledson, John. 1986. *Machado de Assis: Ficção e história*. Rio de Janeiro: Paz e Terra.

Gledson, John. 2006. *Por um novo Machado de Assis*. São Paulo: Companhia das Letras.

Guimarães, Hélio de Seixas. 2004. *Os leitores de Machado de Assis: O romance machadiano e o público de literatura no século 19*. São Paulo: Nankin Editorial; Editora da Universidade de São Paulo.

Guimarães, Hélio de Seixas. 2008. O escritor que nos lê: A figura e a obra machadianas através da recepção e das polêmicas. In *Cadernos de Literatura Brasileira: Machado de Assis*, nos. 23 and 24 (July), 273–292. Rio de Janeiro: Instituto Moreira Salles.

Instituto Moreira Salles. 2008. *Cadernos de Literatura Brasileira: Machado de Assis*, nos. 23 and 24 (July). Rio de Janeiro: Instituto Moreira Salles.

Jackson, K. David. 2015. *Machado de Assis: A literary life*. New Haven: Yale University Press.

Magalhães Júnior, Raimundo. 1981. *Vida e obra de Machado de Assis*. 4 vols. Rio de Janeiro: Civilização Brasileira.

Jean-Michel Massa. 1971. *A juventude de Machado de Assis, 1839–1870: Ensaio de biografia intelectual*. Rio de Janeiro: Civilização Brasileira.

Maya, Alcides. 1912. *Machado de Assis: Some Notes on Humor*. Rio de Janeiro: Jacintho Silva.

Meyer, Augusto. 1958/2007. *Ensaios escolhidos*. Rio de Janeiro: José Olympio Editora.

Mignolo, Walter. 2001. Coloniality of power and subalternity. In Rodriguez, Ileana, ed. *The Latin American Subaltern studies reader*. Durham: Duke University Press.

Neto, José Raimundo Maia. 1994. *Machado de Assis, the Brazilian Pyrrhonian*. West Lafayette: Purdue University Press.

Passos, João Luiz. 2007. *Machado de Assis: Romance com pessoas*. São Paulo: Nankin/Edusp, University of São Paulo Press.

Pereira, Astrojildo. 1944. Machado de Assis, Romancista do Segundo Reinado. In *Interpretações*. Rio de Janeiro: Casa do Estudante.

Pereira, Astrojildo. 1959. Crítica política e social. In *Machado de Assis: ensaios e apontamentos avulsos*. Rio de Janeiro: São José.

Pereira, Lúcia Miguel. 1950. *História da Literatura Brasileira: Prosa de Ficção de 1870 a 1920*. Rio de Janeiro: José Olympio.

Piza, Daniel. 2006. *Machado de Assis: Um gênio brasileiro*. 2nd revised ed. São Paulo: Imprensa Oficial do Estado de São Paulo.

Rocha, João Cezar de Castro. 2005. Introduction: Machado de Assis—The Location of an Author. In *The Author as Plagiarist: The Case of Machado de Assis*, ed. João Cezar de Castro Rocha, xix–xxxix. Dartmouth: Tagus Press.

Romero, Sílvio. 1882. O naturalismo em literatura. In *Literatura, história e crítica*. Org. Luiz Antonio Barreto. 2002. Rio de Janeiro/Aracaju: Imago/ Universidade Federal de Sergipe: 341–367.

Romero, Sílvio. 1888. *History of Brazilian Literature*. Rio de Janeiro: Garnier.

Romero, Sílvio. 1897. *Machado de Assis: Estudo Comparativo da Literatura Brasileira*. Rio de Janeiro: Laemmert.

Rouanet, Sérgio Paulo. 2007. *Riso e melancolia: A forma shandiana em Sterne, Diderot, Xavier de Maistre, Almeida Garret e Machado de Assis*. São Paulo: Companhia das Letras.

Rouanet, Sérgio Paulo, ed. 2008–2015. *Correspondência de Machado de Assis*. 5 vols. Rio de Janeiro: ABL/Biblioteca Nacional.

Schwarz, Roberto. 1988. *Ao vencedor as batatas*. 3rd ed. São Paulo: Livraria Duas Cidades.

Schwarz, Roberto. 1990. *Um mestre na periferia do capitalismo: Machado de Assis*. São Paulo: Livraria Duas Cidades.

Schwarz, Roberto. 2014. *As idéias fora do lugar*. São Paulo: Companhia das Letras.

Senna, Marta de. 2008. *O olhar oblíquo do bruxo: Ensaios machadianos*. 2nd ed. Rio de Janeiro: Lingua Geral.

Sontag, Susan. 1990. Afterlives: The case of Machado de Assis. *New Yorker*, May 7.

Starobinski, Jean. 1975. The inside and the outside. *Hudson Review* 28: 331–51.

Verissimo, José. 1892. Um novo livro do sr. Machado de Assis. *Jornal do Brasil*. Rio de Janeiro, 11 Jan 1892: 1–2.

Verissimo, José. 1903. *Estudos de Literatura Brazileira, Terceira Série*. Rio de Janeiro e Paris: H. Garnier.

Contents

CONTRIBUTORS

Lamonte Aidoo is the Andrew W. Mellon Assistant Professor of Romance Studies at Duke University. He received his Ph.D. in Portuguese and Brazilian Studies from Brown University. Aidoo is a cultural historian and interdisciplinary scholar who specializes in nineteenth- and early twentieth-century Brazilian history and culture with a focus on the construction of race, sexuality, law, medicine, and nation in Brazil and Lusophone Africa. He is author of *Slavery Unseen: Sex, Power, and Brazil's Myth of Racial Democracy* (Duke University Press) and is the coeditor of *Lima Barreto: New Critical Perspectives* (Lexington Books, 2013).

Sidney Chalhoub is Professor of History at Harvard University. He taught history at the University of Campinas, Brazil, for 30 years. He has published three books on the social history of Rio de Janeiro: *Trabalho, lar e botequim* (1986), on working-class culture in the early twentieth century; *Visões da liberdade* (1990), on the last decades of slavery in the city; and *Cidade febril* (1996), on tenements and epidemics in the second half of the nineteenth century. He also published *Machado de Assis, historiador* (2003), about the literature and political ideas of the most important nineteenth-century Brazilian novelist, and co-edited five other books on the social history of Brazil. His most recent monograph is *A força da escravidão: ilegalidade e costume no Brasil oitocentista* (2012), on illegal enslavement and the precariousness of freedom in nineteenth-century Brazil.

G. Reginald Daniel is Professor of Sociology at University of California, Santa Barbara; Affiliated Faculty, Department of Black Studies, Latin American and Iberian Studies, and Asian American Studies. His books include *More Than Black? Multiracial Identity and the New Racial Order* (Temple University Press, 2002); *Uncompleted Independence: The Creation and Revision of Racial Thinking in the United States*, edited with Paul R. Spickard (University of Notre Dame Press,

2002); *Race and Multiraciality in Brazil and the United States: Converging Paths?* (Pennsylvania State University Press, 2006); and *Machado de Assis: Multiracial Identity and the Brazilian Novelist* (Pennsylvania State University Press, 2012). These are a culmination of much of his thinking on the relationship between social structure and racial identity formation—especially, multiracial identities. He has received significant media attention and participated as a panelist at various conferences as an expert on the topic of multiracial identity. He is also a member of the Advisory Board of AMEA (Association of MultiEthnic Americans) and the Advisory Council of the Mixed Heritage Center of MAVIN Foundation, and a former Advisory Board member of Project RACE (Reclassify All Children Equally). These have been the most prominent organizations involved in bringing about changes in the collection of official racial and ethnic data, as in the decennial census, which makes it possible for multiracial-identified individuals to acknowledge their various backgrounds.

M. Elizabeth [Libby] Ginway is Associate Professor in the Department of Spanish and Portuguese Studies at the University of Florida, where she teaches undergraduate and graduate courses on Brazilian and Latin American literature. She is author of *Brazilian Science Fiction: Cultural Myths and Nationhood in the Land of the Future* (Bucknell, 2004), a collection of essays *Alien Vision* (Devir 2010), and co-editor of *Latin American Science Fiction: Theory and Practice* (Palgrave, 2012) with J. Andrew Brown. She has published articles in *Brasil/Brazil,Extrapolation, Femspec, Foundation, Hispania, Luso-Brazilian Review, Modern Language Studies, Revista Iberoamericana,* and *Science Fiction Studies.* Her current book project is a comparative study on the science fiction and fantasy of Brazil and Mexico.

Camilo Gomides is Associate Professor of Portuguese at the University of Puerto Rico-Río Piedras. He specializes in ecocriticism and evolutionary approaches in literary theory. He teaches Portuguese language and Brazilian literature and cinema. He is co-author of Amazônia in the Arts: Ecocriticism versus the Economics of Deforestation, with Joseph Henry Vogel. He has published in *Romance Notes, Interdisciplinary Studies of Environment and Literature, OMETECA Sciences and Humanities,* and the *Tulane Environmental Law Journal* on diverse themes, ranging from homoaffectivity to ecological debt and Columbus's Diary.

Hans Ulrich Gumbrecht is the Albert Guérard Professor in Literature at Stanford University. He teaches Romance and Comparative Literatures and has convened an ongoing "Philosophical Reading Group" at Stanford since 1989. His publications have been translated into more than 20 languages, and the most recent of his many books is "After 1945 -- Latency as Origin of the Present." Gumbrecht is a member of the American Academy of Arts and Sciences, Professeur attaché au Collège de France, and has been a visiting professor at numerous academic institutions worldwide. He writes regularly for the "Frankfurter Allgemeine Zeitung" and the "Estado de São Paulo." In preparation is a book on Denis Diderot and the French Enlightenment philosophers.

Earl E. Fitz is Professor of Portuguese, Spanish, and Comparative Literature Affiliated faculty: Center for Latin American Studies at Vanderbilt University. Earl E. Fitz received his PhD in Comparative Literature from the City University of New York in 1977. His principal languages of concentration were Portuguese, Spanish, French, English, and German while his primary national literatures were those of Brazil, Spanish America, the USA, and Canada. Fitz is the author of a number of articles and books, including *Machado de Assis and Female Characterization: The Novels* (2014); *Rediscovering the New World: Inter-American Literature in a Comparative Context* (1991), *Ambiguity and Gender in the New Novel of Brazil and Spanish America: A Comparative Assessment* (co-authored with Judith A. Payne) *Sexuality and Being in the Poststructuralist Universe of Clarice Lispector* (2001), *Brazilian Narrative Traditions in a Comparative Context* (2005), and *Translation and the Rise of Inter-American Literature* (co-authored with Elizabeth Lowe). His most recent projects involve the completion of a comparative history of inter-American literature, a study of the Borges translation of Faulkner's *The Wild Palms*, and an essay on Machado de Assis, Borges, and Clarice Lispector that offers a new, more comparative evaluation of Latin America's renowned "New Narrative."

Richard Miskolci is Associate Professor of Sociology at the Federal University of São Carlos in São Paulo, Brazil, where he is also founder and chair of Quereres: Núcleo de Pesquisa em Diferenças, Gênero e Sexualidade. He is also a researcher with the Núcleo de Estudos de Gênero Pagu at UNICAMP. He is author of the books *O desejo da nação: masculinidade e branquitude no Brasil de fins do Século XIX* (2012) and *Teoria Queer: um aprendizado pelas diferenças* (2012). He is also co-editor of *Diferenças na Educação: outros aprendizados* (with Jorge Leite Júnior) and *Discursos fora da ordem: sexualidades, saberes, e direitos* (with Larissa Pelúcio). He has published articles in *Sociologias, Revista Brasileira de Ciências Sociais, cadernos pagu, Revista Estudos Feministas, Lua Nova, Revista de Sociologia e Política, Tempo Social,* and *Gênero.* In 2013, he was a research fellow at the University of California-Berkeley.

Pedro Meira Monteiro is Professor of Spanish and Portuguese at Princeton University. He teaches courses on Brazilian literature, Latin American essays, music and poetry, and cultural and intellectual history. His books include *A queda do aventureiro* (1999), *Um moralista nos trópicos* (2004), *Mário de Andrade e Sérgio Buarque de Holanda: Correspondência* (2012),*Cangoma Calling: Spirits and Rhythms of Freedom in Brazilian Jongo Slavery Songs* (2013, co-edited with Michael Stone), and *O futuro abolido: Machado de Assis e o* Memorial de Aires (forthcoming). With João Biehl, Lilia Schwarcz and Antonio Sérgio Guimarães, he co-directs Princeton's Global Network on "Race and Citizenship in the Americas."

He was the editor of *ellipsis*, the journal of the American Portuguese Studies Association, from 2010 to 2014. His current research focuses on re-readings of Shakespeare's *The Tempest* in Latin America.

Paulo Moreira is Associate Professor of Spanish and Portuguese at Yale University. His main areas of interest are American, Brazilian, and Mexican Twentieth-Century Literatures, Comparative Literature, Cinema, Poetry, Short Story, Modernism, Regionalism, and Translation Studies. He has published scholarly articles and reviews on poetry, the short story, Lima Barreto, Machado de Assis, Afro-Brazilian literature, Contemporary Brazilian Film, Faulkner, Guimarães Rosa, and Rulfo. Paulo Moreira has also published a poetry volume (*Quatro Partes*) and his poems have appeared in renowned Brazilian literary magazines (*Inimigo Rumor* and *Coyote*). His first book, *Modernismo Localista das Américas: Os contos de Faulkner, Guimarães Rosa e Rulfo*, was published in January 2013, and his second book, *Literary Relations Between Mexico and Brazil—Deep Undercurrents* was published by Palgrave Macmillan in December 2013.

Marta Peixoto is Associate Professor of Brazilian literature at New York University. She has worked primarily on twentieth-century Brazilian literature. Author of *Poesia com coisas* (1983), on the poet João Cabral de Melo Neto and *Passionate Fictions: Gender Narrative and Violence in Clarice Lispector (1994)*, she has also published several essays on these writers, as well as on others, mainly poets. She has recently written on Brazilian cinema, with a focus on documentary film.

Giulia Ricco obtained both her BA (2010) and MA (2012) in Foreign Languages and Literature at the University of Bologna, Italy, with an emphasis in English and Portuguese. Her MA thesis analyzed the representation of violence in the short stories of Brazilian writers Machado de Assis and Rubem Fonseca. The chapter in this collection is an excerpt of this larger work. She is a PhD candidate in Romance Studies at Duke University, working on both Brazil and Italy. Her main interests are violence and literature; politics of memory; meta-fictional cinema; and Atlantic studies. She is also the co-founder of the working group "Ocean Crossings" and the organizer of many Brazil-related events on campus.

Fernando de Sousa Rocha is Associate Professor of Portuguese and Chair of the Department of Spanish and Portuguese at Middlebury College. He is the author of *Subaltern Writings: Readings on Graciliano Ramos's Novels* (2013). He obtained a Master's and a PhD degree in Comparative Literature from the University of Southern California, Los Angeles. He also holds a Master's degree in Letters (Brazilian Literature and Literary Theory) from the Pontifícia Universidade Católica do Rio de Janeiro (PUC-Rio). His present research interests focus on slavery and its representations in Brazilian culture. He has articles published in journals such as *Luso-Brazilian Review, Itinerários* and *ArtCultura*.

Sônia Roncador is Associate Professor of Spanish and Portuguese at UT Austin. She has published three books: *Domestic Servants in Literature and Testimony in Brazil (1889–1999)* (Palgrave Macmillan, 2014); *A doméstica imaginária: literatura, testemunhos, e a invenção da empregada doméstica no Brasil (1889–1999)* (Editora Universidade de Brasília, 2008); and *Poéticas do empobrecimento: a escrita derradeira de Clarice Lispector* (Annablume, 2002). Additionally, her articles have appeared in a number of peer-reviewed journals, such as *Revista de Crítica Literaria Latinoamericana, Afro-Hispanic Review, Luso-Brazilian Review, Ellipsis: Journal of the American Portuguese Studies Association,* and *Revista de Letras.* Her current book project discusses the overlap of discourses on immigration and slavery and servitude in order to reveal the cross-currents of the Portuguese and African Diasporas in Brazil.

Lilia Moritz Schwarcz is Full Professor in Anthropology at the University of São Paulo. Her main interests are the history of slavery, racial theories, history of the Brazilian Court, academic art, and history of anthropology in Brazil. She has published several books, two of which are in English: *Spectacle of Races: Scientists, Institutions and Racial Theories in Brazil at the End of the XIXth Century* (Farrar Strauss and Giroux, 1999) and *The Emperors Beard: D. Pedro II a Tropical King* (Farrar Strauss and Giroux, 2004). She was a curator of exhibitions such as *The Great Travel of the King's Library* (2006) and *Nicolas-Antoine Taunay: a French Translation of the Tropics* (2008). She is also the editor of a complete collection of Lima Barreto's short stories, *Contos Completos de Lima Barreto* (Companhia das Letras, 2010). She was a fellow at the Guggenheim Foundation (2006–2007) and at the John Carter Brown Library at Brown University (2007), was a visiting professor at Oxford and Leiden Universities, a Tinker Professor at Columbia University (2008), and since 2011, is Global Professor at Princeton. She is a Member of the Advisory Group for the Harvard Brazilian Office since 2006.

Daniel F. Silva is Assistant Professor of Spanish and Portuguese and Comparative Literature at Middlebury College, having received his PhD from Brown University in Portuguese and Brazilian Studies. His research interests include Lusophone literatures and cinemas, comparative visual cultures, imperial discourses, and urban space. He is author of *Subjectivity and the Reproduction of Imperial Power: Empire's Individuals* (Routledge, 2015) and co-editor of *Lima Barreto: New Critical Perspectives* (Lexington Books, 2013), a collection of multidisciplinary essays on the life and oeuvreof Brazilian writer Lima Barreto, the first of its kind in English. His work has been published in peer-reviewed journals such as *Hispania* and *Chasqui.*

Luiz Fernando Valente Professor of Portuguese and Brazilian Studies at Brown University, was educated in Brazil and the United States. His teaching and research interests include Brazilian narrative of the nineteenth and twentieth centuries, with special emphasis on José de Alencar, João Guimarães Rosa, João Ubaldo Ribeiro,

Euclides da Cunha, and Lima Barreto; the relationship of fiction and history; the construction of national identity and the representation of the nation; comparative literature, particularly the modern historical novel and the literature of the Americas; theory of literature, particularly the narrative; and Brazilian poetry since 1945. Some recent publications include *Mundividências: Leituras Comparativas de Guimarães Rosa*; "History, Fiction and National Identity in J. U. Ribeiro's 'An Invincible Memory' and R. Coover's 'The Public Burning'"; "'Estrelas indecifráveis': ciência e literatura em Euclides da Cunha"; "Distopia e utopia nas letras brasileiras da pós-modernidade"; "Paulo Freire: desenvolvimento como prática de liberdade"; "O romance brasileiro de revisitação colonial: o caso de Luiz Antônio de Assis Brasil"; and "DeLillo's Techno-Humanism."

Nelson H. Vieira is University Professor of Portuguese and Brazilian Studies and Judaic Studies and Chair of the Department of Portuguese and Brazilian Studies at Brown University. He is American founding editor of the literary journal *Brasil/Brazil*, and former President of Latin American Jewish Studies Association (1995–2002). Besides numerous articles on Brazilian fiction, his major publications are *Contemporary Jewish Writing in Brazil*, Ed. & Trans, (2009); *Anonymous Celebrity* by Ignácio de Loyola Brandão, Trans. (2009); *The Prophet and Other Stories* by Samuel Rawet [Intro & Trans.] (1998); *Jewish Voices in Brazilian Literature: A Prophetic Discourse of Alterity* (1995); *Construindo a imagem do judeu: algumas abordagens téoricas* [Editor] (1994); *Brasil e Portugal: a imagem recíproca* (1991); *Roads to Today's Portugal* [Editor] (1983); and *The Promise* by Bernardo Santareno, Trans. (1981). He is working on a book manuscript dedicated to the oeuvre of Brazilian writer Dalton Trevisan.

CHAPTER 1

Introduction

Lamonte Aidoo and Daniel F. Silva

Joaquim Maria Machado de Assis, who wrote in the last half of the nineteenth century and into the first decade of the twentieth, has left an indelible mark on Brazilian literature as well as the letters of Latin America. In recent decades, his oeuvre has gained increasing relevance in world literature, reaching new audiences. His nuanced plots and characters—along with his innovations in terms of narration—have influenced innumerable writers and cultural talents of his generation and those that followed, including Gabriel García Márquez, Carlos Fuentes, Susan Sontag, Woody Allen, and José Saramago.

Machado de Assis, as he is better known, or even simply Machado, was born in Rio de Janeiro in 1839, seventeen years after the official independence of Brazil from the Portuguese crown. Although historian Lilia Moritz Schwarcz's essay will cover his biography and his milieu in more detail, to understand the depth of his impact on national and international literature and culture, it is worth noting a few particular points regarding his life. He was born in the Morro do Livramento neighborhood of Rio to

L. Aidoo (✉)
Duke University, Durham, North Carolina, USA

D.F. Silva
Middlebury College, Middlebury, Vermont, USA

© The Editor(s) (if applicable) and The Author(s) 2016
L. Aidoo, D.F. Silva (eds.), *Emerging Dialogues on Machado de Assis*, DOI 10.1057/978-1-137-54174-1_1

1

Francisco José de Assis, a mulatto son of freed slaves, and Maria Leopoldina da Câmara Machado, an Azorean working-class immigrant. Francisco was a painter and Maria, a washwoman. The family resided in the home of their employer, Dona Maria José de Mendonça Barrozo Pereira, wife of the then-deceased Senator Bento Barroso Pereira, as dependent workers, or *agregados*. Dona Maria José would become Machado's godmother, giving him his middle name. Throughout his childhood, Machado experienced two vastly different worlds in terms of race and class: the poverty and deplorable conditions facing the then capital city's enslaved population, and the privilege and abuses of slaveholders of the nation's elite. Machado climbed the social ladder, rising from the poverty of his childhood to become one of the nation's most celebrated writers, intellectuals, and critics. His personal experience of witnessing and navigating these two worlds deeply affected his life and hisliterary endeavors. This complex reality would be a recurring theme in many of his works, as many of the chapters in this book will show. Moreover, Machado had frail health throughout his life. He suffered from epilepsy, often having seizures in public. Machado died on September 29, 1908, at the age of 69, of cancer.

During his lifetime, Machado witnessed great sociopolitical shifts. As some chapters in this volume will elaborate, 1888 brought the formal abolition of slavery in Brazil and the following year marked the end of the Brazilian Empire and the beginning of the republic. However, while the nation experienced these monumental political changes, as Machado underscores in his later work, always with his emblematic wit and irony, the more things changed, the more they stayed the same. From the racial meanings central to slavery in some of his early short stories to a society entrenched in relationships of dependence evident in *Dom Casmurro* (Lord Taciturn) and the complex voice of the patriarchal elite in *Memórias Póstumas de Brás Cubas* (Posthumous Memoirs of Brás Cubas), it is impossible to separate Machado's work from his life and time.

The sheer quantity of his work and its great profundity across genres of writing and art—novels, short stories, journalism, theater, and poetry—have yielded over the years a no less substantial amount of scholarship regarding his life and oeuvre in Brazil, the USA, and across the globe. He is one of the most heralded literary figures of Brazil and one of the most acclaimed writers to produce literature in Portuguese, and there is no shortage of books, articles, and courses in Portuguese dedicated to Machado. Significant work has also been published in English in the USA and Great Britain by scholars such as Helen Caldwell, Earl Fitz, G. Reginald Daniel,

Paul Dixon, and John Gledson. Machado has undoubtedly become an established presence in anglophone academia, from classrooms to libraries, from Lusophone Studies departments to courses in world literature. As this trend continues, new Machado students and scholars continue to emerge, shifting our perceptions of the past (of both Brazil and history in general) and our understandings of literature.

Despite Machado's growing reputation among anglophone readers and in academic circles, there had yet to be a collection of essays published in English dedicated entirely to his life and work. The closest project to such a volume was *Machado de Assis: Reflections on a Brazilian Master Writer* edited by Richard Graham and published in 1999. A more broad-ranging collection can be found in volumes 13 and 14 (2005) of the journal *Portuguese Literary and Cultural Studies*, which bring together essays from noted and emerging scholars from Brazil, the USA, Italy, and Portugal. Scholarship from Brazil and around the world, in a myriad of languages, has continued to offer new interpretations and insights into Machado, often shifting established readings.

Emerging Dialogues on Machado de Assis, while revisiting some previously studied topics, presents new and innovative perspectives on Machado's life and work that can help us understand social and political issues of nineteenth-century Brazil in new ways. We hope, with the publication of this volume, to generate more interest in Machado and to place his works in dialogue with emerging theoretical concerns such as the politics of hybrid racial identity and the connections between homosociability and masculine institutional power. Many of the chapters in this book ask new questions. For instance, how does a nuanced exploration of an unreliable narrator shed light on experiences of sexuality in turn-of-the-century Brazil? Or, what can Machado's deployment of fantastic elements, or incipient magical realism, reveal regarding the reproduction of political power over othered bodies?

Reading Machado over a century after his death inevitably produces new meanings in his texts, offering new understandings of his work and historical context while allowing his oeuvre to enrich our understanding of the present. In this regard, Machado, whether at the level of narration, plot, or even his own personal experiences, can help us grapple with such urgencies of the present as the construction of race, performance of identity and ego totality, the conflicts between gender and desire, and the intersections of historicization and power. In the chapters that follow, we can think of Machado as not only the political critic or keen, biting social observer of his time, but also as a sort of queer theorist, feminist thinker, postcolonial critic, and even psychoanalyst.

Emerging Dialogues on Machado de Assis is divided into five sections that approach different facets of Machado's work, life, and legacy. Many chapters dialogue with one another while exploring unstudied motifs, extrapolating new insights from Machado's works, and reevaluating how we read Machado today vis-à-vis his own lifetime and the present. Sections will focus on Machado's place in literature and philosophy, racial discourse and the politics of identity, the construction of womanhood, his problematization of masculinity, and his intertwining of political concerns with narrative form. These will offer us new ways of thinking through his literary innovations as well as the discourses that structured society in Machado's era and continue to impact societies today.

The collection opens with three chapters situating Machado within the historical events of his time and within literature, in terms of both his literary influences and his impact on letters. Lilia Moritz Schwarcz's chapter, "Machado de Assis: Creator and Character in a Troubled Scene," functions as a historical introduction to Machado and the political and social environment in which he lived and with which he dialogued through his work. His life spanned seven decades that saw substantial political changes during the formative years of Brazilian nationhood. The Paraguayan War, the abolition of slavery, and the declaration of the republic are merely a few of the landmark events that impacted Machado's life and work as a Brazilian writer. Schwarcz also traces his life from his *agregado* childhood to the cementation of his literary and cultural acclaim, and from his beginnings as a typographer apprentice and teenage poet to founding the Brazilian Academy of Letters.

The following chapter, "Machado de Assis and Realism: A Literary Genealogy," by Hans Ulrich Gumbrecht, aims to locate Machado's place in the development of literature, more specifically realism, in Brazil. This exploration of the aesthetic mode of realism in Brazilian literature focuses on Machado and his often-contentious place within literary movements. More importantly, Gumbrecht addresses how Machado reconfigured realist aesthetics to the demands of his time, engendering a new brand of realism—in stark contrast to the European realist tradition—founded upon a firm philosophical questioning of placing reality into representation. Gumbrecht interrogates Machado's relationship with realism, centering on the writer's singular narrative form of instability and self-reflexivity. From this, Machado creates a form of realism that fundamentally questions representational authority. The chapter closes by establishing a critical dialogue between Machado's realism and that of Brazilian writers who have followed him, offering a heightened understanding of not only the realist aesthetic in Brazil, but of Brazilian literature overall.

Chapter three, "Machado de Assis and Pascal," by Pedro Meira Monteiro, revisits Machado's dialogues with the seventeenth-century French philosophers he was known to have read. Monteiro aims to understand how the French moralists enabled Machado to explore the limitations and shortcomings of the modern conception of an autonomous subject, most strikingly, in his late work. Blaise Pascal has been often referred to as a main philosophical source for the Brazilian writer. This chapter studies the influence of the moralists in how Machado portrays individuals who cannot escape from the mundane mechanics of passions and self-interest. Thus, a difference between the Brazilian and the French writers emerges: where Pascal proposes a leap of faith, Machado invents a narrator who is stuck in those mechanics and whose characters can be the victims of a meaningless, purely material world.

Part 2, "Machado on Race, Identity, and Society," begins with Sidney Chalhoub's chapter, "The Legacy of Slavery: Tales of Gender and Racial Violence in Machado de Assis." Chalhoub explores how the themes of slavery, gender, and racism, seen as intertwined, were manifested in the work of Machado de Assis throughout his career. Chalhoub identifies three moments, successive but also to some degree coeval, in the way in which Machado approached and interrelated these subjects. In the first moment, in texts written mainly in the 1860s and 1870s, he denounced the seigneurial custom of resorting to sexual violence against free and enslaved black women, and depicted these women's dignity in dealing with the problem. Next, in the 1880s, in a very allegorical fashion, some of his works offer nuanced reflections on the relations between division of labor, scientific ideologies, and racial injustice. Finally, in his work spanning the 1890s until his death in 1908, Machado turned to the legacy of slavery and its consequences for Brazilian history and society at a time – after abolition – when national elites sought to erase the violence of Brazil's slaveholding past.

G. Reginald Daniel's chapter, "Machado de Assis: From 'Tragic Mulatto' to Human Tragicomedy." Critics have been historically ambivalent regarding Machado's degree of interest in slavery, race relations, and other social concerns, some going so far as to argue that he sought to deny his racial background. Drawing from Machado's own statements as well as his prose fiction, Daniel provides an alternative interpretation of how Machado's writings were inflected by his life—especially the experience of his racial identity. He argues that Machado endeavored to transcend rather than deny his racial background by embracing his greater humanity. Machado presents a challenge to the notion that the most important thing about one's personhood is one's community of descent. Daniel maintains that Machado sought to universalize the experience of racial ambiguity and duality regarding the mulatto condition in Brazil into a fundamental mode of human existence. Accordingly, the conception of the hybrid human subject erodes the very foundation of "raciological" thinking. As a multiracial individual of African and European descent in a society that prized whiteness and stigmatized blackness, Machado viewed the challenge of achieving upward mobility and public success without compromising his own personal integrity as merely one of the myriad epiphenomena of universal duality and ambiguity confronting all of humanity.

In chapter six, " 'Father Versus Mother': Slavery and its Apparatuses," Fernando de Sousa Rocha uses Machado's short story to reinterpret the structuring role of slavery in nineteenth-century Brazil, tracing how, in a microcommunity of Afro-descendants, even those who were free continued to experience slavery as it permeated all aspects of everyday life. Machado's story begins with the assertion that with slavery there came occupations and apparatuses that were specific to it, such as slave catching (the protagonist's occupation), and masks and iron collars, which might be used on Arminda, the runaway slave whom the protagonist catches. What interests Rocha is the extent to which occupation and apparatuses constitute fields in which this microcommunity moves. By means of these apparatuses and this occupation, Machado elaborates a close struggle between Afro-descendants who, being socially so close, clash due to their liminal proximity with the subjugation and death instituted by the "slavocracy."

The final chapter of this section, by Sônia Roncador, titled "The 'Chinese Question' in Machado's Journalism," adds further nuances to Machado's racial politics. This chapter adds one further (and unstudied) layer to the controversy surrounding Machado's racial identity by analyzing his contributions to late nineteenth-century debates regarding Chinese immigration to Brazil. In order to examine Machado's ambivalent position on this question, Roncador relies on his *crônicas* (chronicles), reflecting on the visit of Mandarin Tong King Sing and his African American assistant, G.A. Butley, to Brazil in October 1883. As Roncador argues, by ambiguously embracing the popular Sinophobia of his time, Machado ends up addressing the contentious overlap of nonwhite immigrant servitude and black slavery in Brazil. Such chronicles, as well as his later 1888 column, "Bons Dias!," on the controversial proposal of compulsory naturalization, reveal Machado de Assis's strategy of using by-proxy black(ened) servants to denounce the whitening ideology that would soon give rise to the republican regime.

Part 3 of this volume, "Women in Machado's Work," shifts the focus to the writer's construction of female characters. In chapter eight, Earl E. Fitz's essay, "Writing Womanhood in the New Brazil: Machado's *Lição de Botânica*," offers an analysis of Machado's representation of female characters through critical readings of his short stories and his understudied theatrical works, particularly *Lição da Botânica* (Botanical Lesson). Fitz's argument is that Machado's female characterizations, in his narratives and in his theater, are much more important to his overall sense of literary art than we have long believed. More than mere props or foils for his more famous male characters, Machado's fictional women possess their own narrative logic and their functions are quite distinct from those of his better-known male characters. Machado's fictional women are also the mechanism by which he shows his reading public (made up largely of women) that a new, more socially conscious woman is part of what the new Brazil needs as it creates its postemancipation and postempire era.

In the following chapter, "Capitu's Curiosity: Undecidability and Gender in *Dom Casmurro*," Marta Peixoto revisits one of Machado's most emblematic, if not controversial, characters, Capitu. Raising new questions, Peixoto offers a new reading of Capitu's radically undecidable moral substance, in relation to the position of women on the brink of change in nineteenth-century Brazil. If we read the novel in full awareness of the undecidability of some of its key components, as a literary character, Capitu remains both extremely devious and deceitful, and a proper wife— to the extent that her possible villainy is camouflaged as perfect submissiveness. Peixoto places this characterization in the context of Machado's other female characters, of ideologies of proper female behavior in the nineteenth century, and, considering that intelligence is her salient trait, also in the context of Machado's writings about education for women, of which he was a proponent. Taking into account the long history of reception of this perhaps most written about Brazilian novel, Peixoto considers the undecidability of Capitu's character as a starting point and asks how we can interpret Machado's intricately worked out refusal to settle this issue with certainty, while making it the novel's most urgent question.

If part three is centered on Machado's female characters, positing them as the lens through which to explore other political and social topics, part four, "Machado on Masculinity and Queer Relations," offers readings on the nuanced construction of Machado's male characters, how their identities are performed, and how these are tied to prevalent discourses on masculinity and sexuality. This section of the volume begins with the updated republication of the essay that arguably paved the way for in-depth queer analyses of Machado's male characters, Luiz Fernando Valente's "Machado's Wounded Males." Valente's seminal chapter explores the relationship between patriarchal power and its rigid expectations of heteronormative male identity by analyzing the ways in which Machado's male characters are haunted by specters of inadequacy and impotence, inflicting painful psychological wounds on them. Valente demonstrates how Machado's works, particularly the short stories "Wedding Song" (1883) and "Midnight Mass" (1894) and novel *Lord Taciturn* (1899), reveal wounds that dictate masculine identities and permanently distort these characters' relationships. Although Machado's analysis is grounded in the social and historical context of nineteenth-century Brazil, Valente argues that it contains a modern treatment of gender issues and reveals an understanding of questions of masculinity that is far ahead of its time.

Following up on Valente's reading of *Lord Taciturn*, Camilo Gomides's chapter, "Homoaffectivity Exemplified in *Dom Casmurro*," offers a queer-inflected analysis of the novel's plot, particularly the ambiguous relationship between Bento and Escobar. Gomides explores the homoeroticism and homosocial bonds that go beyond the jealousy of a husband who believes himself cuckolded. According to Gomides, Capitu, the enigmatic wife of Bento, the protagonist and narrator, accused of betraying him with his best friend Escobar, can also be thought of as the conduit for Bento's relationship with Escobar. In the homosocial bond between the two, Capitu becomes an object of exchange for the performance of masculinity central to heteronormative relationships between men at the turn of the twentieth century. Part of the love triangle's complexity resides in Capitu's position as a married woman within patriarchy, enabling the homosocial and homoerotic bond between the two men.

In chapter twelve, Richard Miskolci's "Masculinity and Matrimonial Secrets in *Dom Casmurro*" further problematizes the novel's love triangle by centering on the nascent institution of marriage in Brazilian society. In this regard, the issues of masculinity and homoerotic desire that haunt Bento cannot be divorced from the intersecting discourses of republicanism, national whiteness, "civilizing" Rio, and eugenics. As Miskolci argues, at the turn of the century, marriage aimed at exercising control over desire, reinforcing rigid gender binaries and placing strict limits on relationships between people of the same sex. Miskolci thus interrogates Bento's impossible attempt to reconcile transgressive sexual desire with the desire to consolidate his social standing as an elite white male through marriage. At another analytic level, Miskolci further problematizes Bento's relationship with masculinity by exploring how homoerotics intermingle with patriarchal power over women in the postabolition structuring of Brazilian society.

The volume closes with three chapters comprising its final section, "Machado, Allegory, and the Narration of Violence." The complexity of Machado's narrative techniques has garnered significant academic attention over the past decades. The final chapters consider how Machado uses such techniques in his representations of violence—at the institutional and everyday levels—as constitutive of society.

M. Elizabeth Ginway's chapter, "Machado's Tales of the Fantastic: Allegory and the Macabre," analyzes three largely unstudied works in order to explore a fairly ignored facet of Machado's oeuvre: his gothic short stories. These stories predating his mature period (1880–) have been analyzed as flawed examples of the fantastic genre. Here, Ginway examines three such stories, "O capitão Mendonça" (Captain Mendonça 1870), "A vida eterna" (Eternal Life 1870), and "Os óculos de Pedro Antão" (Pedro Antão's Glasses 1874), to suggest that these are actually political allegories disguised as tales of the macabre. All three stories conjure up images of death and decadence and take place in settings associated with the past. In this sense, Machado's use of allegory in his tales of the fantastic brings us back to history, slavery, melancholy, and loss during the 1870s, precisely the images of ruin and devastation that are central to Benjamin's concept of allegory. If the stories do indeed contain implied critiques of Dom Pedro II and the imperial regime, what better place to hide them, as in Edgar Allan Poe's "The Purloined Letter," than in plain sight in these seemingly frivolous stories appearing in the *Jornal das Famílias*? Disguised as titillating tales of the quasimacabre, Machado's stories incorporate his typical arsenal of intertextuality, allegory, and literary and historical references—techniques that he would continue to refine in his later work.

"Machado de Assis and the Secret Heart of Literature," by Paulo Moreira, proposes a nuanced reading of Machado's short story "A causa secreta" (translated as "The Secret Heart" or "The Hidden Cause").

Moreira uses the story to explore one familiar motif present in several of Machado's stories: the ambitious young man negotiating favors in order to ascend socially and being dragged by unexpected twists of fate into violent and tragic moral circumstances. "A Causa Secreta" is also typical in its subtle choreography of carefully calibrated, shifting points of view and narrative voices that invariably invite the reader to engage with the text. Moreira argues that in this particular short story, these two rich elements combine in a daring examination of voyeuristic and sadistic pleasure ("no anger, no hatred; just a vast pleasure, quiet, and profound") as "something like a pure aesthetic sensation." The chapter fundamentally demonstrates how Machado de Assis decisively links this particularly cruel mode of aesthetic sensation to literary representation.

The final chapter, "Framing Violence: Narrator and Reader in 'Father versus Mother,'" by Giulia Riccò, reads Machado's famed short story as a rich case study for analyzing the ways in which Machado strategically includes and excludes violence through the act of narration. This leads Riccò to also reflect on how the reader collaborates with the narrator in this process. She begins by examining the opening preamble, where Machado inserts the reader into the frame of the story. Riccò's analysis then moves into the plot to explore how the narrator sustains the frame of violence through irony and careful word choices. Lastly, she explores the role of the reader in Machado's narrative by looking at points of comparison between the short story and photography. Riccò ultimately aims to demonstrate that Machado's ability to connect to the present lies precisely in the dialogues that his short stories spark between the narrator and the modern reader when representing the forms of violence that are still intrinsic in Brazilian society.

We hope that this volume offers new perspectives on one of the world's literary giants while dialoguing with existing scholarship and offering new takes on the literature, culture, and history of Brazil and Latin America. From a variety of analytical and theoretical approaches, the contributors of this volume invite us to use Machado de Assis as a reader of the past engaging with issues that continue to impact the present.

Lamonte Aidoo, Durham, North Carolina, July, 2015
Daniel F. Silva, Middlebury, Vermont, July, 2015

PART I

Situating Machado de Assis in History, Literature, and Philosophy

CHAPTER 2

Machado de Assis: Creator and Character in a Troubled Scene

Lília Moritz Schwarcz

INTRODUCTION: LIGHTING THE SCENE

Joaquim Maria Machado de Assis was a wonderful witness to his time, although not in the traditional sense of the word "witness," as if he were a simple and predictable product of his historical context. If we are certain that he saw and experienced the political and cultural consolidation of the Second Reign in Brazil, that of Pedro II, as well as the birth of the First Republic, we cannot then consider him a typical witness in the sense of passively watching the historical periods of his life. Nor can we regard him as a simple reflection of such moments.

Borrowing Carlo Ginzburg's (2005) terminology from his *The Cheese and the Worms*, in which Menocchio, a miller from Friuli, is persecuted by the Inquisition for his supposedly heretical ideas, we can think of Machado de Assis as a "thermometer" of his time. We can argue that both Machado de Assis and Menocchio did more than echo the events that they each experienced. Instead, Machado translated, in his own way, all that he observed, and only then did he tell about it.

We must also keep in mind that we cannot expect literature to simply reflect its time. We know that the most provocative writers are those

Translated by Daniel F. Silva and Lamonte Aidoo

L.M. Schwarcz (✉)
University of São Paulo and Princeton University, São Paulo, Brazil

© The Editor(s) (if applicable) and The Author(s) 2016
L. Aidoo, D.F. Silva (eds.), *Emerging Dialogues on Machado de Assis*, DOI 10.1057/978-1-137-54174-1_2

who dialogue with their historical context, usually in a critical and unexpected fashion. Furthermore, the literary genre owes little to the historical period that formed the writer. This is not to say that we search for the writer's absolute autonomy vis-à-vis the writer's historical context. Attempting to explain one through the other is, nonetheless, overly reductive (Baxandall 2006).[1]

If literature is a product of its time, it also produces its time, making the task in this introduction an arduous one. Therefore, more than searching for the ways that Machado's oeuvre mirrors his time, my goal here is to set the stage for the contributors of this collection to offer in-depth analyses of the writer's life and work. In other words, I will merely trace the historical context in which the writer dwelled, without the intent to establish mechanical bonds between the two. Ultimately, Machado is the context that surrounded him, but he is also one of its main craftsmen. This introduction is thus not a biography of Machado de Assis, nor is it an attempt to give context to the writer. Perhaps the intention here is very much the opposite: to give more of the writer to the context.

BACKSTAGE

Joaquim Maria Machado de Assis, known commonly as Machado, was born in Morro do Livramento, in the city of Rio de Janeiro, on June 21, 1839. The political context of the time was informed by the Regency period (1831–1840), marked by the tempestuous transition of power from Pedro I to his preadolescent son, Pedro II. This was also a period of considerable experimentation in republicanism and political decentralization. The neighborhood where Machado's family lived was largely poor, and his parents were no exception. His father, Francisco José de Assis, was the son of freed slaves and earned his living as a painter, selling pastries in the streets. His mother, Maria Leopoldina da Câmara Machado, was of Portuguese origin from the Azores and worked as a washerwoman. Together, they were *agregados*—workers who resided in their landowners' homes—of Dona Maria José de Mendonça Barroso Pereira, widow of senator Bento Barroso Pereira, whose family owned the land of the Livramento neighborhood.

Dona Maria José would become Machado's godmother, underscoring how bonds of dependency were formed and favors were exchanged. As Roberto Schwarz (1977, 16–17) has pointed out, "favor is our quasi-universal form of mediation," in many ways masking the violence that permeated the deep-rooted system of slavery, for instance. Relations in the public sphere often intertwined with those of private networks.

Godparents, on the surface, were part of one's affective relations. If they offered sentimental advantages on the one hand, they also brought political and economic advantages on the other. This is to say nothing of the practices of dependence they created, in addition to obscuring the arbitrariness of clientelistic practices. For these very reasons (among others), such favors would then have to be returned in the future, often in the form of loyalties and financial contributions.

The story of Machado's parents also highlights the plights of many mixed-race families. As the grandson of slaves, though, he was born free. Naturally, the history of slavery had a significant impact on Brazil's Afro-descendants, forcing them to deal with such a past along with the obstacles they faced after attaining freedom.[2] This ultimately led to some black families that negotiated social mobility during Pedro II's reign to ignore their past, and to even redefine their skin color. Nonetheless, the renegotiation of one's skin color was not seen as a moral problem at the time. Lighter skin color, after all, has long been a marker of social agency in Brazil, aside from underscoring a strict social hierarchy that was itself only unofficially and informally lived.

LIFE IN THE ROYAL COURT

Machado was only one year old when, in 1840, the *Declaração da Maioridade* (Declaration of Adulthood) placed a fourteen-year-old boy on the Brazilian imperial throne. Our writer would eventually be part of that generation, which, being somewhat close in age to the young monarch, participated in the political culture of the Second Reign, itself controlled by the imperial palace. Although Machado did not move within the emperor's intimate circle, since they were separated by age, among other social factors, he did nonetheless attain the vaunted imperial patronage that effectively served to include or exclude representatives of the artistic and intellectual class.

Biographers generally argue that Machado avoided—as far as he could—living in Rio's outskirts in order to live in the court. He would also gradually begin mingling with the capital's literati circles, often frequenting, in the ides of 1855, Francisco de Paula Brito's bookstore. Brito was a well-known journalist and typographer as well as an established humanist who also sold pigs, tobacco rolls, and medicines. Bookstores were a scarce phenomenon during this period, and those that did exist had to be eclectic in order to survive as a business (Bastos 2008). Brito would also offer his library to host the meetings of the *Sociedade Petalógica*, where debates touched on topics as varied as politics, literature, culture, and gossip.

Machado in fact forged a relationship with that social stratum, which increasingly enjoyed the privileges of the Brazilian imperial capital with its public plazas, theaters, balls, and newspapers. This relationship was always ambivalent, however. If on the one hand, he made it a point to reside near these elegant spaces, on the other, he often critiqued the emergence of modernization that significantly characterized them. A notable example is his reflection on the substitution of the cabriolet for the tilbury, supposedly better adapted to the new and paved avenues of Rio de Janeiro: "There is the *Cabriolet*, yes, sir, said the black man that had come to the church of Saint Joseph to request the vicar anoint two corpses. Today's generation did not witness the exit of the *cabriolet* in Rio de Janeiro. They will also not know that the *cab* and the *tilbury* were once part of our plaza cars. The *cab* did not last long. The *tilbury*, prior to the other two, is promised a place in the city junkyard" (Assis 1990, 28). With the urbanization of the time, plantation owners and local elites began moving to the cities, enchanted by the new world of consumption and pavement. The mystique of Ouvidor Street was thus born, where store after store opened—clothing boutiques, florists, jewelers, and cigar vendors, along with restaurants. For the new elegant commerce, Direita Street—which blended fashion establishments with small warehouses and vulgar shops—no longer sufficed. The humble past of the streets, the odor of sewage, the slave-based urban labor, and the ocean smell all had to be left behind. In opposition to the limited commerce of yore, afternoon strolls, teatime in elegant cafés, and fancy clothing made of English and French fabrics quickly emerged. Ouvidor Street symbolized the desire to imitate the royal cultural life and boulevards of Europe while residing in the tropics.

Reading some of Machado's short stories, we get a sense of the frivolity and artificiality, the gap between reality and representation that characterized the city. His short story "Fulano" is arguably the most emblematic of this. The story is centered on Fulano Beltrão, a simple man whose social mobility and politics led to profound changes in his daily habits. One such habit became "showing off on Ouvidor Street." Another was the original way in which he mourned his wife's passing: "He shared his pain with the public; and if he buried his wife discreetly, he did not stop himself from ordering a magnificent mausoleum sculpted in Italy and exhibiting it on Ouvidor Street over the span of a month" (Assis 1989, 119).

Machado would also earn a living by writing for a few of Rio de Janeiro's newspapers, including the *Diário do Rio de Janeiro*, *O Jornal das Famílias*, and *Semana Ilustrada*. He slowly began making a name for himself, to the point that in 1865, he founded an artistic-literary organization called Arcádia Fluminense. Such sociability was very much in vogue at the time, and the organization became a place where young intellectuals would gather, discuss literature, and hold readings and other social events. At this juncture, Machado became publically known as a theater critic. In this way, he grew socially closer to imperial cultural circles, so much so that he was nominated assistant director of the *Diário Oficial* through Pedro II's intervention. Years later, near the end of the Empire in 1888, the monarch would name Machado an official of the Order of the Rose. It is also worth recalling Machado's promotion to the royal court's chief of staff on December 7, 1876, by Princess Isabel.

What is of interest here is that Machado was increasingly becoming involved in the restricted group of urban literati, which implied for him a lifestyle of moderation. This sort of transition is also evident in his residential movements across Rio's neighborhoods: he resided first in Catete and then Cosme Velho, the latter eventually lending him the nickname "Bruxo do Cosme Velho" (the Wizard of Cosme Velho).

Along with his moderated lifestyle—which conferred on him the reputation of a well-behaved writer vis-à-vis the emergent bohemian generation of the time—came a career as a public functionary. As a true legion of the empire, functionaries constituted a type of battalion of stable employment supported by the state. Machado's professional life became yet another example of personal proximity and literary distance. That is, if on the one hand his state employment ensured his societal existence among Rio de Janeiro's elites, he did not resist criticizing the profession that was becoming seen in the public sphere as an "inflated" (Chalhoub 2003) part of the State.

CLOSING AND OPENING CURTAINS: ABOLITION AND THE FIRST REPUBLIC

Machado's lifetime would not be characterized solely by tranquility. Following the Paraguayan War (1870), pressure to end slavery began taking up the nation's political, social, and cultural agenda. The issue inspired large rallies, recitals, and evenings of theater. The Paraguay conflict effectively marked the apex and the decline of the empire

(Carvalho and Schwarcz 1989). If at the beginning of the war, King Pedro II and his empire were cast as examples of civic diplomacy—"o voluntário número 1" (volunteer number one), as he was publically labeled—with the rising death toll and financial costs of the war, Pedro II's legacy grew increasingly tarnished. The public controversy over the war directly sparked the organization of groups openly opposed to the regime, particularly the Republican Party and the Abolitionist Movement, that would eventually spread across the country.

Machado seemed uninclined toward the nation's political realm, systematically turning down invitations to act as senator or delegate, claiming that he preferred to dedicate himself to literature. Nonetheless, this period was not without incident for Machado. With the abolition of slavery in the United States (1863) and Cuba (1866), Brazil was left isolated as the only nation of the Americas to maintain the internationally condemned institution.

Machado wrote little about slavery, the great contradiction of the Second Reign. Even though Pedro II abolished slavery for his domestic slaves, attempted to quell the controversy with the 1870 Law of Free Birth granting freedom to "enslaved wombs," and declared the Sexagenarian Law freeing any slave 65 or older in 1885—considered a conservative move even by his contemporaries—the complete demise of the institution was increasingly late in coming. Thus slavery and the empire became intimately bonded, on both the national and international stages. Although Machado does not openly rail against slavery, the institution is nonetheless portrayed in a particularly perverse light in his short story "Pai contra Mãe" (Father versus Mother 1966). In the story, an expecting father facing the impossibility of providing for his growing family turns to slave catching, a deeply stigmatized line of work even at the time. After a prolonged lack of success, he pursues, via wanted ads, a runaway female slave, eventually apprehending her. The slave, who is also expecting, ultimately loses the child. Machado closes the story with a memorable line delivered by the narrator, reflecting the perversity of slavery: "Not all babies have the luck to be born" (1966, 112).

While opposition to slavery and the empire began taking shape, it is worth noting that, as Brazil approached the official end of slavery, theories of social determinism and scientific racism gained increasing notoriety. Such discourses essentially articulated human difference not as a social matter, but as a biological fact. Theories inspired by Cesare Lombroso, Agassiz, Lapouge, and Gobineau were particularly successful at the time, and were responsible for transforming the concept of race into an essential and immutable fact. Worse than "pure races"—which may have been inferior, but at least predictable—were those that were products of miscegenation and therefore susceptible to all forms of degeneration.[3]

It should come as no surprise that individuals like Machado, from mixed-race families, would attempt to obfuscate their racial origins in public spaces. Ultimately, writers were not obliged to produce literature from the point of view of color or class origin. We must, instead, understand the limited possibilities and options afforded to people of color in a race-based society, in terms of both social mobility and social contestation.

It is, therefore, difficult to ignore Machado's skepticism in general, but particularly vis-à-vis the aforementioned theories of scientific racism and social determinism. A significant example would be his famous short story "O Alienista" (The Psychiatrist), originally published in 1882. The narrative is centered on the story of Simão Bacamarte, a noted psychiatrist who erects a psychiatric asylum (the "Casa Verde" or Green House) and eventually detains the entire city including his wife under suspicions of madness. He then releases all detainees and admits himself to the asylum, making himself his own object of scientific inquiry:

> It was decided. Simão Bacamarte bowed his head in a combination of happiness and sadness, more happy than sad. He proceeded to retire to the Green House. In vain, his friends and wife asked him to stay, telling him he was in a perfectly stable mental state. Neither pleas nor suggestions nor tears made him hesitate even for even a second.
>
> "This is a scientific matter," he said. "This is about a new science, and I am its first example. I have united, in my very person, both theory and practice."
>
> "Simão! Simão! My love!" his wife would say, her face washed with tears. But the famed doctor, his eyes fired by scientific conviction, closed his ears to his wife's pleas and gently pushed her away. Closing the door of the Green House, he began working on the study and cure of himself. (Assis 1882, 42, my translation)

We know that in the late nineteenth century, the "alienation" was considered a symptom of degeneration, most prevalent among the mixed-race population, according to the theories of racial determinism of the time. The issue was as public as it was controversial, so much so that in 1894, the medical doctor of the Bahia Tropical School published *As Raças Humanas e a Responsabilidade Penal no Brasil* (*The Human Races and Criminal Responsibility in Brazil*) proposing to separate penal codes for the nascent republic: one for whites and another for blacks—all in the name of science.

Machado, by scrutinizing scientific discourses of exclusion in the early 1880s, appeared to be ahead of his time.

As we can see, this was a period marked by the sociological emergence of various determinisms. The abolition of slavery in 1888 may have finally brought the promise of lawful and universal freedom, but in no way did it imply equality. The very notion of a universal humanity for all was ultimately compromised by scientific discourses that brought forth new forms of social exclusion.

THE OLD EMPEROR'S EXIT AND BEGINNING OF CUSTÓDIO'S REPUBLIC

The Ilha Fiscal Ball on November 9, 1889, came to be known as the monarchy's last event before the rise of the republic. In *Esau and Jacob* [published in 1904], Machado recalls the procession of royal gala uniforms, decorated blazers, and the finest dresses through the court. Machado was not the only writer to address the empire's last breath with such sarcasm. Many journalists of the time chronicled the moment as one of nervousness within court life. Many rumors pertaining to that night circulated in the nation's newspapers. One stated that Pedro II tripped upon entering the ball, joking, "The monarchy trips, but does not fall." The monarch was ultimately wrong: the court was truly about to fall.

On November 15, a coup d'état led by the nation's displeased military would overthrow the empire, bringing to a close a nearly century-long political experience. By that time, the monarchy had grown ideologically isolated, having lost its last group of supporters, concentrated among the coffee growers of western São Paulo state.

Despite national dissatisfaction, the emperor maintained his popularity and his place in the national imaginary as a good father (to the country), almost as a gray-bearded grandfather whose thoughts were largely outside of politics. Nonetheless, the harsh political facts that characterized the Empire could no longer be ignored, and quickly dissipated the emperor's popular mystique. Having learned of the coup, Pedro II attempted to negotiate with the military and the republicans, but promptly abandoned the court in the early morning hours.

The republic was officially declared, but was far from being fully consolidated. The emperor was uncertain of his continuity in power until the last minute, as were his confidants. We can once again turn to Machado for political perspective, namely the hilarious moment in *Esau and Jacob* involving Custódio, the owner of the Confeitaria do Império (Confectionery of the Empire). Mr. Custódio had just ordered a new signboard for his confectionery when he learned of the coup: "Only a few letters had been painted—the word *Confeitaria* and the letter *d*. The letter *o* and the word *Império* were still only traced in chalk" (138).[4] To his great despair, the painter ignored his request to change the planned lettering. Confronted with the need of a new signboard, Custódio sought the advice of Counselor Ayres, who suggested the name "Confeitaria da República" (Confectionery of the Republic). They feared, however, that, in a few months, there would be yet another coup and the name of the establishment would once again have to change. The counselor then suggested a name that could apply to any regime: "Confeitaria do Governo" (Confectionery of the Government). After further thought, they concluded that all governments have their antagonists, and that such opposition could express their political dissatisfaction by destroying the signboard. Ayres then suggested leaving the original name—"Confectionery of the Empire"—and merely adding "founded in 1860" in order to dispel any doubts as to the establishment's origins. The owner, however, felt that such a detail would connect him too strongly to a foregone past, which in that era of modernity would not be good for business. Finally, they opted for the name of the owner: "Custódio's Confectionery." The two thus concluded their complex conversation: "Money would be spent on substituting one word for another, *Custódio* instead of *Império*, but revolutions always incur costs" (142).

Revolutions "are laborious and incur costs" (Assis 1988, 142). More than a joke, the historical moment was one of collective concern and agitation. The republic emerged with the promise of universal citizenship, social inclusion, and new models for greater political participation. However, the reality was very different: the coup had been orchestrated by an elite, as connected to the rural economy as to the court; theories of social determinism deeply compromised the utopia of equality; and local revolts would soon take over the streets. The coup promised a redemptive future, but the reality was, in its many facets, dystopian, much like Custódio's signboard.

SECOND ACT WITH THE BRAZILIAN ACADEMY OF LETTERS: FINALLY A REPUBLIC OF LETTERS

While real changes were slow to arrive, others became part of everyday life in Rio de Janeiro. The substitution of terms—the imperialists leave and the republicans enter; "federal capital" replaces "court"—was a source of estrangement and curiosity among the public. Machado is once again a reliable thermometer of the period, pointing to the artificiality of the situation:

> There is a vacancy in the cabinet of the Federal Capital.... I say "Federal Capital" as a simple way of describing this city, without its proper name, due to it being the city's constitutionally adopted name. Before November 15, people would say "Court," even though the court was really only the emperor's palace and its respective personnel; the city nonetheless retained its name, Rio de Janeiro, which is neither beautiful nor precise, but it was a name, Guanabara, *carioca*, were only used in poetry.... Our only hope is that the capital can be remade. What would naturally follow would be the return of our old name or the decree of another. (Assis 1892a, n.p., my translation)

As always, more than simply reiterating what was already known, Machado, by means of sarcasm, showed himself to be ahead of the times. He criticized the new republican hero, Tiradentes,[5] and humorously described the quotidian of new titles, as well as shifts in vocabulary. The supposed substitution for the French term "citizen" coexists here with imperial titles of the past:

> Everything loses part of its greatness. I met two old and esteemed neighbors who had their daily artistic merriment. One was a knight of the Order of the Rose, for service in the Paraguayan War; the other was a lieutenant in the national guard reserves, to which he dutifully lent his services. They would play chess and fall asleep between moves. They would wake each other up in this manner: "My dear major!" "Ready, Commander!" Sometimes they would alternate: "My dear commander!" "Here I go, Major." Everything loses certain status. (Assis 1892b, n.p., my translation)

It was through poignant reflections such as this that Machado truly became a figure of and for his time, as well as a sort of symbol of a particular place and its historical projection. It is no wonder, then, that in the early years of the republic, Machado aspired to partake in a different brand of politics: literary politics. In 1897, inspired by the French Academy, Machado—alongside other intellectuals like Medeiros e Albuquerque, Lúcio de Mendonça, and Joaquim Nabuco—founded the Academia Brasileira de Letras (Brazilian Academy of Letters). The ultimate goal of the academy was, as Alessandra El Far argues, to worship Brazilian culture and especially national literature (El Far 2004).

The initiative of creating the academy came from Lúcio de Mendonça, but the preparatory meetings that began on December 15, 1896, were presided over by Machado, elected and acclaimed by his fellow founders. The meetings were held at the *Revista Brasileira*'s editorial office. There, the academy's statutes were approved and Machado was elected its "perpetual president." The famed writer thus became an assiduous academic, leading the presidency for a span of 10 years until his death in 1908 at the age of 69. Machado would, in fact, become a symbol of the institution, less a brand of literature than a type of posture.

It is said that in 1901, he created the "Panelinha" (literally small pot), a sort of brotherhood where writers and artists would meet for friendly get-togethers. Legend has it that the name of the brotherhood, which even today is a metaphor for a closed group, was created during those meetings, since guests were served from a silver pot (Matos 1939; Fonseca 1968). True or not, the formation of the group, which distinguished itself through closely moderated customs, represented a break from another group led by Emílio de Menezes. Through this counterposition, Menezes's group began referring to itself as bohemian. We know, nonetheless, that dichotomies are merely positions and that nothing is naturally fixed. Such identities are constructed and embodied as relations between binary oppositions.

What matters is that Machado was experiencing his time; as he deconstructed it, he also impacted its formation. Moreover, in the so-called second phase of his oeuvre, he denounced in many ways the quid pro quo of ideas and the dissonance between our modern culture and the realities of a slave-based society. Such a gap created a void and Machado was masterful in denouncing, in his own way, the emptiness of that void, without simply mirroring the historical context.

It is no mere coincidence that Rubião, the memorable character from *QuincasBorba* (1891), felt compelled to trade his slave for a French or Spanish cook, or that the protagonist of "Father versus Mother" was ultimately humiliated in persecuting a runaway pregnant slave. It is these minor and great improprieties, these dissonances between representation and realities, this ambiguity between the lie of liberal thought in Brazil and its painful truth that become Machado's inspiration. He was, after all, as complex as the greater historical period of his time. Despite beginning his literary trajectory as a combative journalist, he would go on to write verses for royal elites. At times, he would receive imperial medals and honorariums while also founding an institution in his own way, equally marked by an elite profile and a particular social composition.

We cannot, nonetheless, demand from a literary character, anything more than his time. His literature is written in a manner that is very different from the ornamental approach to literary production. Through various series of displacements within his plots, Machado was able to create an intellectual experience that opened new approaches and interrogations of the ideas that affected his present.

What I have endeavored here, in a few pages, is merely the tracing of the historical stage that Machado inhabited. In this space, he made himself into a fundamental and inescapable tool for anyone interested in understanding what Tom Jobim later called "the enigma named Brazil."

NOTES

1. I suggest Baxhandal (2006), who critiques the notion of "influence."
2. Maria Helena Machado shows, for example, how the freeing of slaves through the "Lei Áurea" (Golden Law) became known as "the 13th of May." See Machado 1999.
3. I have explored this question in greater detail in Schwarcz 1987.
4. Translator's note: All translations of Machado 1988 are my own.
5. For more information on Tiradentes as a national hero, see Carvalho 1999 and Murilo 1999.

REFERENCES

Assis, Joaquim Maria Machado de. 1882. O Alienista. In *Papéis Avulsos*. Rio de Janeiro: Lombaerts.

Assis, Joaquim Maria Machado de. 1892a. "24 July 1892." *A Semana*. http://www.machadodeassis.ufsc.br/obras/cronicas/CRONICA,%20A%20semana,%201892.htm#C1892

Assis, Joaquim Maria Machado de. 1892b. "24 April 1892." *A Semana*. http://www.machadodeassis.ufsc.br/obras/cronicas/CRONICA,%20A%20semana,%201892.htm#C1892

Assis, Joaquim Maria Machado de. 1966. Father versus mother. In *The psychiatrist and other stories*. Trans. Helen Caldwell, 101–112. Berkeley: University of California Press.

Assis, Joaquim Maria Machado de. 1988. *Esaú e Jacó*. Rio de Janeiro: Livraria Garnier.

Assis, Joaquim Maria Machado de. 1989. Fulano. In *Papéisavulsos*, 118–120. Rio de Janeiro: Livraria Garnier.

Assis, Joaquim Maria Machado de. 1990. *Relíquias da Casa Velha*. Rio de Janeiro: Livraria Garnier.

Bastos, Dau. 2008. *Machado de Assis: Num recanto, um mund ointeiro*. Rio de Janeiro: Garamond.

Baxandall, Michael. 2006. *Padrões de intenção*. São Paulo: Companhia das Letras.

Carvalho, José Murilo de. 1999. *A formação das almas*. São Paulo: Companhia das Letras.

Carvalho, José Murilo de, and Lila Schwarcz. 1989. *As barbas do Imperador*. São Paulo: Companhia das Letras.

Chalhoub, Sidney. 2003. *Machado de Assis, historiador*. São Paulo: Companhia das Letras.

El Far, Alessandra. 2004. *Páginas de Sensação*. São Paulo: EditoraCompanhia das Letras.

Fonseca, Gondin da. 1968. *Machado de Assis e o hipopótamo*. Coleção Brasileira de Ouro, vol. 924. Rio de Janeiro: Ed. de Ouro.

Ginzburg, Carlo. 2005. *O queijo e osvermes: O cotidiano e as idéias de um moleiro perseguido pela Inquisição*. São Paulo: Companhia das Letras.

Machado, Maria Helena. 1999. Teremos grandes desastres se não houver providências enérgicas. In *História do Império*, 371–373. Rio de Janeiro: Record.

Matos, Mário. 1939. *Machado de Assis: O homem e a obra, os personagens explicam o autor*. In *Brasiliana*; vol. 153 of *Biblioteca Pedagógica Brasileira*.Companhia editora nacional.

Murilo, José. 1999. *A formação das almas*. São Paulo: Companhia das Letras.

Schwarcz, Lília. 1987. *Espetáculo das raças*. São Paulo: Companhia das Letras.

Schwarz, Roberto. 1977. As ideiasfora do lugar. In *Ao vencedor as batatas: Forma literária e processo social nos inícios do romance brasileiro*, 16–17. São Paulo: Livraria Duas Cidades, Editora 34.

CHAPTER 3

Machado de Assis and Realism: A Literary Genealogy

Hans Ulrich Gumbrecht

Realism in Brazilian literature, from a philosophically argued position, can be seen as a series of five novels, published between 1881 and 1908, and all written, after a good number of poems, stories, and other novels, by the same author, Joaquim Maria Machado de Assis. Machado was born on June 21, 1839, in Rio de Janeiro, where he died on September 29, 1908—a few months after the last of his five novels appeared. From an aesthetic point of view, those texts are considered to be the early culminating moment within the historical emergence of Brazilian literature as a national discourse, within the "formation of Brazilian literature" (Candido 1997), to use a key concept from the local debates about literary historiography, launched in 1975 by Antônio Cândido, the undisputed figure of authority in this field.

Much of the international prestige of Brazilian literature hinges on the "classical" works of Machado who, for example, is the only Brazilian writer included by Harold Bloom in his canon of the one hundred all-time literary geniuses and whom Susan Sontag frequently mentioned as one of her favorite authors. Despite such particularly visible appreciation and translations (some of them outstanding) into many Western languages, Machado de Assis's work has never reached the same intense popularity among global literary readerships as other South American authors of the nineteenth and twentieth centuries, most of whom wrote in Spanish.

H.U. Gumbrecht (✉)
Stanford University, Stanford, California, USA

© The Editor(s) (if applicable) and The Author(s) 2016
L. Aidoo, D.F. Silva (eds.), *Emerging Dialogues on Machado de Assis*, DOI 10.1057/978-1-137-54174-1_3

Why Machado's five most canonized novels should be subsumed under the concept of "realism" is not an easy question to answer. The everyday usage of this noun, referring to a supposed closeness between artworks and reality as their environment, does not stand the test of even the mildest philosophical critique—because both what is considered to be real and what can be seen, in an artwork, as corresponding to or close to reality, have been proven to be variable over time. Rather than as a metahistorically and transculturally valid concept, therefore, it seems adequate to use the word "realism" as a name, referring to a specific body of texts (and artworks) from different Western cultures that largely belongs to the nineteenth century. More precisely, the term refers to a body of texts (and artworks) that documents an unprecedented concern about their closeness to reality, both in their sometimes obsessively broad descriptions of the social quotidian (in this very sense, Balzac wanted to be "the secretary of French society") and in their lingering doubts about whether this task could be achieved (the position occupied by Flaubert and his work in the larger historical context).

But what would such a literary concern with reality have to do with an objectively existing extratextual reality itself? In his book *The Theory of the Novel*, written in 1914–15, Hungarian philosopher Georg Lukács gave an answer that has remained present in contemporary discussions. His starting point was Hegel's conviction that the ancient Greek epic had provided, for many generations, a homogeneous image of their world, allowing them to experience the world as an existential home. From postmedieval times on, by contrast, Lukács continued, the "productivity of the (human) spirit" (Lukács 1963, 33) through "work and investigation," had made the world "larger" and "more complex" (*reicher* in the original German text) (Lukács 1963, 62) to a degree that excluded the possibility of finding an adequate literary form—and the subsequent feeling of finding a home in the epic. This impression of an inevitable tension between reality and its descriptions, according to Lukács, was the condition for the novel's emergence as a dominant genre, a genre that reacted to the new world complexity with a general instability and with specific experiments in its textual forms.

For all of its brilliance and well-deserved influence, Lukács's approach shares a Hegelian premise that many intellectuals today have come to judge as epistemologically and ontologically problematic. It is the assumption that a relation between world and text, between world complexity and textual form, can exist at all, and can be judged as adequate or inadequate. Due to our doubts, we are now confronted with the challenge to find an alternative historical explanation for the (often productive) formal instability that we observe in realistic novels throughout the nineteenth century. During that time, one could argue, the novel as a literary genre was overcome, from outside, by a concern that had first presented itself roughly 200 years earlier as a philosophical problem and had then progressively conquered cultural life and even the pragmatic everyday business of many professions. It was the double question of whether the human mind was sufficiently equipped to produce an appropriate picture of the world by which it was surrounded and of which it was a part, and whether there was a position available from which the problem of representation could be solved, or at least be analyzed. If Kant, and to a certain degree Hegel also, had been struggling with this agenda and had reached altogether optimistic philosophical answers, the chronologically earliest authors of European realism arrived at equivalent literary positions. In many different ways, Balzac's *La Comédie humaine* [The Human Comedy], for example, staged the problem and often led, quite literally, to visions of society that were supposed to be truthful because they were visions attributed, by the third-person narrator, to morally impeccable protagonists. Stendhal produced a similar "effect of reality," mostly by inserting quotes from philosophical and literary authorities as a commentary to his descriptions and plot narratives, whereas in Flaubert's novels the different worldviews of different protagonists appeared to be centrifugal, and thus further undermined the hope that an adequate representation of social life might be possible at all.

The point of convergence for all these varieties of literary realism— a point of convergence, too, between Lukács's "Theory" and our alternative historical explanation of literary realism—lies in the observation that the primary epistemological challenge led to an impressive variety of experiments in textual form. As long as we continue to worry about the human capacity for "adequately capturing the reality outside of our mind" (1963, 78), we will probably associate such literary forms with a sense of reality. In nineteenth-century Brazilian literature, and even within his own work, Machado de Assis's five canonical novels stand out because they very actively participate in this specific tendency of formal experimentation—although it is not obvious at all from the available sources that the author was interested in the epistemological challenges that had led to the rise of the realistic novel in Europe.

In order to understand and appreciate Machado's realism as a distinctively early moment of culmination within Brazilian literature, a larger panorama of the preceding national culture is required. Different from most other former colonies, especially in South America, where the early nineteenth-century threshold of political independence marks the transition from colonial to national literatures, Brazil's independence occurred as a protracted process of gaining distance from Portugal in the political form of an empire under the Portuguese Bragança monarchy. Until the declaration of the Brazilian Republic in 1889, which consolidated the abolition of slavery as a legal institution (and even after this moment of positive discontinuity), economic, social, and cultural change occurred at a very slow pace and without any incisive events. Within the empire—and even with its second monarch, Dom Pedro II (since 1831), who saw himself as an enlightened and, at least from an intellectual viewpoint, constitutional authority—Brazilian society continued to be dominated by the relation between wealthy landowners and their slaves, while the Brazilian economy was based on the export of agricultural products (mainly coffee), gold, and precious stones. Between the landowners and the slaves, a middle class slowly emerged, especially in Rio de Janeiro and São Paulo, whose members had neither political rights nor economic strength and thus remained dependent on favors from the more privileged families, while middle-class behavior was shaped by a traditionally patriarchal mentality.[1] At the same time, ideas and discourses originating in the Enlightenment and in the bourgeois revolutions were circulating in imperial Brazil but, until the late nineteenth century, there was neither a social basis nor a political framework within which they could have produced any transformative consequences.

For all of these reasons, Brazilian literature as a national literature began to emerge slowly and almost belatedly within its continental context, and it mostly did so in several waves and schools of romantic poetry during the fourth and fifth decades of the nineteenth century. One of the few romantic novelists was José de Alencar (1829–77), a friend of Machado de Assis and a lawyer by training (like many of the early literary authors in Brazil), whose works such as *O Guarani* (1857) and *Iracema* (1865) are still on every reading list for academic introductions to Brazilian literature. Both of them combine three components: the flavor of melodrama and love narratives from the historically romantic legacy; a level of ongoing commentary and interpretation through which the plots tended to become allegories of Brazil's precolonial past and future (Iracema, the name of the main female protagonist, symbolizes America); and a set of liberal ideals that permeated the allegorical and mythological layer. Roberto Schwarz, one of the most widely read historians of Brazilian literature, emphasizes the quality of Alencar's descriptions, in particular of landscapes (1977). At the same time, he believes, according to the critical tradition founded by Georg Lukács, that the free-floating status of the liberal discourse in mid-nineteenth-century Brazil was the reason why Alencar just recycled its concepts and structures, never engaging in any formal experiments or innovations. In other words, the allegorical level of Alencar's novel emerged too smoothly and flawlessly for them to ever become associated with the literary realism of their time.

The four early novels by Machado de Assis, *Ressurreição* [Resurrection] (1872), *A mão e a luva* [The Hand and the Glove] (1874), *Helena* (1876), and *Iaiá Garcia* (1878), share this distance vis-à-vis all stylistic and structural innovation, while their thematic range differs from Alencar's. In the descriptive passages and in the narrative development, they concentrate on the affluent middle class of Rio de Janeiro. Nothing tropical, exotic, or political, no landscapes, pre-colonial cultures, or scandalous effects of slavery are mentioned, and the logic of the narratives mostly seems to correspond to the moral constraints of the prevailing patriarchal mentality. During a very early stage of his life, Machado had been exposed to the patriarchal layer of contemporary Brazilian society. He was the son of a mulatto wall painter and an Azorean Portuguese washerwoman in a house owned by Dona Maria José de Mendonça Barro Perreira, the widow of a wealthy senator, who became Machado's godmother. After her death, the sickly child's upbringing and the adolescent's professional trajectory career as a typographer's apprentice, a journalist, and later as a literary author finally brought him back to the dignified middle class. It thus seems altogether plausible that, different from his friend Alencar, Machado was committed to the abolitionist cause in many of his early writings destined for the emerging public sphere, while his literary texts remained distant from the political tensions and battles as well as from the contemporary, rather ideological concept of realism embraced by not a few contemporary authors. He was an honest admirer of the enlightened monarch Dom Pedro II, and this attitude may have contributed to earning him a reputation and status as an outstanding national author during his lifetime.

The only remarkable discontinuity in Machado's life concerns the form of his literary work and separates *Iaiá Garcia*, the novel published in 1878, from *Memórias Postúmas de Brás Cubas*, which appeared in 1881. There are no evident events or reasons that could explain this sudden change in his writing. Toward the end of a note directed to "the reader," Brás Cubas, the title protagonist of the 1881 novel, as if in passing, mentions that his "Memories" were "elaborated here, in the other world" (2006, 16), the world after death. He adds that he would well be able to explain how he achieved this way of communicating with his posthumous readers but renounces to do so because such an explanation would turn out "hugely extensive," without being "necessary for the understanding of the work" (16). In the previous (and first) paragraph, Brás Cubas refers to the "free form" of the eighteenth-century British novelist Lawrence Sterne as a decisive influence, although he claims to have "added" some nuances of "pessimism" (16). These and a number of other elements from the intrafictional prologue, all of them heterogeneous without being in tension or even in contradiction, produce an impression of narrative instability and even a nervousness that not only accompanies the entire plot of this novel but increasingly captures the reader's fascination, to a point where the zigzagging content line of this fictional autobiography becomes secondary. Its ending is undramatically pessimistic. If the novel started with a dedication to "the worm that was first eroding the cold flesh of my corpse" (17), its final sentence expresses Brás Cubas's relief about having remained childless, which means that he does not "transmit to any creature the legacy of our misery" (176), referring to an essential and generalized human misery rather than to the fictional Brás Cubas's individual fate.

In his four subsequent novels, Machado maintained and probably even augmented this mood of narrative volatility without ever cultivating any stable formula, which, on a more abstract level, became part of the same instability. Quincas Borba, from 1889, according to an introductory note (this time signed by the real author) is the story of Rubião, an "existentially shipwrecked" protagonist who already had a short appearance in *Memórias Póstumas de Brás Cubas*, a "beggar, a poverty stricken heir, an inventor of a philosophy" (2006, 137). The name Quincas Borbas belongs both to the parody of a philosopher who tries to combine positivism and high-flying ethical values, and to the philosopher's dog. By virtue of taking care of the dog, Rubião becomes the heir of Quincas Borbas's philosophy and fortune while a cynical third-person narrator tells his life story instead of him doing it himself. This third-person narrator finishes the novel by mentioning the dog's death and by "anticipating" the reader's question as to whether the novel's title refers to the philosopher or to the dog. But he refuses to give an answer, encouraging the reader to mourn both the dog and his master, to cry and to smile because "seen from the stars there is no way to distinguish between human tears and human laughter" (2013, 477).

Dom Casmurro from 1899 is another fictional autobiography, this time told during the protagonist's lifetime and without any prefatory remark attributed to either the author or his hero. Here, the impression of narrative instability results from the hero's (and fictional author's) growing obsession with his wife's possible infidelity. A son who resembles the narrator's friend triggers it, and endless critical speculations have been wasted trying to figure out whether Dom Casmurro's suspicion is justified or not—although it was obviously the intention behind Machado's narrative strategy to make any clear answer impossible. There is a question more worthwhile to ask because it concerns Machado's tendency to blur the difference between his own and his protagonists' worlds. During the author's lifetime a rumor existed that a son of José Alencar was indeed Machado's, whose otherwise happy marriage with a woman from the Portuguese upper class had remained childless. But for a lack of biographical information, rather than due to a narrative strategy, this question, too, will forever remain unresolved. Finally, in *Esaú e Jacó* (1904), a story of twin brothers who become passionate political enemies during the years of transition between empire and republic, the Counselor Aires is introduced—a retired Brazilian diplomat and third-person narrator whose posthumous papers Machado claims to publish in two installments—so to speak, as his final novel from 1908 will feature the same Aires as an autobiographical narrator.

Machado's last novel, *Memorial de Aires*, published in 1908 shortly before his own death, brings the changing configurations of narrative instability both to a final extreme point and to an atmosphere of harmonious melancholia. The entries in Aires's diary are irregular and of different lengths. He frequently apologizes for not writing about events or conditions that his reader might be particularly interested in, and he has admittedly no reason or good excuse for these gaps. Aires seems to increasingly focus on, the fate of his friends, the Aguiares, another childless couple in the well-to-do middle class of late imperial and early republican Rio. Aires himself is childless: "I have a wife under the earth of Vienna, and none of my children ever emerged from the cradle of Nothingness. I am alone, absolutely alone" (1988, 104). The Aguiares, by contrast, seem to be lucky enough to enjoy "two quasi adoptive children" (90), older adolescents: Tristão, the son of friends who have decided to spend a larger portion of their lives in Portugal, and Fidélia, a young widow from a good family who cannot return to her parents' home after the death of her husband because her parents had never approved of their marriage. Both names are evidently ironic because loquacious Tristão (meaning "very sad") never feels any sadness, whereas Fidélia (meaning "loyal") forgets about all her promises of posthumous fidelity as soon as she encounters Tristão. Fidélia and Tristão get married in their adoptive parents' home, and the wedding is a day of great happiness for the Aguiares. Soon, however, the young couple leaves under the pretext of meeting Tristão's true parents, and only a few weeks later, he will send the adoptive parents a letter confessing that he has decided to stay in Portugal to pursue a political career.

The novel—and the trajectory of Machado's literary work—ends with a scene in which Counselor Aires goes to the Aguiares's house and ends up deciding not to talk because he finds them on their porch "melancholic of their own melancholia" (the Portuguese word translated here by "melancholia" is *saudade*, related to the Latin *solitudo*, "lonesomeness") (1988, 174). But shortly before this concluding moment, a few days before Tristão and Fidélia's wedding, Aires can no longer repress the certainty that he, the retired old widower, has fallen in love with the beautiful young widow: "Aires, my friend, confess that, when you heard Tristão talk about the pain of not being loved, you felt a certain pleasure that neither lasted long nor ever came back. You did not wish her for yourself but you would not want her to be passionate about him; explain this to yourself if you can—but you cannot" (171). What this novel makes apparent for its readers, more through the narrative form than by explicit descriptions and interpretations, is a mood of being distant—distant from the fulfillment of individual desire—but distant also from the European world that, in the late nineteenth century, still appears to be the true center of life. In more subtle ways than other Brazilian novelists of his time, like Lima Barreto or Aluísio Azevedo, Machado's narrative form thus also preserves for us early twenty-first-century readers a value of historical documentation. This realistic value, however, is not identical with what I am referring to as the literary realism of his work.

Given that the concern with grasping reality, as it had emerged in Western culture since the late eighteenth century, has endured until the present day, it is well possible to apply the concept of realism to later texts in all national literatures that have struggled to offer solutions to the lasting problem by means different from nineteenth-century realism's experiments with narrative form. In Brazil, still during Machado's lifetime, Euclides da Cunha (1866–1909) used discursive techniques and techniques of documentation adopted from the contemporary state of the natural sciences to describe a revolt of masses excluded from Brazilian society and its brutal repression by the national military. After multiple newspaper essays and diaries covering these events, *Os Sertões* (1902), his attempt at an objective description, turned into a manifesto of compassion and a pledge for political change. Nothing could have been further from Machado's playful instability than this gesture of objectivity and the pathos of existential seriousness with which Euclides was writing. For different reasons, the same is true for the realistic discourse in the northeastern Brazilian novel of the 1930s and authors like Rachel de Queirós, Jorge Amado, José Lins do Rego, or Graciliano Ramos.

With João Guimarães Rosa (1908–67), the great Brazilian novelist of the mid-twentieth century, the genre was overcome by a deeply transformed dimension and ambition of form. His *Grande Sertão: Veredas*, published in 1956, renders the landscape and the tough life in the country's interior, far away from the big modern cities of the Atlantic coastline. Antônio Cândido, Luiz Costa Lima, and, from a Marxist basis, Roberto Schwarz, the great Brazilian critics of our time, have all made it clear that Guimarães Rosa's text presupposes and further develops a profound transformation of Western literary writing, a transformation emblematically condensed in James Joyce's novels *Ulysses* (1922) and *Finnegan's Wake* (1939). The necessarily metonymical way of describing this literary innovation highlights the creation of a lexically and syntactically different new language (full of neologisms and word plays, truly difficult to read and perhaps impossible to translate) that was supposed to emerge from a direct confrontation with reality, with the material world that wanted to skip or to bracket all historically specific and socially constructed cultural worlds. Ultimately, this new language would reach a degree of convergence with the advanced tradition of nineteenth-century literary realism because they both sprang from the intuition that none of the available discourses could do justice to reality. Different from Machado's classical novels, however, the discourse of *Grande Sertão: Veredas* is neither ironic nor playful. Nor does it fully correspond to the Spanish Latin American gesture of magical realism, where elements and effects heterogeneous to institutionalized views of reality are seamlessly included in literary descriptions.

And yet, in spite of the double discursive discontinuity vis-à-vis Euclides da Cunha and João Guimarães Rosa, there is one level on which Machado's novels have been a foundational legacy for Brazilian literature as a national literature. They have elevated its texts to a level of aesthetic quality by which they became a potential part of world literature. This potential, however, still awaits redemption through an intense international resonance and recognition.

NOTE

1. For more on favor and *clientelismo*, see Lília Moritz Schwarcz's historical introduction to this volume.

REFERENCES

Assis, Machado de. 1988. *Memorial de Aires*. Rio de Janeiro: Livraria Garnier.
Assis, Machado de. 2006. *Memórias póstumas de Brás Cubas*. São Paulo: Editora Ática.
Assis, Machado de. 2013. *Quincas Borba*. Rio de Janeiro: Obliq Press.
Candido, Antonio. 1997. *Formação da literatura brasileira*, 8th ed. Belo Horizonte: Editora Itaia.
Lukács, György. 1963. *The theory of the novel: A historico-philosophical essay on the forms of great epic literature*. London: Merlin Press.

CHAPTER 4

Machado de Assis and Pascal

Pedro Meira Monteiro

When referring to Pascal, Brazilian poet, essayist, and cultural critic Augusto Meyer recalls the Muslim roots of his beliefs. Here, the critic describes medieval poet Abu'l al-Ma'arri in terms that might well suit Machado de Assis: "In contrast with plodding apologetic reasoning, the words of the poet are as lightweight as a murmur, lasting no longer than a sigh. We feel that this tranquility bears the light of an ironical smile—the inner light of a blind man defying the gloom of the world" (2008, 83).

But let us set blind writers and the apologetic tones of Pascal's writings aside, turning to the idea that in order to understand the "light" of that ironical smile, one ought to evaluate how the author illuminates his characters. What do these portraits reveal, and what do they hide?

There is an art of the portrait in Machado's works. The author uses the medium to cast an uncertain light on his characters, allowing him to both say and not say, affirm and just as quickly cast doubt. The topic is as old as the sun for those who study Machado. But it may be worthwhile to return to it as we consider Machado's Pascalian inspirations.

This is not the place for a synthesis of what has already been said about Machado and Pascal. That task would force us to return to the insights of Lúcia Miguel Pereira (1936) and, of course, the key study on the topic by

---

Translated by Flora Thomson-DeVeaux

P.M. Monteiro (✉)
Princeton University, Princeton, New Jersey, USA

© The Editor(s) (if applicable) and The Author(s) 2016
L. Aidoo, D.F. Silva (eds.), *Emerging Dialogues on Machado de Assis*, DOI 10.1057/978-1-137-54174-1_4

Afrânio Coutinho (1959), winding up at Alfredo Bosi and the more recent rediscovery of Machado's moralist wellspring. These reflections lend a broad scope to the theme of the intersections between Pascal's Jansenism and the despair of the Brazilian writer, demonstrating just how relevant and critically productive Machado's observation in a letter to Joaquim Nabuco—that Pascal was never read "out of distraction"—remains (Assis 1997, 939).[1]

Nor do I intend to delve into the countless interpretations of Machado's pessimism, suggestive of rich parallels that flow into authors such as Schopenhauer and Leopardi. Rather than restating or revising the topic, I would like to outline a few reflections on the fount of French moralism, including Pascal, from which Machado seems to be drinking when he cuts down the notion of autonomy or the apparent integrity of the subject. A mature Machado will cast a doubting eye on that integrity, when not beholding it with a sarcasm that is both powerful and subtle, posted behind the diaphanous veil of his irony.

I should say that the discussion of this fount does not imply a new consideration of the philosophy of Machado de Assis. The analyses of historians and sociologists, as well as literary criticism based in sociology, have already shown how Machado is constantly engaging with the philosophical trends of his time. With that in mind, however, we must recall that human autonomy is not an abstraction, nor is Machado a philosopher in the strict sense of the word. Sapping the foundations of a conception of humans as sovereign masters of themselves and their actions may, at first blush, seem a philosophical task. But it is also a Machadian way of establishing a truly ideological critique, forging a text that reveals unspeakable desires and drives hidden beneath the noblest actions and their ostensible motivations, often opaque to the subject (or to society itself) as they may be. It is as if the author were sketching portraits of what is not apparent precisely because that is what escapes the perception and understanding of those who restrict their attention to the surface of speech and gestures.

I shall take portraits, then, as my starting point. They are curious objects in and of themselves. Though they seek to capture a tiny moment—a snapshot, in photographic terms—they ultimately portray a duration. This is an interesting debate in the field of photography (with which Machado was not unfamiliar), because duration has to do with what can be captured in motion, what the portraitist is able to or wishes to capture. It is in the duration that something can be captured.

The portraitist's desire is a vast topic, however. In the mature Machado's prose, the narrator's desire is often difficult to locate; it may be diffuse, elusive, frequently attenuated by a standoffish tone. That attenuation makes the issue of absenteeism even more interesting, situating the question, "What does Machado de Assis want?" in terms that are both unresolvable and ripe for critical examination. There is, however, a desire sprung of the narrator—just as in the duration there is something of the photographer's will—that sets off the camera in response to a curiosity that is boundless but sparked by something that will find itself in focus, the ultimate proof of an attempt (so often in vain) to capture the sought-after object.

But desire is not the exclusive province of the portraitist. Even when a portrait is static, it contains—whatever the materials of its execution—the circulation of some desire. Fidélia, Capitu, Helena, Bento, and even Brás Cubas (a more complicated case) are all, at some point, caught in the act of beholding their desire, captured in the portrait. It would be reasonable to suppose that some drive overtakes them, or may be ever poised to overtake them. This dizzying desire that readers can only begin to make out ultimately makes them less static.

As an exercise in clarification, think of a canonical painting, a portrait so iconic that it practically begs for a Duchampian moustache. But some circumspection is due here: I am referring to Rembrandt's series of self-portraits. We know that this sequence is representative of a variety of conquests within Italian Renaissance painting, without which Flemish painting simply cannot be understood. There is chiaroscuro here, and the perspective that allows the subject of the portrait to emerge and come close to the spectator, as well as a certain imposing aspect to the man—a modern man who seems pleased to find himself free from the allegorical frames (and frameworks) of the Middle Ages. Rembrandt is cut loose from the heavens; hence the fundamental pride underpinning the subject, which exerts such fascination for Pascal and Machado. But Rembrandt is also a man who gazes at us. We are left with a question that is both simple and complex: what do we see in Rembrandt's gaze? What can we make out in those pupils? What does that inimitable mass of hues evoke?

Everything is there. Everything that we intuit as the motives of the subject, what we suppose to be his inner world, the private sea of passions and sentiments that drive them, their designs and their failures lie in that gaze upon which we gaze.

But what can this teach us about Machado? And why Pascal?

The interplay of the static nature of the portrait and those elements that assume or suggest movement can teach us plenty about the art of these two authors, understood here as portraitists.

Wherever there is that inner movement, there is also an unknown entity. After all, more or less tumultuous as it may be, we can glimpse in the portrait some movement of the subject, containing something that is often beyond what we can describe, beyond what pencil or brush can suggest, beyond what the viewer can understand, and beyond the understanding of the first person to behold any character—to wit, the author. The opacity of Machado's characters, their degree of allegorical potential notwithstanding, is also a massive area of investigation, and this time not one as old as the sun. This is a field of research still replete with possibilities and space to be explored.

The idea of characters with a will and story of their own would seem, at first, to support the assumption of an autonomous subject. That said, if subjects desire, it is because they are overtaken by a stream of passions, bending to a logic that is not their own. Subjects are not merely cleaved; rather, they appear as creatures with something unknown inside. In pagan terms, we might understand this inner nucleus as the zone where our demons run rampant. In Christian terms, we could say that we are looking at a subject tormented by a lack of internal control. We know that the topos of demons, when dragged into the net of Christian rhetoric, is the key to the world of temptation. Hence the importance of evil in understanding Machado's characters, who every so often find themselves faced with the opportunity to destroy the Other (Passos 2009; Moraes 2009). They are ethical subjects with wills of their own, but they are also operating within a truly minimal field of possible agency.

Here we have the modern side to a Machado who takes the moral laboratory inaugurated by the Enlightenment to its ultimate consequences, investigating the limits of human autonomy as imposed by an internal confluence of passions, and, of course, by a constellation of cultural and historical elements. Humans, in short, do not exist outside of limits and internal and external pressures. This view frees us up for fictional experimentation, which may test the autonomy and integrity of the subject. In testing these traits, however, fiction also postulates them, or presupposes them as a logical possibility.

Autonomy is, for all intents and purposes, an a priori assumption that is not always laid out clearly, but rather surreptitiously postulated whenever characters are complex, able to keep themselves within a zone of indefinition, with inner worlds of varying degrees of inscrutability that defy deep exploration. Machado brings us to the antipodes of naturalist literature; his characters are born of a contradictory duration, never a preset story that might determine them in absolute terms. Hence the importance of the development of the self throughout time, in the process that, as José Luiz Passos has ably described, lends ever greater depth to his characters:

> To go backwards, in this case, is to go even deeper. One way of ensuring the verisimilitude of characters' motivations is to set up seams among them that make it possible for the past to break through into current events. This is not retrospection for purposes of characterization, the old flashback used so often by 19th-century novels. On the contrary: Machado's heroes are constantly faced with the danger that the shadows of the past may rear up before them, marring their designs on autonomy, deception, or satisfaction. The weight of the past lends emotional baggage to the hero, deepening his composition, enlivening his character with the convincing appearance of lived experience. (2007, 79)

Here I must introduce my own concerns: the presumed autonomy of the subject, as tested in Machado, is negated by many of the sources that may plausibly have informed his conception of humanity. While Machadian fiction can be said to develop characters with moral plausibility, capable of actions that strike us as sufficiently complex as to seem real, on the other hand, the concept of "person" is founded on a dissimilarity within the subject; and this would seem to shatter any fantasies of a wholeness for which the subject will always be searching (Passos 2007, 172).

There can be no antidote more powerful against belief in the autonomy of the subject than the portrait of the individual from the brush of the French moralists of the seventeenth century, with Pascal leading the pack. To recall a long-standing theological dispute, which he addressed at length, unconditional belief in free will can be nothing more than proof of human pride, incapable as we are of feeling humility before the power of Nature the creator, a mysterious and distant entity altogether greater than human creatures.[2] Pascal speaks of the smallness of humans, both as a theologian and an observer of society.

There is something paradoxical in the modernity of an author like Machado—peculiar modernity, informed by a cohort of authors who lived and wrote before the Enlightenment, and hence, before the great fable of the liberty of the subject took on clearer form. I cannot help but note the influence of Pascal on one of Pierre Bourdieu's last books—*Pascalian Meditations*. But why did Bourdieu return, at the end of his life, to the Pascalian source of his own reflections? The question takes us to the heart of the effort made by modern French sociology to knock down precisely the notion (or the fantasy) of the absolute freedom of the subject.

Bourdieu's turning to Pascal should come as no surprise. After all, the sociologist's obsession with the definition of "field" led him to imagine that the action of individuals was ever overshadowed by opinion, that indispensable pillar without which the subject simply does not exist, as readers of Pascal—and of Machado—are well aware.

There is an often neglected bridge between the array of reasons that shape the actions of an individual and the individual's own foundations: namely, a collective belief in the correctness and necessity of those reasons. In other words, the reasons that guide me as a subject are only sustained because a belief in them is shared by those around me, creating a blind spot that is the very source of that belief, the deeper reasons for which become invisible, and hence natural, for all. In Bourdieu's Pascalian take, this springs from the necessary connection between *nomos* and *illusio* (which may be translated as "rule" and "illusion"). From this perspective, humanity, as a delirious Brás Cubas once hallucinated, is running in the same direction, ensnared by the fleeting figure of happiness. That happiness, as readers of Machado may suspect, boils down to the full acceptance of the Other, or the profound and inescapable drive behind any and all action: recognition. We are free, then, but only insofar as we can move within the cramped field of our shared illusions. This is a bitter realization in opposition to notions of human progress and the guiding power of reason behind history.

From the perspective of sociological critique, these illusions only vary within fields—or as Bourdieu, echoing Pascal, would have it, within different orders: "each field, like the Pascalian 'order,' thus involves its agents in its own stakes, which, from another point of view, [that] of another game, become invisible or at least insignificant or illusory" (2000, 97). The revelation of the "illusory" aspect of human goals also reminds us that we are moved forward by a natural principle, which seventeenth-century French moralists would call amour propre (echoing the Augustinian *amor sui*), and which the scientific imagination of the nineteenth century would come to define as a survival instinct embedded in our very nature. "Survival above all," we might well hear in one of the deranged tirades from poor demented Quincas Borba, a merciless parody of the modern sage, given to generalizations and a childish glee at his own discoveries. But behind each one of Machado's jokes there lies an important fact: when seen through a disenchanted glass, we are no longer the participants in a mysterious higher plan. In a Machadian worldview, we are creatures bereft of any otherworldly aid, and it is only down here (*ici-bas*, in Pascal's Jansenist jargon) that we act, driven principally by passions, among which, once again, self-love reigns supreme.

We have come to an aporia. On one hand, the absence of any belief in the powers of the beyond to provide any ultimate solution (the death of God, in Nietzsche's metaphor) would initially suggest that humans might be revealed the masters of themselves, sovereign and free, ready to act in ways that, from an Enlightened perspective, feed into other actions toward the improvement of the species. Here we see an unshakeable faith in secular progress, in the power of Enlightened thought (the point at which Nietzsche veers violently away from Enlightenment faith, of course). On the other hand, if we seek to block out the age of lights and, in seeking to understand Machado, slide back at least a century in the history of ideas in Europe, we will find that the classic French moralists, merciless analysts of humanity as they were, also portrayed creatures bereft of divine aid. We should recall that the mundane world of, say, François de La Rochefoucauld—the author of the most cutting maxims—has its religious parallel in Pascal's anguish, as the latter refuses to abandon his belief, although he admits that faith is, ultimately, a wager. And if it is a wager, that is because we can find no more explanations to comfort us and fill the void of existence; we cannot say, for example, that all that is happening bends to a veiled, transcendent reason. We are left with an immanent reason, which the modern philosopher ludicrously portrayed by Machado will reduce to the scramble for survival ("to the victor, the potatoes" to quote the oft-repeated phrase in *Quincas Borba*), and which Pascal, less given to sarcasm and in any case, with a broader array of interests, sought out and recognized in the natural world, through his scientific investigations.

In terms of moralist interpretation (of *mores*, customs), critics tend to note that the difference between pious Pascal and mundane La Rochefoucauld becomes considerably less acute whenever we recall the common cradle of their thought: Jansenism, which has been defined as a "Reformation within the Counter-Reformation" (Maire 1998, 14). The Jansenists of the *grand siècle* were persecuted, among other reasons, because they insisted that the distance between man and God was infinite and unsurpassable. This echoed deeply Augustinian heresies, anchored in the idea of the abyss between the city of God and the city of humans.

But where does the recognition of this infinite distance between us and the beyond leave us?

It brings us to the notion that, having been abandoned by the force of transcendence, we are all alone, and tragically solitary. Once we see that a higher force will never intervene in this realm (there are no miracles in the modern world), action becomes exclusively focused on the universe down here, with its own mechanics and nature to be unraveled and examined. From here on out, the observation of humanity would skirt around any investigation as to the higher causes of action. To observe humans would merely be to see them in action, on a stage upon which bodies move through space guided by forces of preservation, conquest, and glory. The differences between the scientist and the theologian begin to blur here, as both recognize that whatever they observe is here, never beyond. What stands beyond our view can be nothing more than a matter for speculation and wagering.

Among moralists, this becomes an issue of capturing what nature can offer us in its immense living laboratory. When Augusto Meyer imagined a bridge connecting the seventeenth-century moralists to Machado, he tried to imagine a hunter resting his finger on the trigger, ready to fell his prey with a cutting maxim. Machadian literature, then, is the universe glimpsed through the eyes of this hunter:

> The great sensuality in Machado de Assis is that of ideas. For the monster of lucidity that had slowly grown within him—eyes wide open, nostrils flaring—could there be any pleasure more keen than this joy of hunting down the essences that come through in the works of moralists and psychologists? Those who open a La Rochefoucauld or a La Bruyère soon feel the contagious pleasure of a well-aimed strike, of the still-humming arrow in the center of the target. They are born hunters, and their passion is an abstract sport played with words, but it provides sensations just as violent as any muscular exercise on a sun-beaten field. (Meyer 2008, 177)

Meyer's interest in Machadian "sensuality" speaks clearly to a world in which bodies are governed by powerful forces of preservation and conquest, revealing a veritable complex of motivations that are often obscure to humans themselves. In the wake of Lúcia Miguel Pereira's classic study, Meyer places Machado alongside the "pre-Freudian meanderings" that point toward the labyrinth of instinctive forces shaping humanity. The resulting universe "begins in the half-light of the background and winds up in an unfathomable shadow" (Meyer 2008, 179).[3] We might suppose that this shadow conceals the hunter waiting in ambush, ready to spring forth at any moment with a sharp observation that can cut through the skin and soul of a character (or of us readers), revealing that even the most magnanimous of acts (and especially those) have, at their root, the desire to be recognized and loved.

The moralists have frequently been dubbed excellent psychologists. Lacan adored La Rochefoucauld, just as Nietzsche admired the cutting perfection of the *Maxims* (Monteiro 2004). And literature, after all, has the gift of penetrating into the psychology of its characters, inquiring into the deepest roots of their actions. In this it goes beyond sociology, which asks after the meaning of actions, but does not necessarily penetrate the turbulent interior of the subject, wherein acts are formed and reformed as pure virtual possibilities until they can be consummated in observable activity. Given the division of intellectual labor, sociology can content itself with the visible result of actions, while it is left to literature to dive into what takes place before an action is carried out. Once again, the question is, what lies in those eyes that gaze upon us? What can we expect of them?

The critical clash between a historical-sociological interpretation of Machado's fiction and a more strictly literary approach is fairly unproductive, recalling a recurring football match where two teams test their muscles and morale, to the glee of their respective fans. Behind the sterility of the fixed opposition, however, we can make out a profound truth related to Machado's focus, and to the fact that his characters are ultimately both perfect allegories of historical subjects and, at the same time, profound investigations into what exactly makes human beings act and think (Bosi 2009). Above all, Machado's characters can reveal that the recognition sought by humankind can only exist when there is an overlap between (1) what the subject who acts is seeing and (2) what is seen by those who see the subject act. Here we have the (very Pascalian) bridge between *nomos* and *illusio*.

It is all a matter of convention and shared illusions in the end. As a result, the only freedom left to us is apparently the freedom to play with conventions. But in order to do so, we must recognize that even as we believe ourselves to be free, at the precise moment when we feel ready to act as autonomous subjects, we are captured by the illusions that surround us. When subjects imagine themselves to be free, they suddenly find themselves carrying out not what Enlightenment fantasies had cast as sovereign will, but rather, the will of others. The will of others becomes the will of subjects, who now deceive themselves, in keeping with a baroque topos that runs through the reflections of the moralists of the *grand siècle*.

At the center of it all is human action, keeping us from seeing the difference between the will of the agent and the will of another. When we act, whom do we obey: ourselves, or a spectral Other? This is not the modern Rimbaudian schism, however, of the *I* who is an *Other*. In the mirror of the Machadian soul, which can be understood through a Pascalian worldview, we can make out an *I* that moves away from itself, falling into the web of a constant, deceptive reconstruction of its self-image. An exemplary case is that of Jacobina, the protagonist of Machado's famous short story, "The Mirror."

When, in his analysis of "The Mirror," Alcides Villaça posed the question, "Who are we, if no one sees us?," we can see him delicately tracing the Pascalian problem of *divertissement*. Note that, although he does not invoke Pascal in his essay, with the author of the *Pensées* in mind Villaça uses the same term ("order") as Bourdieu:

> The process of the constitution and manifestation of the soul, which Jacobina does not hesitate to locate in *gaze*, makes us permanently subjects and objects of attributed signification. This ample gaze, seeming to take in all material perceptions, conditions and limits the projection of the body, which is both relationship and function. The primitivism of the human horde resists the symbols and sophistications of civilization, never letting us forget the brutal ties of an inexorable interdependence. We can see, once again, why metaphysics can find no space in skeptical Jacobina: he has felt viscerally, in the fullest sense, that the absence of the other is the absence of oneself. Who are we, if no one sees us? What are we, when we find ourselves in the anomalous position of being outside any and all hierarchies? This is all the more urgent for a recently promoted second lieutenant, who has just put on the uniform that all recognize and make be recognized, the relevance of the post shining in the gold buttons that conjure up the admiration of others, just as it makes them participants in the order of that social relevance. (Villaça 2009, 101–2)

But what is *divertissement*? Given the multiplicity of meanings of the term in Pascal, it would be both rash and reductive to translate it as *divertimento*, in Portuguese—unless, of course, we pay attention to the root, *divertere*, which draws our attention to the constant *desvio* (diversion) that marks our inability to remain alone. Or we might say, using Pascal's words, the impossibility of "sitting quietly in one's own chamber" (1992, 358). Or perhaps, with our thoughts given over to the concision of the aphorism and a revealing arithmetic, we might say that "we hide ourselves away in the countryside for eight months so that we can shine at court for four." (1992, 583)

The inability to "find pleasure in oneself" recalls the moment in which the Machadian character (from Jacobina to Bento Santiago and a plethora of others) finds that being left alone is an unattainable aim, as it would mean fleeing from the happy thrum of the world and diving into the condition that Pascal repeatedly refers to as "miserable." *Divertissement* is thus tied to people who swerve away from themselves, distracting themselves (diverting themselves, or diverging) from their true misery.

For those who have read Machado, the word "misery" conjures up the image of the last will and testament of Brás Cubas, where both authors, Pascal and Machado, come together, to the extent that we can identify author and narrator, or to the extent that, in the dated but still provocative terms of critic Lúcia Miguel Pereira, we can say that Brás Cubas is "the first of the morbid types through which Machado lets his own neuropathic strangenesses flow out" (1936, 220). The comment encapsulates Oliveira Lima's talk at the Sorbonne, when, a year after the novelist's death, he declared that Brás Cubas had been "a photograph of his [own] soul" (quoted in Pereira 1936, 217).

We should go beyond the overly simple observation of a pessimistic vision of the human condition and note that Pascal's misery evokes the Christian profession of faith in the simplicity that a Jansenist will see as linked to the suffering and universal expiation of guilt—the guilt of all the human race, which lies outside Machado's view. To follow a path blazed by sociological criticism, we might suppose that Brás Cubas is constantly seeking to excuse himself, shedding the burden of guilt for the atrocities committed by his social class. But let us focus, for a moment, on an understanding that predates Roberto Schwarz's seminal readings.

In the case of Sérgio Buarque de Holanda, for example, I believe that he went too far in his stinging critique of Afrânio Coutinho's important study on Pascal and Machado. Even so, there is something to be said for the text where he recalls that Machado "knows no tragedy," because in his works, "the tragic dissolves into the absurd, and the ridiculous has a bitter taste to it" (Holanda 1996, 311). Compared to Pascal, Holanda suggests, the world of Machado

is a world without a beginning, a world without Paradise. Hence the incurable insensibility to all explanations based on sins and the Fall for understanding the way in which things have been arranged in the world. His amoralism is rooted in this fundamental insensibility. Moral law is born of a willful, insipid demagogy, best suited for soothing human vanity. Our acts have no clear end, and the spectacle offered by the agitation of men inspires much the same feeling as the speeches of a lunatic. (1996, 1: 308)

Perhaps Holanda's imagination is projecting a Machado who is more Machadian than Machado himself. In any case, it seems clear to me that the future author of *Visão do paraíso*, writing in 1940, is heavily influenced by the theses of Lúcia Miguel Pereira. But we must ask, in the end, whether Machado's fiction is truly and irrevocably distant from the suggestion of a lost paradise, an end that awaits us as a collectivity.

The end for Pascal, seen from his ecstatic Christianity, is death, awaited and redeeming, as well as the jubilant encounter with the tears of humanity. In Machado, however, there are no capital letters, and the Bible is simply one more source in an interminable mesh of inaccurate, entertaining quotations. It may be most productive, in terms of understanding the Machadian oeuvre, to set aside the absence of God for the moment and ask what it might mean, in his time and given his context, to construct a narrative that situates humankind in a space that has never been nor will ever be perfect. What broken promises is Machado writing about? What anguish before human misery (both real and historic) are his texts responding to?

To go back to the start—now with the arguments from the Pascalian counterpoint—we can only say that, in the gaze that is cast on human action, there lies a question as to the meaning of action, which here should be taken more in a historical than a sociological sense, as if we were asking after the direction, and, ultimately, the utility of human action. But can we make out a utilitarian perspective in Machado? Evidently, the answer is no.

He is observing humans, of course, but seeking out the utility of their actions, as Mandeville did in the seventeenth century, is not his aim, nor is it the source of his pleasure. Machado takes joy from abandoning us in the instant before the meaning of his characters' actions become fixed, leaving us before a cunningly constructed indeterminacy, but also with a question as to what is constructed, if anything at all, out of the accumulation of the actions of humans living in society.

Giving the first push to a movement that would transform moral science into a modern secular science (political economy), Mandeville imagined that in obeying the most basic individual drives, seeking out the satisfaction of our own intimate needs, we would be building the future of society. Hence the paradox of the fable of the bees: acting by themselves and for themselves, they construct the hive in its collectivist virtue. Following a similar line, but still wrapped up in the theological mentality of Scottish moralism, Adam Smith would envision an even higher drive acting like a hand (an invisible one, of course), directing action so that society might rise, in the end, beautiful as a finally realized promise. The ideological side to this never fulfilled promise is precisely one of the favorite targets of the critique behind Machado's texts.[4]

Although also an heir to the great moralist thinking of the seventeenth and eighteenth centuries, Machado would not go so far. After all, in his prose, we never glimpse that promised better society, not utopian or divine but within our reach, the attainment of which would be simply a matter of following the designs of a reason that is no longer transcendent, but immanent, within society itself. Here we have the raw ideological foundations of economic liberalism: why change the course of the social body if, once left to operate on its own, it will move in the direction of a superior society?

While the utilitarian moralist sees a good society in construction, meanwhile, the *Bruxo do Cosme Velho* (The Wizard of Cosme Velho), as Machado would be later known, stops short and simply observes humankind, an intractable plaything in the hands of absurd forces—none of which leads to anything palpable, as a delirious Brás Cubas would remind us. For Brás, after all, slavery is just another detail, practically a minor one, in a system whose ultimate and unquestionable aim is the satisfaction (to remain on a sociological and historical plane) of a social class and its children as they enjoy themselves to the utmost.

If Machadian literature does not, indeed, point to the future, it is because it speaks of a present littered with unrealized promises, inhabited by individuals who, in struggling to invent something that may serve as a counterweight to their own impotence, let themselves be guided by brilliant illusions, shared with a joy that is as absolute as it is deceptive.

Machado's tone is certainly not that of Pascal, who oscillates between the most somber sentiment of Christian humility and the most extreme of mystical solutions: belief itself.

Machado refuses to place wagers. That said, even when we consider the complexity and the variety of his narrators, we may still imagine that in them, or around them, we can always find, despite the perennially proclaimed death of the author, Machado himself, casting a keen gaze on his surroundings. With properly adjusted lenses, we can make him out, crouched in ambush in the dark corner devoid of faith, sharing with us the ironic smile that lights up his face.

NOTES

1. Here I refer to Machado de Assis' reaction, in a letter from August 1906, to a book of aphorisms published by Nabuco, his friend and colleague: "From an early age I have read Pascal often, to mention no others, and I can say that it was never to distract myself. Even today, when I turn to those readings and console myself in the disconsolation of *Ecclesiastes*, I find in them the same savor as I did then. If I should ever disagree with what I read, I am always pleased by the way in which that divergence is expressed" (Assis 1997, 939). For a recent reexamination of the intersection between the two, see Sneed, Azevedo, and Senna.
2. On Pascal's polemics with the Jesuits, and his attempt to reconcile Thomism and Augustinism, see Sellier, and also Marin.
3. On the "pre-Freudian" shadows in Machado de Assis, see Pereira, *Um narrador incerto*, and *O conto machadiano*.
4. On the path that leads from moral science to political economy, including the Jansenist debates that informed Pascal, see Lafond. On the prehistory of economic liberalism, see Hirschman.

REFERENCES

Assis, Machado de. 1997. *Obra completa*. 3 vols. Rio de Janeiro: Nova Aguilar.

Bosi, Alfredo. 2009. Rumo ao concreto: Brás Cubas em três versões. *Luso-Brazilian Review* 46(1): 7–15.

Bourdieu, Pierre. 2000. *Pascalian Meditations*. Stanford, CA: Stanford University Press.

Coutinho, Afrânio. 1959. *A filosofia de Machado de Assis e outros ensaios*. Rio de Janeiro: Livraria São José.

Holanda, Sérgio Buarque de. 1996. *O espírito e a letra: Estudos de crítica literária*. Edited by Antonio Arnoni Prado. 2 vols. São Paulo: Companhia das Letras.

Maire, Catherine. 1998. *De la cause de Dieu à la cause de la Nation: Le jansénisme au XVIIIe siècle*. Paris: Gallimard.

Meyer, Augusto. 2008. *Ensaios escolhidos*. Rio de Janeiro: José Olympio.

Monteiro, Pedro Meira. 2004. *Um moralista nos trópicos: O visconde de Cairu e o duque de La Rochefoucauld*. São Paulo: Boitempo.

Moraes, Eliane Robert. 2009. Um vasto prazer, quieto e profundo. *Luso-Brazilian Review* 46(1): 75–92.

Pascal, Blaise. 1992. Pensées. In *Moralistes du XVIIᵉ siècle: De Pibrac à Dufresny*, ed. Jean Lafond. Paris: Robert Laffont.

Passos, José Luiz. 2007. *Machado de Assis: O romance com pessoas*. São Paulo: Edusp.

Passos, José Luiz. 2009. O mal e a metamorfose em Machado de Assis. *Luso-Brazilian Review* 46(1): 57–74.

Pereira, Lúcia Miguel. 1936. *Machado de Assis: Estudo crítico e biográfico*. São Paulo: Companhia Editora Nacional.

Villaça, Alcides. 2009. 'O espelho': Superfície e corrosão. *Luso-Brazilian Review* 46(1): 93–105.

PART II

Machado on Race, Identity, and Society

CHAPTER 5

The Legacy of Slavery: Tales of Gender and Racial Violence in Machado de Assis

Sidney Chalhoub

The themes of slavery, gender, and racism, seen as intertwined, were present in the work of Machado de Assis throughout his career. It is possible to identify three moments, successive but also to some degree coeval, in the way in which Machado approached and interrelated these subjects. First, he denounced the seigneurial custom of resorting to sexual violence against free and enslaved black women and depicted these women's dignity in dealing with the problem (in texts written mainly in the 1860s and 1870s). Second, in very allegorical mode, he analyzed the relations among division of labor, scientific ideologies, and racial injustice (1880s). Finally, he turned to the legacy of slavery and its consequences for Brazilian history and society (1890s and 1900s).[1]

First Moment: 1860s and 1870s

In 1864, Machado published a short story titled "Virginius" in the periodical *Jornal das Famílias*, a lawyer narrates the story. One of the main characters is Pio ("pious"), a powerful plantation owner, known as "the Father of All."[2] Depicted as very generous, caring, and just, he represents the convergence of judicial, local, and police authorities, since his opinion is decisive on whatever happens in the county, and everyone obeys his

S. Chalhoub (✉)
Harvard University, Cambridge, Massachusetts, USA

© The Editor(s) (if applicable) and The Author(s) 2016
L. Aidoo, D.F. Silva (eds.), *Emerging Dialogues on Machado de Assis*, DOI 10.1057/978-1-137-54174-1_5

orders. The pious plantation owner has a son, Carlos, seemingly a good young man, who returns home changed after some years away to study.

Julião, a farm laborer who is a faithful dependent of the plantation owner, lives nearby within Pio's jurisdiction. Julião has a daughter, Elisa, whom he considers the prettiest *mulatinha* (young mulatto girl) in the locality. Although younger, she had grown up close to Carlos, the plantation owner's son. Perhaps readers of the time would have been able to guess the rest of the story. Upon returning from his studies, Carlos spends his time on the plantation hunting or doing nothing. He begins to regard Elisa from the perspective of the sexual predator, an alleged prerogative of people of his social status. Elisa resists his advances, which only strengthens his resolve to have her. Carlos hires a group of thugs to go to the dependent's house with him, overwhelm Elisa's resistance, and allow him to rape the girl. Julião is able to prevent the gang's first onslaught, but realizes that he would not be able to deter the young master's impetus for long. Desolated to see his daughter's despair facing imminent rape, he decides to kill her and put an end to her agony. The narrator of the story is the lawyer hired by Pio to defend Julião, his dependent, in the jury trial.

Despite its paroxysms of evil and virtue, its sentimental and moralizing tone, the story conveys a clear message: the alleged good intentions of a powerful plantation owner produce disgrace and social injustice. In relation to the people he seeks to protect, such as Julião, Pio can only contribute, perhaps unwillingly, to the experience of structural vulnerability of dependents in that society. The story, taken as a whole, destabilizes the Manichaeism of vices and virtues that constitutes its parts. The planter is unable to keep his favorite dependent free of harm. Julião, the dependent, does not feel safe despite his unflinching devotion to the powerful landowner. Pio's love for his son results in Carlos's laziness, the unnecessary killing of animals, and cruelty, which go unpunished, whereas the dependent's love for his daughter kills her. In the end, Machado's narrator lays bare the injustices and inequalities that characterize paternalist ideology, slavery, and personal dependence.

According to the lawyer and narrator of the story, Elisa tenaciously resists the young master's advances and, therefore, the notion that he holds sexual rights over slave and dependent free girls who live on his father's property. As the girl continues to refuse his advances, Carlos becomes angry and vows to have her no matter what. In the passage describing the attempted rape, the girl cries for help and fights back until her father arrives and succeeds in keeping the thugs away momentarily, but they overwhelm him soon afterward. As father and daughter are forced to wait for the return of the rapist, Julião manages to reach for a knife and kill his daughter.

There are at least two other stories that belong to this first approach that Machado adopted to gender and racial violence in nineteenth-century Brazilian society. In "Mariana" (1871), the protagonist is a domestic slave girl raised as a favorite of the household. She falls in love with the young master, provoking his interest in sexually abusing her. Toward the end of the story, Mariana runs away from her masters' household. When the young master tries to recapture her, she commits suicide in front of him. A similar story is told in the poem "Sabina," published in *Americanas* (1875). The main character is again a slave girl raised as a favorite of the household who falls in love with the young master. Coming home from his studies for a vacation, the young man finds the girl bathing in a nearby river and rapes her. While the dandy returns to his affairs unperturbed and soon finds a girl of his race and social status to marry, Sabina, pregnant and desperate, considers suicide by drowning in the same river where she was raped. However, she decides to live. The drama and violence of these tales can perhaps be seen now as unlike the Machado of later writings that we learned to appreciate. Nonetheless, the author would return to the theme of unrelenting gender and racial violence throughout his career, mostly in allegorical and somewhat abstract fashion, belaboring the same message repeatedly: white males thought that women of slave or subaltern condition were there for them to exploit their labor and, if they pleased, violate their bodies. In case of resistance, they could resort to violence, seeking to overcome by force or eliminate women who showed a rebellious, or sometimes simply autonomous, disposition.

SECOND MOMENT: 1880s

In 1881, Machado de Assis published what some consider to be his magnum opus—*Memórias Póstumas de Brás Cubas* [*Posthumous Memoires of Brás Cubas*]. The titular character is a defunct narrator that, from the tomb, pieces together his life through a series of self-reflective fragments. In a particularly illustrative passage, Brás Cubas recalls sitting in his bedroom when a large black butterfly enters, flutters about, and finally alights on his head. He shakes it off, causing the insect to land on the window. Chased off again, the butterfly settles on an old portrait of Brás's father and stays there, moving its wings softly. Brás remarks that the insect has "a certain mocking way ... that bothered me a great deal" (1997, 61).[3]

He turns away and leaves the room, returning shortly afterward to find the butterfly on the same spot, displaying the same attitude. Brás then takes a towel and kills the insect. He becomes a little upset and wonders whether the insect's fate would have been different if it were blue.

The large black butterfly in Brás's bedroom happened to be the second he saw in a short period. The day before, he had been visiting Dona Eusébia and her daughter, Eugênia, old acquaintances of his family, when a black butterfly appeared on the veranda and began to fly around the women. Dona Eusébia became upset. The old lady seemed to believe that a butterfly of such color meant misfortune, or perhaps it was a mischievous witch in the form of a winged insect. Brás took control of the situation, telling her that she should not be afraid, and shooed the butterfly away. Brás narrates, "Dona Eusébia sat down again, puffing, a little embarrassed. Her daughter, pale with fear, perhaps, concealed that impression with great will power. I shook hands with them and left, laughing to myself at the two women's superstition, a philosophical, disinterested, superior laugh" (61). This episode illustrates a claim that the narrator would repeatedly make to demonstrate his alleged superiority over other people: he was rational, "philosophical"; others were superstitious, hence inferior to him.

There was a wider context for Brás's portrayal of Dona Eusébia and (perhaps) Eugênia's superstition regarding the butterfly. Brás and Eugênia had been courting, and it seems that the dandy felt he could eventually come to love the young lady. The narrator articulates ruthlessly the reasons why Eugênia is unfit to marry him. First, there are her social origins, which the narrator deems inferior and even morally unsound. Dona Eusébia initially appeared in Brás's narration in a banquet to celebrate Napoleon's defeat. The boy was then kept from eating compote because Dr. Vilaça, a lawyer, had been expounding endlessly. Brás swore he would take revenge on the glosser, and thus started to follow him all around in the banquet. He became determined to do something to make him look ridiculous. Suddenly, he saw the man, who was married and a father, talking to Dona Eusébia, a maiden; the boy also noticed that they had gone behind a little thicket. Minutes later, there was "the smack, very light, of a kiss" (31). Young Brás then jumped out of his hiding place shouting, "Dr. Vilaça kissed Dona Eusébia!" (31). Despite the scandal, the affair proved inevitable, and Dona Eusébia soon gave birth to a daughter, Eugênia.

Brás remembered all these events as he felt himself leaning toward the girl. In fighting back his inclination, he conjured up the notion that Eugênia, being an illegitimate child, was not morally worthy of him. The girl's origins made her unsuitable for marriage. In order to demean her further, Brás thought of her as "the flower from the shrubbery" (60). This resort to seigneurial prejudice and moralizing regarding social origins did not suffice to thwart Brás's inclination toward the girl. Thus, the next step was to highlight Eugênia's physical disability; she was "lame from birth" (63). As usual, the narrator confronted the question philosophically:

> The worst of it was that she was lame. Such lucid eyes, such a fresh mouth, such ladylike composure—and lame! That contrast could lead one to believe that nature is sometimes a great mocker. Why pretty if lame? Why lame if pretty? That was the question I kept asking myself on my way back home at night without hitting upon the solution to the enigma. The best thing to do when an enigma is unresolved is to toss it out the window. That was what I did. I laid hand onto another towel and drove off that other black butterfly fluttering in my brain. (64)

Brás kills the butterfly because it is black—"Why the devil wasn't it blue?" (62) he asks. He deems Eugênia unfit for marriage because she is lame. The butterfly's blackness and the girl's birth defect are natural characteristics, not social constructs. Brás sorts them out for extinction and humiliation, however, because these markers are socially constructed as naturally inferior, apparently unequipped to survive life's necessary struggles. Brás's final discourse as he "tossed out" Eugênia seems to fuse allegations of gender, class, and biological superiority:

> Eugênia's first kiss came on a Sunday.... Poor Eugênia! If you only knew what ideas were drifting out of my mind on that occasion! You, quivering with excitement, your arms on my shoulders, contemplating your welcome spouse in me, and I, my eyes on 1814, on the shrubbery, on Vilaça, and suspecting that you couldn't lie to your blood, to your origins. (65)

This passage conveys Brás's usual representation that women with whom he interacted were always at his feet. He happens to have been invariably wrong in this regard, though for different reasons. In the cases of Marcela, Virgília, and Dona Plácida, Brás deals with women who make him think he is in control so as to dissimulate their objectives and achieve them without openly confronting him. In contrast, "Eugênia's look didn't limp but was straight"; she "looked at me with frankness, without timidity or false modesty" (64). Eugênia does not allow herself to be delved into by Brás's mental habits; she does not negotiate, but rather chooses autonomy at any cost. Actually, it is the narrator who consistently struggles to reach any certainty regarding Eugênia. When the black butterfly flutters around mother and daughter, Brás refers to both women as being afraid and sharing the superstition: he left "laughing to myself at the two women's superstition" (61). But the assertion contradicted a previous comment, in the same chapter, that makes it clear that he remained unsure: "Her daughter, pale with fear, *perhaps*, concealed that impression with great will power" (61; italics added). Elsewhere he remarks, "At the feet of that so artless creature, a spurious, lame daughter, the product of love and disdain, at her feet I felt good, and she, *I think*, felt even better at my feet" (65; italics added). Despite his demeaning attitude, he is unsure as to whether or not he is in the dominant role. Toward the end of his narration, Brás relates that many years later, he went to a slum to distribute alms and met Eugênia there. He found her "as lame as I'd left and sadder still," but ready to stand up to him: "She immediately raised her head and looked straight at me with dignity. I understood that she wouldn't accept alms from my pocket" (201).

Brás's formulation that Eugênia "couldn't lie" about her "blood" and "origins" is ambivalent. "Origins" refers to her illegitimate birth and inferior social status. "Blood" may refer to social status as well, for Brás is allegedly of traditional, illustrious descent: he would like to think of himself as a blue-blooded aristocrat, thus perhaps fond of blue butterflies. Nonetheless, "blood" may also convey natural superiority. After all, Eugênia was "lame from birth," (63); thus her blood appeared degenerate. Eugênia, black butterflies, slaves and other dependents: they all seem to exist to be used as needed and then discarded. It is significant that when Brás decides that he should run away from Eugênia because of her birth defect, he says that he "drove off that other black butterfly fluttering in my brain" (64).

Eugênia's resistance to Brás encourages him to offer embattled rationalizations for his alleged superiority over her. He struggles to explain the reasons why it would not have been appropriate for him to marry her. He resorts both to traditional, paternalist reasons for social prominence and to new, "scientific" renderings of "life as struggle" in which the fittest survive. Therefore, it became undesirable to marry a girl who was lame and, presumably, unfit for sound biological reproduction. If we proceed a little further using this type of twisted reasoning, we find an explanation for the international division of labor and its implicitly racist justification. As Quincas Borba, the philosopher of Humanitism from *Posthumous Memoires of Brás Cubas* and later his own titular character, says,

I don't need any other documentation of the sublimity of my system than this chicken right here. It nourished itself on corn, which was planted by an African, let us suppose imported from Angola. That African was born, grew up, was sold. A ship brought him here, a ship built of wood cut in the forest by ten or twelve men, propelled by sails that eight or ten men sewed together, not to mention the rigging and other parts of the nautical apparatus. In that way, this chicken, which I have lunched on just now, is the result of a multitude of efforts and struggles carried out with the sole aim of satisfying my appetite. (163)

Machado de Assis understood perfectly well how this Atlantic concert for the subordination of people of African descent in the international division of labor reverberated in the national context. In Rio de Janeiro, in the second half of the nineteenth century, blacks—slaves, freed, or free-born—seemed increasingly excluded from the most advantageous positions in the urban labor market. *Quincas Borba*, a novel that appeared in book form in 1891, takes up Borba's proposed school of thought, itself a parody of the emergent discourses of Scientism and Darwinism, through Rubião, Borba's disciple, who puts Humanitism into practice. Rubião feels uneasy with the (blatantly racist) pressure that Cristiano Palha—a capitalist he meets and by whom he is manipulated—places on him to employ white domestic servants:

The servant was waiting, stiff and serious. He was Spanish, and it had only been after some resistance that Rubião accepted him from the hands of Cristiano, no matter how much he argued that he was used to his blacks from Minas Gerais and didn't want any foreign languages in his house. His friend Palha insisted, pointing out the necessity of having white servants. Rubião gave in regretfully. His good manservant, whom he wished to keep in the parlor as a touch of the provinces, couldn't even stay in the kitchen, where a Frenchman, Jean, reigned. The slave was downgraded to other duties. (1998, 29)

In the original Portuguese—in the above passage—Machado uses the word *pajem* (page) rather than *escravo* (slave) to describe the domestic servant in question. A page could be enslaved, freed, or free. The context makes clear that the page was a black man, but his condition remained uncertain, which is of interest in the passage. The story returns to the circumstances in which Rubião and Palha first met—that is, to a period well before the one referred to in the passage above—and the narrator mentions that Rubião intended to grant freedom to the page "as soon as he came into possession of his goods" (29). Therefore, if the page of African descent referred to is always the same, his passage from slavery to freedom coincided with his being "downgraded to other duties."

THIRD MOMENT

Páginas recolhidas [*Collected Pages*] a volume first published in 1899, is mostly a collection of short stories, although it also features a play (a comedy), passages of homage to people Machado appreciated—such as Alencar, Henriqueta Renan, and Garnier—plus an account of his times as a journalist covering the debates of the Senate. Despite the diversity of the content, the volume deals mostly with the process of the construction of memories—that is, the attribution of retrospective meanings to events, characters, and institutions.

"O caso da vara" ["The Cane"] the short story that opens the volume, appeared for the first time on February 1, 1891, in the daily *Gazeta de Notícias*. The two versions of the story are very similar, except for the omission, in 1899, of a very long passage that started a few lines after the opening of the tale—a very telling omission, as we shall see. Right at the outset, the narrator explains that he could not say with precision when the story took place, but it was certainly "well before 1850" (2008c, 221). If we suppose that the time of the narration is the same as the date of publication of the text—the 1890s—then the reader is immediately invited to adopt a retrospective gaze, to seek the meaning of things past. The story describes the misfortunes of Damião, made a seminarian because his authoritarian father decided that he was to become a priest. Alleging lack of vocation, the young man runs away from the seminary and decides to seek the protection of Sinhá Rita, an intimate friend of his godfather. The runaway thinks that Sinhá Rita would have the means to convince the godfather to intervene on his behalf with his father. The maneuver seems skillful, since the godfather was the one who took the young man to the seminary in the first place.

As the plot moves to Sinhá Rita's house, two tales develop in parallel trajectories, converging occasionally. The first one—which seems predominant until the last lines of the story, when the perspective is completely reversed—concerns the conversations between Damião and Sinhá Rita and the latter's attempt to engage the boy's godfather to help him. The other tale, which occupies a much smaller number of lines but was indeed the story Machado wanted to tell, deals with labor relations in Sinhá Rita's house and the fate of Lucretia, one of the children present there. Sinhá Rita lives mostly from teaching lace-making and embroidery to black girls, most probably enslaved, both belonging to the house and from outside.

Although the narrator focuses on the conversations between Damião and Sinhá Rita most of the time, readers know that the girls are around, toiling without respite. The world of child labor sometimes pops up, unwelcome and inopportune, interrupting the supposedly main line of the story. Thus, when Damião enters the house unexpectedly and breathless, all the girls "stopped their hands and their bobbins" to look at him; Sinhá Rita promptly orders them "to go on working." A little later, seeking to dispel the young man's worries and cheer him up, Sinhá Rita tells stories, asks him to tell some as well, and they end up laughing together. One of Damião's stories, accompanied by comic gestures, makes one of the girls laugh: "She'd forgotten her work to look at the lad, and listen to him. Sinhá Rita picked up a cane at the side of the settee, and threatened her: 'Lucretia, mind the cane!'" (224). The girl lowers her head waiting for the blow that would usually follow. This time, however, perhaps because there is a visitor, it turns out to be just a warning. In the evening, if the task were not concluded, Lucretia would receive the customary punishment. As a consequence of the episode, Damião observed Lucretia: "She was a black girl, skinny, a little waif with a scar on her forehead and a burn on her left hand" (224). Besides these signs suggesting regular beatings and other forms of torture, the 11-year-old girl "was coughing, but inwardly and muffled" (224), as if she were afraid of being noticed. Damião immediately feels sorry for Lucretia and decides that he would protect her in case she does not finish her task. After all, the girl had gotten into trouble because she thought him funny, an idea that strengthens his resolve to plead on her behalf if necessary.

Thus the narrator returns to what appeared to be his main interest: the godfather came and went and Sinhá Rita kept him under pressure. Damião seemed, or pretended, to be close to a nervous breakdown. Five neighbors arrived to chat and drink coffee. Damião's skills as an entertainer served Sinhá Rita well this time around; although the boy hesitates to tell jokes again because he is afraid Lucretia might laugh and get into trouble. He is eventually asked to recount the exact tale that had made the girl laugh. But he "didn't forget Lucretia and looked at her, to see if she'd laughed too. He saw she had her face close to her cushion to finish her task. She wasn't laughing; or maybe she'd laughed inwardly, just as she coughed" (227).

The narrator resumes the supposed main story: The godfather sent news of his ongoing efforts with Damião's father; he described the man's fury so as to enhance his sacrifice and efforts; and so on. It seemed that the story would close with readers satiating their curiosity about the destiny of the runaway seminarian.

Damião grows nervous, oppressed by his father's tyranny, feeling perhaps a connection with those enslaved girls all around him, especially Lucretia, that skinny creature of 11 years, full of scars, coughing, "weaving her bobbins in and out, unable to see" (228). When the time comes to gather the day's work, only Lucretia hadn't finished hers. Sinhá Rita, full of seigneurial rage, grabbed her by the ear, saying she was a "little good-for-nothing" (229). Lucretia struggles, weeps, asks for forgiveness, has a fit of coughing, and implores for Damião's intervention. At this point, holding the girl firmly by the ear, Sinhá Rita looks for the cane and sees that it is close to Damião: "Senhor Damião, pass me the cane, if you please." The boy hesitates, remembering that "he had sworn to give the girl his protection." However, "He needed to get out of the seminary so badly!" So he "picked up the cane and handed it to Sinhá Rita" (230).

In the original 1891 version of the story, there is a long passage at the beginning that described in detail Damião's arrival at the seminary, taken there by his godfather and received by the rector with a peroration about ecclesiastical vocation. The episode, amounting to almost 20% of the text, was entirely omitted by Machado for the version that appeared in *Páginas Recolhidas*. It seems to me that the intent of the passage in the original version was to emphasize the oppressions that weighed on Damião, who was hampered by the religious prejudices of his family, the authoritarian nature of patriarchy, and the expectations of society. He had run away from the oppressions of the seminary as enslaved people ran away from slavery. In the 1891 version of the story, the intention to approximate the plights of Damião and Lucretia is more explicit. The elimination of the passage arguably increases the visibility of the world of child labor, thus focusing exclusively on the events within the house and workshop belonging to Sinhá Rita. The theme of slavery and the social interests that sustained it for so long come to the fore, forcing readers situated in the late 1890s to reckon with the realities of bonded labor and its legacy: intense economic exploitation—including widespread use of child labor—torture of workers, routine seigneurial arbitrariness and abuse of laborers, ample social backing, and connivance with the institution. Moreover, suppressing the long passage at the beginning may show that Machado, in 1899, had come to think that the original parallelism between religious oppression and racial oppression was exaggerated. After all, as we know despite the fact that the narrator did not tell us, Damião's fate would have nothing to do with Lucretia's. Things would end up all right for him.

Relíquias de casa velha [*Relics of the Old House*], the last volume of collected short pieces that Machado edited, appeared in 1906. As was the case with *Páginas recolhidas*, the volume contained texts of different genres. Although short stories predominated, there was a poem dedicated to his recently deceased wife, "A Carolina" ["To Carolina"], which opened the volume, and there were further homages to figures the author appreciated such as Eduardo Prado, critical pieces, and two plays.

"Father against Mother," the first short story in the volume, had never been published before, unlike "The Cane." Again, it seems that Machado had decided it was necessary to remind readers, in detail, of the violence of slavery; thus, the first two paragraphs of the story contain the description of objects routinely used to torture slaves. "When slavery ended, it took with it certain trades and tools; the same must have happened with other social institutions" (2008, 255), starts the narrator. Without further warning, the following sentence mentions the "neck iron," "leg irons," and "tin-plate mask." The mask "cured the slaves of the vice of drunkenness by shutting their mouths. It had only three holes in it, two to see, one to breathe, and it was fastened behind the head with a padlock" (255). The narrator adds, "The mask was grotesque, but order in the human and social realm is not always achieved without grotesquery—cruelty, even, sometimes" (255). After remarking that tinsmiths had the habit of hanging the masks up for sale in the doorways of their shops, the storyteller seems to signal that he might shift topics: "But let's not think about masks" (255).

Actually, the previous sentence serves as indication that the narrator was not willing to hide anything. On the contrary, he seems determined to force the reader to remember aspects of the history of slavery in Brazil—an insistence on the need to remember that is a bit startling, considering that less than two decades had elapsed since the abolition of slavery in 1888. Therefore, the next subject is the neck iron, which "was applied to slaves with the habit of running away" (256). Apparently surmising that readers would not be familiar with such a tool and its uses, the narrator explains, "Imagine a thick collar, with an equally thick shaft on the side, left or right, which went up to the top of the head, and which was locked behind with a key. It weighed a lot, naturally, but it was less a punishment than a sign. A slave who fled with one of these showed that he was a repeated offender, and wherever he went was easily caught" (256).

After these introductory paragraphs, the rest of the story moves swiftly. Cândido Neves ("snow") and Clara, whose names highlight their whiteness to the point of caricature, are married and live in the company of a relative, aunt Mônica. The two women work hard and survive on sewing jobs for a long time. Nothing changes after Clara's marriage, since Cândido keeps moving from one profession to another, from one job to another, without ever finding any steady means to earn a living. Clara becomes pregnant, to the elation of the couple and the dismay of aunt Mônica, who believes that the family cannot grow under such deprivation and predicts that the child will starve to death. The situation worsens when the landlord demands the payment of three months' rent he is owed, threatening to kick them out of the house. Cândido seeks to avoid the eviction but to no avail, and the three of them seem headed toward homelessness until aunt Mônica finds temporary lodging for them in a friend's house. However, the aunt no longer tolerates the couple's intention to raise a child under those circumstances. She had previously suggested an abortion, a piece of advice that the narrator found "difficult to write down, though less difficult than it was for the father to hear it" (261). The child is born right after their eviction and move to temporary lodging, which is a "basement at the back of the stables" (266) in the house of a rich old woman. Aunt Mônica now insists that the child be given to the Orphans' Wheel for abandoned babies, in the wall of a convent, where the nuns would take care of it and find someone with means to raise the child. The situation becomes so desperate that the parents ultimately agree. Cândido grows desolate, tries to gain some time, and promises to go to the convent the next day.

While events leading to the birth of the child and the decision to take it to the Orphans' Wheel followed their course, readers also learn that Cândido, after failing in different professions and jobs, has invested his last hopes in the business of catching runaway slaves. The option appeals to him because he does not have to work long fixed hours. Furthermore, "all it needed was strength, a sharp eye, patience, courage and a bit of rope" (258). Cândido copies the advertisements for fugitive slaves and memorizes the distinguishing marks and habits of the runaway. He acquires some experience in the trade, although the increasing competition makes profits dwindle. He finds himself having no luck as of late, exactly when he seemed most in need of it. The next day, as he walks slowly to the convent with his son in his arms, he sees a mulatta, Arminda, who he believes to be a runaway he had been seeking. He recalls that her master had offered handsome compensation for her recapture. Cândido leaves the baby in a pharmacy nearby and goes after Arminda.

The last two or three pages of the short story are of a heart-wrenching violence, unique in the whole body of Machado's writings—except, perhaps, for the passages depicting the torture of animals in "A causa secreta" (The Hidden Cause). Arminda begs Cândido to let her go, explaining to him that she is pregnant and that the punishment her master would certainly inflict upon her would be dangerous in her present condition. A detailed description of the struggles between Cândido and Arminda, father and mother, follows, with the slave catcher succeeding in taking the woman to the master's house. The proprietor recognizes the slave immediately and, while he is paying Cândido the reward, Arminda has a miscarriage: "The product of a few months' growth came lifeless into the world, amid the groans of the mother, and the owner's gestures of despair. Cândido Neves saw the whole spectacle" (269). Later, after retrieving his son and returning home, Cândido tells the story to his wife and to Aunt Mônica, the latter apparently reconciled to the idea of the couple keeping the baby boy. Cândido kisses the boy, "blessed the escape and was unconcerned about the miscarriage" (270). He concluded, "Not all children make it" (270).

Why did Machado decide to open his two last volumes of collected short pieces with these two strong tales, "The Cane" and "Father against Mother," about the violence of slavery? An appropriate answer to this question would probably require another text, but I offer the following tentative explanations. The first aspect to bear in mind is that the theme of violence associated with slavery—especially violence against black women—as I have argued here, was not at all a novelty in Machado's writings. He simply returns to it in different moments of his oeuvre where he found it necessary. Thus, the second point is that Machado noticed a tendency to produce silence about slavery and its legacy in the 1890s and 1900s. Not only did Brazilian society refuse to reckon with the consequences of slavery for people of African descent, but authorities and politicians actively engaged in rewriting or reinterpreting its meaning, as was clear, for instance, regarding the efforts to promote the yearly commemoration of abolition as merely an occasion for strengthening friendship and fraternity among all Brazilians. On the occasion of the first celebrations of abolition, in May 1888 and May 1889, the event had been more commonly referred to as "the liberation of a race" (Moraes 2012,

303) Finally, as I showed elsewhere, Machado de Assis, in his long career as a public employee, had been intensely involved in the question of slave emancipation. He worked for it in the Ministry of Agriculture, studied legal means to promote and enlarge the rights of enslaved people, and struggled for the enforcement of legislation and other government decisions regarding the subject (Chalhoub 2003). He had a lifetime commitment to the question, and this fact helps to explain the sense of urgency and engagement showed in these two short stories and in other pieces that he wrote in this period.

NOTES

1. Several recent books have contributed much to the understanding of Machado's views on the questions of slavery, race, and gender. On race, see Duarte (2007), Vital (2012), and Daniel (2012). On gender, see Megid (2014) and Fitz (2015).
2. Unless otherwise indicated, translations of Portuguese phrases and short passages cited are my own.
3. In this paragraph and in the following ones, I summarize the argument I originally presented in "What Are Noses For? Paternalism, Social Darwinism and Race Science in Machado de Assis," *Journal of Latin American Cultural Studies* 10, no.2 (2001): 171–191.

REFERENCES

Assis, Machado de. 1899. *Páginas recolhidas*. Rio de Janeiro: Editora Garnier.
Assis, Machado de. 1906. *Relíquias de casa velha*. Rio de Janeiro: Editora Garnier.
Assis, Machado de. 1997. *The Posthumous Memoirs of Brás Cubas*. Trans. Gregory Rabassa. New York: Oxford University Press.
Assis, Machado de. 1998. *Quincas Borba*. Trans. Gregory Rabassa. New York: Oxford University Press.
Assis, Machado de. 2008a. Mariana. In *Machado de Assis: Obra completa em quatro volumes*, vol. 2, 1007–1019. Rio de Janeiro: Nova Aguilar.
Assis, Machado de. 2008b. *A Chapter of Hats and Other Stories*. Trans. John Gledson. London: Bloomsbury.
Assis, Machado de. 2008c. The Cane. In *A Chapter of Hats and Other Stories*. Trans. John Gledson. London: Bloomsbury.
Assis, Machado de. 2008d. Father versus Mother. In *A Chapter of Hats and Other Stories*. Trans. John Gledson. London: Bloomsbury.
Assis, Machado de. 2008e. Sabina. In *Obra completa*, vol. 3, 550–556.

Assis, Machado de. 2008f. Virginius: Narrativa de um advogado. In *Obra completa*, vol. 2. 750–761.

Chalhoub, Sidney. 2003. *Machado de Assis, historiador*. São Paulo: Companhia das Letras.

Daniel, G. Reginald. 2012. *Machado de Assis: Multiracial identity and the Brazilian novelist*. University Park: The Pennsylvania State University Press.

Duarte, Eduardo de Assis (ed.). 2007. *Machado de Assis afro-descendente: Escritos de caramujo (antologia)*. Rio de Janeiro: Crisálida.

Fitz, Earl E. 2015. *Machado de Assis and female characterization: The novels*. Lewisburg: Bucknell University Press.

Megid, Daniele Maria. 2014. *À roda de Brás Cubas: Literatura, ciência e personagens femininas em Machado de Assis*. São Paulo: Nankin Editorial.

Moraes, Renata Figueiredo. 2012. As festas da Abolição: O 13 de maio e seus significados no Rio de Janeiro (1888–1908). Dissertation, Pontifícia Universidade Católica, Rio de Janeiro.

Vital, Selma. 2012. *Quase brancos, quase pretos: Representação étnico-racial no conto machadiano*. São Paulo: Intermeios.

CHAPTER 6

Machado de Assis: From "Tragic Mulatto" to Human Tragicomedy

G. Reginald Daniel

Critics historically interpreted Machado de Assis as a mulatto who broke through the wall of second-class citizenship and studiously avoided any reference to his racial origins (Brookshaw 1986, 179–81; Daniel 2012, 62–76; Massa 1969, I: 55n56, 64–9; Sayers 1958, 385–400). His life and writings reflect a disinterest in slavery and race relations as well as other contemporary social issues. Critics argued that Machado's literary works, far from concerning themselves with questions of race, much less slavery, focus on the upper echelon—the urban bourgeoisie—which was a small and overwhelmingly white segment of Brazilian society (Daniel 2012, 4–5, 62–76).

By the mid-twentieth century, critics discovered that Machado did in fact display an interest in slavery, race relations, and other social concerns (Daniel 2012, 77–100). The plantation on which Brazil's political economy depended appears in its most developed form in the novels *The Posthumous Memoirs of Brás Cubas, Esau and Jacob,* and *Ayres's Memorial,* yet even in those works it is not central (Gledson 1984, 5). Indeed, later scholarship asserted that Machado's public pronouncements, as well as the treatment of slavery and race relations in his writings, seem both meek and

This chapter borrows from material in Daniel, *Machado de Assis: Multiracial Identity and the Brazilian novelist,* 2012.

G.R. Daniel (✉)
University of California, Santa Barbara, California, USA

L. Aidoo, D.F. Silva (eds.), *Emerging Dialogues on Machado de Assis,* DOI 10.1057/978-1-137-54174-1_6

sparse compared to several prominent late nineteenth and early twentieth-century Afro-Brazilian writers such as Luís Gama (1830–82), José do Patrocínio (1853–1905), and Lima Barreto (1881–1922) (Daniel 2012, 48–101; Marins 2004, 36, 40, 45; Wasserman 2008, 85, 97).

Drawing from Machado's own statements, as well as his prose fiction, I provide an alternative interpretation as to how Machado's writings were inflected by the experience of his racial identity. I argue that Machado endeavored to *transcend*, rather than *deny*, his racial background by embracing his greater humanity. In his writings, Machado sought to reflect this by universalizing the experience of racial ambiguity and duality regarding the "mulatto" condition in Brazil into a fundamental mode of human existence. For Machado, the struggle with duality and ambiguity is both personal and universal.

THE TRAGIC MULATTO

Machado's reticence regarding racial concerns, Raymond Sayers tells us, was most likely influenced in part by his marriage into a European Brazilian family of Portuguese descent and by his rise as a functionary in the governmental bureaucracy and increasing literary prominence, which culminated in his election as the first president of the Brazilian Academy of Letters (Sayers 1958, 388–9). Despite the more fluid race relations in nineteenth- and early twentieth-century Brazil—particularly in the state of Rio de Janeiro, where Machado was born and spent his life—mulattos were subject to both covert and overt forms of discrimination (Klein 1972, 309–34; Russell-Wood 1972, 84–133; Spitzer 1989, 102). Machado was not a slave. Yet he was only two generations or so removed from slavery and could not psychologically escape the fact that he was descended from African slaves.

Machado's father was a mulatto whose antecedents had been established in the free classes for at least one generation, and his mother was white (Massa 1969, 1: 33–4, 49). Moreover, a window of opportunity that Carl Degler refers to as the "mulatto escape hatch" (Degler 1971, 225) made it possible for a few exceptional, visibly or socially designated mulattoes in colonial and nineteenth-century Brazil to integrate themselves more easily into the dominant European Brazilian society. This informal social mechanism granted them vertical mobility in accordance with their approximation to a more European phenotype, as well as acquisition of the social, economic, intellectual, and cultural attainments characteristic of the privileged whites (Coutinho 1940, 22–4; Daniel 2006, x, 33–40; Degler 1971, 213–16, 223–2; Hoetink 1973, 21–45, 165–76; Spitzer 1989, 102).

Furthermore, since the beginning of the seventeenth century, Western civilization had come to view writing as the most visible sign of intellect. Individuals of African descent who could write and publish imaginative literature were said to have taken "a few giant steps up" (Gates 1986, 8–9) the ladder of evolution (Mazama 1998, 6, 9). A literary career, especially the new profession of journalism (Costa 2005, 561), was instrumental to the upward mobility of many mulattos in Brazil (Haberly 1983, 74; Needell 1987, 185). Journalism attracted "those whose marginal status, due to race or class, effectively barred them from more traditional careers" (Flory 1977, 213). Christine Costa observes that Machado, like many of his contemporaries, necessarily entered "the great halls of literature through the service entrance of journalism" (2005, 561). David Haberly suggests that a career in letters cosmetically touched up Machado's "real" racial status as a mulatto, by furthering the illusion of his situational status as white (Haberly 1983, 74).

Nevertheless, because his somatic identity was always apparent, Machado remained fundamentally vulnerable in his European Brazilian sociocultural milieu (Daniel 1981, 6; Haberly 1983, 74; Spitzer 1989, 12). Given the prevailing attitudes among the white elite (Skidmore 1974, 44–6), Machado was no doubt privy to their racist attitudes and comments. Indeed, Machado's close associate and prominent abolitionist Joaquim Nabuco (1849–1910) made racist statements publicly in his speeches as federal deputy during 1879. Nabuco expressed openly what he only implied in his books (Murat 1926, 146–8; Santos 2002, 66): his belief that Europeans were superior and Africans and Asians inferior and his fear that Brazil would remain a nation with a black majority. Nabuco was also explicit about his desire for the eventual racial whitening of Brazil, believing that because of their natural inferiority, Afro-Brazilians would vanish either through miscegenation or attrition (Nabuco 1938, 6; 1983, 180–3, 188–91).

Statements like this would certainly heighten Machado's awareness of his vulnerability even if they were not directed at him. Indeed, Haberly contends that Machado is a classic case study of what sociologists have traditionally associated with the condition of marginality, and specifically held to be the source of lifelong personal conflict, divided loyalties, ambivalence, and hypersensitivity. These traits have figured prominently in the literary trope of the tragic mulatto, caught between the white and black worlds without fully belonging to or being accepted by either (Berzon 1978, 99–111; Brookshaw 1986, 21–68; Raimon 2004, 1–25).

Essentially, Machado was an insider who remained to some extent a detached observer—an outsider. As an individual living on the margins of a society where white was an absolute good and black an absolute evil, Machado was surely aware that his mulatto appearance and racially blended ancestry (or "actual" racial identity; Goffman 1963, 2–3) made him inferior to the members of the elite European Brazilian circles in which he moved. At the same time, he realized that these same physical characteristics, in conjunction with his cultural refinement and intellectual accomplishments made him superior to the Afro-Brazilian masses. This racial and cultural capital, along with Machado's white spouse, succeeded in moving his perceived racial identity (or "virtual" racial identity; Goffman 1963, 2–3) closer to the white end of the social spectrum (Brookshaw 1986, 11, 57, 180; Daniel 1981, 6; Haberly 1983, 74).

Moreover, some critics have asserted that photographers retouched images of Machado in order to lighten his complexion, a practice that was common at the time (Duarte 2007b, 135; Santos and Dias 2006). Many contend that to further his rise to social and literary prominence, Machado disguised his mulatto facial features by wearing a thick mustache and a beard and that he also wore his hair closely cropped in his later years to enhance this camouflage (Dixon 1989, 1–3; Pérez 1962, 85). Certainly photographs of Machado indicate a more European appearance later in life. It is not implausible that Machado, seeking to bring as little attention to his origins as possible, may have chosen to hide the fullness of his lips and the waviness of his hair. On the other hand, he may have grown a beard because it was stylish at the time, and a moustache because it was indeed obligatory among men of the elite (Duarte 2007b, 135), and he may have simply chosen to wear his hair short, which coincidently gave him a more European appearance.

That said, it is interesting to note a statement by Nabuco in his response to José Veríssimo (1857–1916) when the latter, some weeks after Machado's death, wrote an article about the deceased author:

> Your article was simply beautiful, but this following sentence caused chills to run up my neck: "A mulatto, he was indeed a Greek of the best epoch." I would have never called him a mulatto, and I think nothing would cause him greater pain than your having concluded this. I beg that you remove this epithet when your article is made part of permanent records: The word is not literary and is pejorative. To me, he was white, and I believe that is what he considered himself: whatever foreign blood he may have had in no way affected his perfect Caucasoid makeup. I, at least, saw only the Greek in him. (Quoted in Massa 1969, 1: 47)[1]

What is noteworthy about Nabuco's remarks is his assumption that Machado considered himself white despite the lack of oral statements or written records that would indicate how he identified racially. Nabuco's reaction should not seem unusual if we consider the contemporary scientific racism that expounded upon the negative consequences of miscegenation and the diminished physical and mental capabilities of mulattoes (Skidmore 1974, 48–69). Although "mulatto" could have a negative connotation, it was more often used simply to designate multiracials of African and European descent. From Nabuco's perspective, any such reference devalued Machado's social and literary prominence and his contribution to Brazilian culture. Regardless of his racial origins, Machado had to be white, a status that was formally and publicly acknowledged in his obituary, which appeared in the newspaper *Correio da Manha* (Morning Mail): "I, Olympio da Silva Pereira, official of the civil registrar and senior notary of the sixth magistrate of the Federal District, on September 29, 1908—do hereby certify that on page 63 of the register of obituary under number 52 is recorded the obituary of Joaquim Maria Machado de Assis: age 69, widower, native of Rio de Janeiro, public functionary, white, death due to arterial sclerosis, at 3:20 a.m." (quoted in Sousa 1958, 168).

The Meta-Mulatto

Machado undoubtedly experienced the ambiguities and conflicts that come with marginality in a society that viewed white identities as dominant and black identities as subdominant, and thus both as mutually exclusive categories of experience. Feeling betwixt and between, he no doubt became adept at what Edwina Barbosa refers to as "selfcraft": a style of self-consciousness in which individuals continuously incorporate and discard aspects of their identity and experience in response to each situation (Barbosa 2008, 175–92, 207–29). Machado may have found it expedient to be silent on the issue of race and to subdue one racial component to the other in his public life to ensure his social survival (Daniel 1981, 6; Moniz 1984, 173–4).

Yet, contrary to David Haberly, I contend that Machado's manner of operating has less to do with feelings of discomfort that sociologists have traditionally attributed to the condition of marginality. This negative view of marginality that has underpinned the image of the tragic mulatto is based largely on misinterpretations of the work of sociologist Robert

E. Park, especially as articulated by Everett Stonequist (1937, 44–8, 139–58, 201–09). The latter distorted or ignored the positive nuances of Park's theory, which argued that marginality could also give individuals a broader vision and wider range of sympathies (Park 1928, 881–93).

In Machado's case, those sentiments traditionally associated with marginality coexisted with another, possibly overriding, desire to transcend all racial ascriptions and embrace a more universal and inclusive self, beyond questions of racial, cultural, or any other specificity. Far from espousing a naive egalitarianism that deflects attention away from—or even denies the existence of—racial inequities, I submit that Machado calls into question the notion that the most important thing about one's personhood is one's "community of descent" (Hollinger 2008, 1034). Notwithstanding the long-held belief that Machado sought at best to camouflage and at worst to deny being a mulatto by masquerading as white, his apparent lack of racial consciousness reflects his underlying desire to become raceless.

Of course, the ability to experience racelessness—a humanity unfettered by racial oppression—is a natural corollary of the ability to claim whiteness, given its privileged status in the racial hierarchy and whites' pervasive and universal status as the hegemonic Other against which all other Otherness is posited (Fanon 1952/1967, 138n24; Young 2006, 22). Seeking to become raceless and to masquerade as white involves the absence of attitudinal and behavioral markers that specifically affirm an affinity with racialized Otherness. Although both reflect integrationist dynamics, they diverge significantly in terms of motivation and operationalization.

Masquerading as white is an assimilationist identity based on inegalitarian integration. Individuals seek to blend into the larger society by covering (Yoshino 2006, 18), denying, or diluting something deemed inferior or undesirable, which, according to Irving Goffman, has a socially discrediting impact because it is stigmatized. Stigma, he argues, is a specific discrepancy between one's "virtual" social identity, which reflects the assumed demands and character imputed to individuals, and one's "actual" social identity, which reflects the category and attributes that individuals can in fact be proven to possess (Goffman 1963, 2–3).

In the extreme, this phenomenon may involve racial "passing," which, for example, has been associated with the adoption of a virtual white racial identity by individuals whose actual identity is African American according to the legal definition of blackness based on the one-drop rule of hypodescent. This device designates as black all individuals with any degree of African American descent (Daniel 1992, 92–4; 2002, 49–55;

Goffman 1963, 48–51). Passers have pirated an identity that allows them to escape racial subordination and gain privileges and status that are not "rightfully" theirs (Daniel 2002, 82–4; Ginsberg 1996, 3–5).

Passing not only can exact a heavy emotional toll but also maintains racial hierarchy even as it subverts normative racial categories. If viewed as part of a spectrum of tactics, however, passing may be viewed as an underground tactic, a conspiracy of silence and resistance that seeks to best oppression at its own game. Passing exposes not only the political motivations behind racial categories (Daniel 1992, 92–4; 2002, 49–55) but also racial difference as a continually emerging distinction devoid of any essential content. It attests to the fact that whiteness can be performed by someone who has mastered the art of racial cross-dressing and disguise (Ginsberg 1996, 3–5).

The absence of racial or cultural specificity (or deracination) that emerges in this process, where the goal is the dilution, denial, or erasure of something that is stigmatized and deemed undesirable, should not be confused with racelessness, which is based on egalitarian or transracial and transcultural integration. The objective of racelessness is to embrace a metaracial philosophy of life—one that seeks a more universal and inclusive identity transcending racial ascription altogether (Daniel 2002, 106–11; Renn 2004, 91–2; Rockquemore and Brunsma 2002, 71–2). Nonetheless, the fact that these two phenomena are mutually exclusive does not preclude them from existing sequentially or simultaneously over the course of an individual's psychological development (Daniel 2002, 106–11; Poston 1990, 52–5).

By striving toward universality—and perhaps what Joaquim Nabuco meant when he said he saw in Machado only the Greek—Machado de Assis may have appeared to be masquerading as white. He endeavored to transcend, rather than deny, his racial background by embracing his greater humanity (Adler 1974, 24–5).

In doing so, Machado's behavior is consistent with the identity paradigms captured by Adler, Ramirez, and others. Indeed, according to Adler, the identity that Machado claims is indicative of an individual who

> has an orientation and view of the world [that] profoundly transcends…his indigenous culture….He is…the timeless "universal" person described…by philosophers through the ages. He [is] the classical ideal of a person whose lifestyle is one of knowledge and wisdom, integrity and direction, principle and fulfillment, balance and proportion….[His] identity…is based, not on

> a "belongingness" which implies either owning or being owned by culture, but on a style of self consciousness that is capable of negotiating ever new formations of reality....He is neither totally a part of nor totally apart from his culture; he lives, instead, on the boundary. (Adler 1974, 24–5)

Machado refrained from explicit discussions of slavery, racial discrimination, Afro-Brazilian themes in general, and the mulatto experience in particular not simply to sidestep controversy, but because he also wished to create enduring works of art that had broader universal human significance. This was apart from any concerns about how being a mulatto and writing about racial matters might affect him personally or his ability to publish his work. It should be noted, however, that only a fraction of Machado's more than nine hundred characters are described in a way that would allow us to clearly infer their race (Daniel 2012, 181–2). It is true that those characters referred to as black or mulatto, directly or indirectly, are few, as compared to those directly or indirectly referred to as white. Nevertheless, the apparent dearth of discernibly Afro-Brazilian characters can be explained in part by the lack of what Machado considered "epidermal descriptions" and "long digressions, which would fill the paper without helping the action of the story" (1962: vol. 2, 27). Thus, it is assumed that those characters lacking racial specificity are white (Fanon 1952/1967, 138n24; Young 2006, 22).

This dearth of discernibly Afro-Brazilian characters may also be explained by the fact that Machado's main characters are primarily drawn from that small segment of Brazilian society that was also his primary audience: the urban bourgeoisie. Due to social stratification and racial demographics, these individuals would have been overwhelmingly white despite the demographic preponderance of blacks and mulattos in the public sphere and their significant presence in the private sphere of most whites. Moreover, as Gizêldo Nascimento and Mailde Trípoli point out, an accurate portrayal of the private lives of the white urban bourgeoisie would, for the most part, require that Afro-Brazilians be characterized as shadowy if not invisible figures, on the periphery of their social milieu (Nascimento 2002, 53–62; Trípoli 2006, 90–1).

However, if Machado chose to depict the urban bourgeoisie in all its splendor, vanities, psychology, and manners, why did he not chronicle the experiences of an important element within that society—the upwardly mobile mulatto? Machado's few mulatto characters, all of them female, do not actually portray the mulatto experience, that is, the conflicts, strains, and ambiguities specifically originating in the status and identity of multiracials of African and European descent in a society that prized whiteness and stigmatized blackness.[2] To understand this void in Machado's works, we need only consider his own firsthand knowledge of the subject matter and another, highly controversial, work of prose fiction, Aluísio Azevedo's *O mulato* (The Mulatto), written in 1879 and published in 1881. The novel is an attack on slavery and the racial bigotry of provincial society. Set in the state of Maranhão prior to the abolition of slavery, it involves a tragic love affair between the mulatto Raimundo, the main character, and his sexually unfulfilled wealthy white cousin, Ana Rosa.[3]

Machado's conspicuous avoidance of the topic of interracial intimacy in his own writings was sharply criticized by Gilberto Freyre (1962, 117–18). Yet, because Machado's writings focused on familial relationships and love among the ruling class, where interracial marriage was socially frowned upon (Expilly 1935, 277–80), it would have been impossible to introduce a mulatto (let alone a black) character into the main plot without forcing his novels to take on an explicitly sociological, polemical, or political cast. That Machado deliberately chose to avoid such an approach in his search for universality can be seen in several journal articles he contributed to *O Espelho* (1859), *O Futuro* (1862), and *Diario do Rio* (1866), where he advises:

> Do not involve yourself in polemics, be they of a political, literary, or any other nature....
>
> Our intentions are to see cultivated by Brazilian muses the literary novel that unifies the state of human passions and feelings ... that will make a mockery of the passing of time, always remaining the same and pure, under the rigid judgment of posterity.... Art destined to march in the vanguard of the people as an instructor must be immortal and relevant to future societies. (1962, vol. 3, 793; Viana Filho 1974, 21, 42–3)

This does not mean that the oppression experienced by blacks and mulattoes in nineteenth-century Brazil could not serve as a source of artistic inspiration by virtue of its historical specificity (Jackson 1988, xv). Indeed, Machado explores such oppression in some of his short stories, his more journalistically oriented chronicles and essays, and a few passages in his novels (Daniel 2012, 77–100). Moreover, his understanding of this and other social issues of the time "was farsighted enough to convey more than their immediate implications" (Nunes 1983, x). Yet, in Machado's opinion, writers who examined the Afro-Brazilian experience risked falling prey to the myopia and tendentiousness of political or social propaganda regardless of the aesthetic or ethical merit of the content—unless they could also bring broader human significance and greater universality to their work (Booth 1961, 118). And, given the weight of racial oppression, Afro-Brazilian writers faced the challenge of tempering their subjectivity and speaking to universal concerns when discussing the topic of race.

Nevertheless, some would argue that Machado's posture reflects his internalization and support of the inherently Eurocentric assumption that universality is a necessary criterion for art, and, in particular, that the literature of the subaltern is worthy only to the extent that it overcomes parochialism. But Machado did not support universality simply because it was part of the European canon. He did so because it was also a guard against the danger of falling into the catacombs of literary history (*Oc*, 3:912–13).

Given this somewhat Olympian vantage point, Machado veiled his mulatto experience in metaphor not simply as a type of camouflage and evasion because of any discomfort he might have felt about expressing that experience in his writings, but in an effort to unveil the basis of societal dis-ease. He attributed this to humanity's own metaphorically mulatto nature—particularly the dual and ambiguous relationship as well as conflict between the subjective and objective dimensions of human experience. The conception of the hybrid human subject erodes the very foundation of raciological thinking (Monteiro 2012).

From his own experience of being a racial blend of both black and white and yet neither, Machado developed an acute sensitivity to even more pervasive dualities and ambiguities. Accordingly, he displayed what has been termed "mestizo consciousness," "radical mestizaje," and "critical hybridity" (Anzaldúa 1987, 77; Ramirez 1983, 6; Daniel 2005, 264; Sandoval 2000, 72) by striving to go beyond the physical limitations of being a mulatto to become a meta-mulatto. Accordingly, Machado sought to universalize the experience of racial duality and ambiguity regarding the mulatto condition in Brazil into a fundamental mode of human existence—miscegenation in a higher sense.

To achieve this, Machado does in his writings what Brás Cubas from *Posthumous Memoirs of Brás Cubas* did in his famous delirium:

> I climbed to the top of a mountain…and from there I saw everything compressed into one…a reduction of centuries into one, a parading of them all, every race, every passion and feeling…the war of avarice and hate, the reciprocal destruction of beings and things….I saw everything…from what

we call glory to what we call misery....There came greed that devours, anger that kindles, envy that enslaves, and glory and grief, humid sweat, ambition, hunger, vanity, melancholy, wealth,—love—and all of them struggled within humanity. (112)

THE HUMAN TRAGICOMEDY

Deeply engaged in probing psychological motivations, Machado seeks to have his readers identify with what is universal in the human experience (Bone 1958, 2–3, 5; Coutinho 2010, 93–100; Daniel 2012, 185; Fitz 1989, 2, 5; Flynn, Calvo-González, and Mendes de Souza, 2013, 3–24; Gayle 1976, ix). Nevertheless, one can argue that racial concerns provide a seething backdrop in Machado's writings, however shadowy their presence (Gordon 1997, 8).[4] Machado drew considerable attention to the contradictions between public appearances and private feelings to a society that for all its virtuous pretenses was in fact cynical, dishonest, motivated by egoism, and sustained by African slavery (Borges 1995, 61; Brookshaw 1986, 179–81; Gledson 1984, 6–7; Sayers 1958, 389–90). Accordingly, Machado's writing provides a scathing, if oblique and masterfully disguised, critique of the European Brazilian elite (and by extension late nineteenth-century Westerners). They were themselves living in a world enslaved by materialist rationalism, egoism, and greed, and characterized by the accompanying lack of reciprocity between the subjective and objective dimensions of human experience. The former is the individual morality or conscience; the latter is the image reflected in the mirror through social interactions and motivated by egoism and the dictates of public success.

Machado considered the dominance of materialist rationalism with its underlying either/or paradigm to be the source of the extremity to which this schism between the subjective and objective dimensions of human experience had progressed in modern Western European consciousness and behavior (Boyd 1975, 45; Caldwell 1970, 125; Daniel 1981, 11; 2002, 180, 189; Haberly 1983, 74–5; Nunes 1983, 12, 82–4, 140, 142–3). As someone highly sensitive to the "space-in-between" (*o entre-lugar*; Santiago 1978, 9), Machado not only challenges the whole notion of exclusive (or dichotomous) and essentialist categories of difference—racial and otherwise—but also calls into question the hierarchical ranking upon which these differences are constructed. He seeks to move away from the modern and Eurocentric either/or paradigm to incorporate concepts of both/neither (Daniel 2002, 180, 189; Daniel 2012, 187–9; Rattansi 1994, 30; Rosenau 1992, 5–7; Seidman 1994, 8–9).

Although Machado's writings are not empirically autobiographical, neither are they, as Brookshaw and others have suggested, divorced from his racial origins. The dualism and ambiguity he experienced (between himself and the dominant Euro-Brazilian culture) was a source of his intense concern with the dual and ambiguous relationship between individual morality or conscience (the internal or subjective self) and the image reflected in the mirror through social interactions (the external or objective self), which is motivated by egoism and the dictates of public success (Daniel 1981, 10, 11–13; Haberly 1983, 74–7). Nowhere is Machado's sensitivity to these questions more explicit than in the short story "O espelho" (The Mirror), where the narrator puts forth the notion that humanity possesses two souls: the subjective self (*alma interior*) and the objective self (*alma exterior*; *Oc*, 2:345–52). The importance of this dual essence is symbolized by Jacobina, a former military officer who needs to parade in front of a mirror in his decorated uniform—alma exterior—in order to reaffirm his existence.

Ideally, the internal and external identities, the individual conscience, and the dictates of public success should work together. Machado's gallery of characters, under the exigencies of materialist rationalist thinking, are more often than not individuals in whom the external self and ambition for public success are at odds with the promptings of the individual conscience and morality, thus impeding—or precluding—a sense of mutuality between the two identities (Daniel 1981, 12; Haberly 1983, 76; Passos 2007, 12, 24, 38, 44–5, 59, 68, 104–05; 2009, 57). Machado's characters are not, however, defined by their moral goodness or badness, notwithstanding their propensity for evildoing. Rather, they are made from a complex and tragicomic blending of doubt with hope; of pride, egoism, and ambition with altruism, social responsibility, and self-sacrifice such that "seriousness stimulates laughter, and pain pleasure," in the words of eighteenth-century German critic Gotthold Lessing (1968, 6:353; Carlson 1993, 170).

Alfredo Bosi considers Machado to be a master analyst of the complicated and often murky relationship between the two identities, which he refers to as "first nature" and "second nature." First nature, which consists of individual inclinations, desires, and drives, is more often than not veiled by second nature, which is composed of conventions, habits, customs, and norms imposed by society. The strategic interplay between essences and appearances results in a host of vices that come masked as virtues through skillful calculation, hypocrisy, arrogance, lying, and other strategies (Bosi 1999, 81; 2004, 366–9).

José Luiz Passos maintains that Machado's protagonists display the tension between these two identities, between their desires and social norms, in the face of factual occurrences, and that the effects of memory play a crucial role in this process by allowing a certain distancing between the actual facts and the consciousness operationalized in the narration. As someone who navigated a racial location intermediate to black and white, Machado became acutely mindful of the liminality (from the Latin *limen*, "boundary" or "threshold") or twilight zone of experience (Turner 1969, 94–130; Whalen 2004, 1) where the absolute truth about fact and fiction is their inherent ambiguity as relative extremes on a continuum of grays (Hansen 1997, 250–1).

More than simply relating the facts, Machado is interested in exposing the conflict between the subjectivity of the characters and their respective objective social personae. This involves a process in which protagonists seek to fashion the public presentation of their selves by imagining alternatives to their actual origins, desires, and social predicaments (Passos 2009, 57). Machado's writings are intricate reflections on how his characters make decisions and how they often seek to camouflage—or mask, according to Bosi—their underlying motivations from themselves and others (Bosi 1994, 79–81; Passos 2007, 44, 52, 68, 73, 79, 104–5, 108–10).

The dialectic between these two identities, according to Passos, is what provides the basis for the disconcerting albeit humorous ambivalence that emerges with Machado's novels, beginning with *The Posthumous Memoirs of Brás Cubas*. As an observer who can distance himself in time, the deceased narrator Brás feels free to speculate—and take the reader along as an accomplice—about the subtle game of intentions he exposes in the events he relates (Passos 2007, 58, 110–14, 123–30, 153–8). Yet, like Brás, most of Machado's main characters are ambivalent, ambiguous, elusive, and contradictory (Moreci 2009; Passos 2007, 52, 58). They straddle the fine margin between reason and sentiment, conscious desires and unconscious motivations, public appearances and private feelings, and the choices they make.

Machado's characters inhabit an absurd existence where the cut of one's clothes, the size of one's bank account, and other such material considerations invariably supersede loving relationships (Nunes 1983, 140–3; Virgillo 1966, 778–86). Instead of being helpless victims of circumstances beyond their control, they fail to choose the one thing that might bring them wholeness—love—pursuing substitutes under the pressures of public success and the dictates of the external self (Borges 1995, 60–1; Daniel 1981, 12; 40, 142–3; Passos 2007, 42–7; Virgillo 1966, 778–86).

Though Machado makes no direct statements or pronouncements, his ironical narration and allusions reflect a criticism of humanity, expressed through the recurring theme in which the external self and ambition for public success are at odds with the promptings of the individual conscience and morality, which impedes—or precludes—a sense of reciprocity between the two identities. Machado hoped to make his readers see themselves and to point the way to a cure, however elusive, by holding up the mirror of his fictions (Haberly 1983, 140; Nunes 1983, 141). Within his sorrows and triumphs as a multiracial individual seeking to achieve upward mobility and public success without compromising his own integrity in a society that prized whiteness and stigmatized blackness, Machado saw a reflection of the struggles confronting all of humanity.

NOTES

1. Unless otherwise indicated, all translations are my own.
2. One possible exception is the mulatto slave girl Sabina. In *Americanas* (American Verses; 1865), a collection of Machado's poetry, the poem "Sabina" tells of a brief sexual escapade between Sabina and Octávio, the master's handsome son, who, during his vacation from school, leaves Sabina pregnant. After returning to school, Octávio falls in love with a white girl. Now a college graduate, he returns home married to this young woman, having forgotten his interlude with Sabina, who is now carrying his child. In desperation, Sabina decides to drown herself and the baby in the river at the place where Octávio had seduced her. But the call of motherhood wins out in the end. The poem ends with Sabina lying stoically on the river's edge, but uncertain of the future (*Poesias completas, Americanas, Oc*, 3:140–5).
3. It is interesting that Azevedo's novel does not appear in Machado's literary criticism. This lacuna is all the more remarkable considering that Machado was engaged in an open and at times acrimonious debate over the merits of Realism-Naturalist aesthetics to which Azevedo subscribed. On April 16 and 30, 1878, writing under the pseudonym "Eleazar," Machado critiqued the aesthetics of Realism-Naturalism, particularly that of Portuguese writer Eça de Queirós, in a two-part essay published in *0 Cruzeiro* (Southern Cross; *Crítica, Oc*, 3:903–13). In December 1879, Machado published an even lengthier critique, "A nova geração" (The New Generation; *Crítica, Oc*,

3:809–34) in *Revista Brasileira*, vol. 2, which was an equally strong attack against Brazilian writers he felt had come under the pernicious spell of Realist-Naturalist aesthetics. Notwithstanding Machado's advice in the 1850s and 1860s that authors avoid polemics, literary and otherwise, this critique from the late 1870s indicates that he may have somewhat shifted his stance on this question at least in terms of literary aesthetics more generally if not specifically the topic of race.

4. See for example, Bim 2010; Borges 1995; Chalhoub 2010; 2003; Duarte 2007a,b; Gledson 1984; Magalhães Junior 1955; Marotti 1982; Nascimento 2002; Schwarz 1977, 1990, and 1992; and Trípoli 2006, among other works.

References

Adler, Peter S. 1974. Beyond cultural identity: Reflections on cultural and multi-cultural man. In *Topics in cultural learning*, ed. R. Brislin, 23–40. Honolulu: Ease-West Center.

Anzaldúa, Gloria. 1987. *Borderlands: La Frontera—The New Mestiza*. San Francisco: Spinsters/Aunt Lute.

Assis, Joaquim Maria Machado de. 1962. *Obra completa*. 3 vols. Rio de Janeiro: Editora José Aguilar.

Barbosa, Edwina. 2008. *Wealth of selves: Multiple identities, mestiza consciousness, and the subject of politics*. College Station: Texas A&M University Press.

Berzon, Judith. 1978. *Neither white nor black: The mulatto character in American fiction*. New York: New York University Press.

Bim, Leda Marana. 2010. Amor e morte: Uma comparação dos contos 'Pai contra Mãe' e 'Mariana.' In *Machado de Assis e a escravidão/Machado de Assis und die Sklaverei* Hamburg Conferences, eds. Gustavo Bernardo, Joachim Michel, and Markus Schaffauer, 115–124. São Paulo: Annablume.

Bone, Robert. 1958. *The negro novel in America*. New Haven: Yale University Press.

Booth, Wayne C. 1961. *The rhetoric of fiction*. Chicago: University of Chicago Press.

Borges, Dain. 1995. The recognition of Afro-Brazilian symbols and ideas, 1890–1940: Luso-Brazilian Review. *Culture and ideology in the Americas: Essays in honor of Richard M. Morse* 32(2) (Winter): 59–78.

Bosi, Alfredo. 1994. *História Concisa da Literatura Brasileira*. São Paulo: Editora Cultrix.

Bosi, Alfredo. 1999. *Machado de Assis: O enigma do olhar*. São Paulo: Ática.

Bosi, Alfredo. 2004. Raymundo Faoro: Leitor de Machado de Assis. *Estudos Avançados* 18(51): 355–376.

Boyd, A. O. 1975. The concept of black aesthetics as seen in selected works of three Latin American writers: Machado de Assis, Nicolás Guillén, and Adalberto Ortiz. PhD dissertation, Stanford University.

Brookshaw, David. 1986. *Race and color in Brazilian literature*. Metuchen: Scarecrow Press.

Caldwell, Helen. 1970. *Machado de Assis: The Brazilian master and his novels*. Berkeley: University of California Press.

Carlson, Marin A. 1993. *Theories of the theatre: A historical and critical survey from the Greeks to the present*, Expandedth ed. Ithaca: Cornell University Press.

Chalhoub, Sidney. 2003. *Machado de Assis: Historiador*. São Paulo: Companhia das Letras.

Chalhoub, Sidney. 2010. What are noses for? Paternalism, social Darwinism, and race science in Machado de Assis. *Journal of Latin American Cultural Studies* 10(2): 171–191.

Costa, C. 2005. Machado de Assis: The apprentice journalist. *Portuguese literary and cultural studies*, special issue, *The Author as Plagiarist: The case of Machado de Assis*, (13–14) (Fall–Spring): 561–569.

Coutinho, Afrânio. 1940. Machado de Assis e o problema do mestiço. *Revista do Livro*, 3rd ser., 3(20): 22–29.

Coutinho, Eduardo de Faria. 2010. A desconstrução de estereótipos na obra de Machado de Assis: A questão da escravidão. In *Machado de Assis e a Escravidão/ Macchado de Assis und die Sklaverei*, Hamburg Conferences, eds. Gustavo Joachim Michel, and Markus Schaffauer, 93–100. Sao Paulo: Annablume.

Daniel, G. Reginald. 1981. Machado de Assis: Racial identity and the Brazilian novelist. Paper presented at the symposium on Portuguese Traditions, University of California, Los Angeles.

Daniel, G. Reginald. 1992. Passers and pluralists: Subverting the racial divide. In *Racially mixed people in America*, ed. Maria P.P. Root, 91–108. Newberry Park: Sage.

Daniel, G. Reginald. 2002. *More than black? multiracial identity and the new racial order*. Philadelphia: Temple University Press.

Daniel, G. Reginald. 2005. Beyond Eurocentrism and Afrocentrism: Globalization, critical hybridity, and postcolonial blackness. In *Critical globalization studies*, ed. Richard P. Appelbaum and William L. Robinson, 259–268. New York: Routledge.

Daniel, G. Reginald. 2006. *Race and multiraciality in Brazil and the United States: Converging paths?* University Park: Pennsylvania State University Press.

Daniel, G. Reginald. 2012. *Machado de Assis: Multiracial identity and the Brazilian novelist*. University Park: Pennsylvania State University Press.

Degler, Carl N. 1971. *Neither black nor white: Slavery and race relations in Brazil and the United States*. New York: Macmillan.

Dixon, Paul. 1989. *Retired dreams: "Dom Casmurro": Myth and modernity*. West Lafayette: Purdue Research Foundation.

Duarte, Eduardo de Assis. 2007a. *Machado de Assis afro-descendente: Escritos de caramujo (antologia)*. Rio de Janeiro/Belo Horizonte: Pallas/Crisálidas.

Duarte, Eduardo de Assis. 2007b. Machado de Assis's African descent: *Research in African Literatures* 38(1) (Spring): 134–151.

Expilly, Charles [Jean-Charles Marie]. 1935. *Mulheres e costumes do Brasil.* São Paulo: Companhia Editôra Nacional.

Fanon, Franz. 1952/1967. *Black skin, white masks.* Trans. Charles Lam Markmann. New York: Grove Press.

Fitz, Earl. 1989. *Machado de Assis.* Boston: G. K. Hall.

Flory, Thomas. 1977. Race and social control in independent Brazil. *Latin American Studies* 9(2): 199–224.

Flynn, Alex, Elena Calvo-González, and Marcelo Mendes de Souza. 2013. Whiter shades of pale: 'Coloring In' Machado de Assis and race in contemporary Brazil. *Latin American Research Review* 48(3): 3–24.

Freyre, Gilberto. 1962. Reinterpretando José de Alencar. In *Vida, forma, e cor*, ed. Gilberto Freyre, 115–133. Rio de Janeiro: José Olympio.

Gates Jr., Henry Louis. 1986. Editor's introduction: Writing race and the difference it makes. In *Race, writing, and difference*, ed. Henry Louis Gates, 1–20. Chicago: University of Chicago Press.

Gayle Jr., Addison. 1976. *The way of the new world: The Black novel in America.* New York: Doubleday.

Ginsberg, Elaine K. 1996. Introduction: The politics of passing. In *Passing and the fictions of identity*, ed. Elaine K. Ginsberg, 1–18. Durham: Duke University Press.

Gledson, John. 1984. *The deceptive realism of Machado de Assis.* Francis Cairns: Liverpool Monographs in Hispanic Studies. Liverpool.

Goffman, Irving. 1963. *Stigma: Notes on the management of spoiled identity.* Englewood Cliffs: Prentice-Hall.

Gordon, Avery. 1997. *"Ghostly matters": Haunting and the sociological imagination.* Minneapolis: University of Minnesota Press.

Haberly, David T. 1983. *Three sad races: National identity and national consciousness in Brazilian literature.* New York: Cambridge University Press.

Hansen, João Adolfo. 1997. *Dom Casmurro,* the fruit and the rind: An afterword. In *"Dom Casmurro": A Novel by Joaquim Maria Machado de Assis.* Trans. John Gledson, 245–258. New York: Oxford University Press.

Hoetink, H[arramus]. 1973. *Slavery and race relations in the Americas: Comparative notes on their nature and nexus.* New York: Harper and Row.

Hollinger, David A. 2008. Obama, the instability of color lines, and the promise of a postethnic future. *Callaloo* 31(4 (Fall)): 1033–1037.

Jackson, Richard L. 1988. *Black literature and humanism in Latin America.* Athens: University of Georgia Press.

Klein, Herbert S. 1972. Nineteenth-century Brazil. In *Neither slave nor free: The freemen of African descent in the slave societies of the new world*, ed. David Cohen and Jack P. Greene, 309–334. Baltimore: Johns Hopkins University Press.

Lessing, Gotthold Ephraim. 1968. In *Gesammelte Werke*, vol. 10, 2nd ed, ed. Rilla Paul. Berlin: Aufbau.

Luiz, Viana Filho. 1974. *A vida de Machado de Assis*. São Paulo: Livraria Martins Editora.

Magalhães Junior, Raimundo. 1955. *Machado de Assis desconhecido*. Rio de Janeiro: Civilização Brasileira.

Marins, A. 2004. *Machado e Lima: Da ironia* a *sátira*. Série Ensaios Brasileiros, no. I. Rio de Janeiro: Utópos.

Marotti, Giorgio. 1982. *Il negro nel romanzo brasiliano*. Rome: Bulzoni Editore.

Massa, Jean-Michel. 1969. *La jeunesse de Machado de Assis (1839–1870): Essai de biographie intellectuelle*, vol. 2. Aix-en-Provence: Rennes.

Mazama, Arna. 1998. The Eurocentric discourse on writing: An exercise in self-determination. *Journal of Black Studies* 29(1): 3–16.

Moniz, Edmundo. 1984. *O espírito das épocas: Dialéctica da ficção*, 4th ed. Rio de Janeiro: Elo Editora e Distribuidora.

Monteiro, Pedro Meira. 2012. *External review of 'Machado de Assis: Multiracial identity and the Brazilian novelist.'* University Park: Pennsylvania State University Press.

Moreci, M. 2009. False truths: How fact is fiction in Machado de Assis. *Quarterly Conversation*, December 7. http://quarterlyconversation.com/false-truths-how-fact-is-fiction-in-machado-de-assis

Murat, Luis. 1926. Machado de Assis e Joaquim Nabuco. *Revista da Academia Brasileira de Letras* 21(54): 146–148.

Nabuco, Joaquim. 1938. *O abolicionismo*. Rio de Janeiro: Civilização Brasileira.

Nabuco, Joaquim. 1983. *Discursos parlamentares*. Brasilia: Câmara dos Deputados.

Nascimento, Gizelda Melodo. 2002. Machado: Três momentos negros. *Terra Roxa e Outras Terras: Revista de Estudos Literários* 2: 53–62.

Needell, Jeffrey D. 1987. *A Tropical Belle Époque: Elite Culture and Society in Tum-of-the-Century Rio de Janeiro*. New York: Cambridge University Press.

Nunes, Maria Luisa. 1983. *The craft of an absolute winner: Characterization and narratology in the novels of Machado de Assis*. Westport: Greenwood Press.

Park, Robert. 1928. Human migration and the marginal man. *American Journal of Sociology* 33(May): 881–893.

Passos, José Luiz. 2007. *Machado de Assis: O romance com pessoas*. São Paulo: EDUSP, Nankin Editoria.

Passos, José Luiz. 2009. O mal e a metamorfose em Machado de Assis. *Luso-Brazilian Review* 46(1): 57–74.

Pérez, Renard. 1962. Esboço biográfico: Machado de Assis e a sua circunstância. In *Obra Completa, 1*, ed. Joaquim Maria Machado de Assis, 65–90. Rio de Janeiro: Editora José Aguilar.

Poston, W.S. Carlos. 1990. The biracial identity model: A needed addition. *Journal of Counseling and Development* 69: 152–155.

Raimon, Eve Allegra. 2004. *The "tragic mulatta" revisited: Race and nationalism in nineteenth-century antislavery fiction*. New Brunswick: Rutgers University Press.

Ramirez, Manuel I.I.I. 1983. *Psychology of the Americas: Mestizo perspectives on personality and mental health*. New York: Pergamon Press.

Rattansi, Ali. 1994. 'Western' racisms, ethnicities, and identities in a 'Postmodern' frame. In *Racism, modernity, and identity: On the western front*, ed. Ali Rattansi and Sallie Westwood, 15–86. Cambridge: Polity Press.

Renn, Kristen. 2004. *Mixed race students in college*. Albany: State University of New York Press.

Rockquemore, Kerry Ann, and David L. Brunsma. 2002. *Beyond black: Biracial identity in America*. Thousand Oaks: Sage.

Rosenau, Pauline Marie. 1992. *Postmodernism and the social sciences: Insights, inroads, and intrusions*. Princeton: Princeton University Press.

Russell-Wood, Anthony John R. 1972. Colonial Brazil. In *Neither slave nor free: The freemen of African descent in the slave societies of the new world*, ed. David W. Cohen and Jack P. Greene, 84–133. Baltimore: Johns Hopkins University Press.

Sandoval, Chela. 2000. *Methodology of the oppressed*. Minneapolis: University of Minnesota Press.

Santiago, Silviano. 1978. O entre-lugar no discurso latino-americano. In *Uma literatura nos trópicos: Ensaios sobre dependência cultural*, 9–26. São Paulo: Perspectiva.

Santos, Sales Augusto dos. 2002. Historical roots of the 'whitening' of Brazil. *Latin American Perspectives* 29(1) (January): 61–82.

Santos, L. and C. Dias. 2006. Carta da redação: História sem retoques. *Raça Brasil* 95 (February). http://racabrasil.uol.com.br/Edicoes/95/arcigo14890-1.asp

Sayers, Raymond S. 1958. *O negro na literatura brasileira*. Trans. Antonio Houaiss. Rio de Janeiro: Cruzeiro.

Schwarz, Roberto. 1977. *Ao vencedor as batatas: Forma literária e processo social nos inícios do romance brasileira*. São Paulo: Duas Cidades.

Schwarz, Roberto. 1990. *Um mestre na periferia do capitalismo: Machado de Assis*. São Paulo: Duas Cidades.

Schwarz, Roberto. 1992. *Misplaced ideas: Essays on Brazilian culture*. Trans. John Gledson. New York: Verso.

Seidman, Steven. 1994. Introduction. In *The postmodern turn: New perspectives on social theory*, ed. Seidman Steven, 1–21. New York: Cambridge University Press.

Skidmore, Thomas A. 1974. *Black into white: Race and nationality in Brazilian thought*. New York: Oxford University Press.

Sousa, J. Galante de. 1958. "Cronologia de Machado de Assis." *Revista do Livro* 3 (September): 141-181.

Spitzer, Leo. 1989. *Lives in between: Assimilation and marginality in Austria, Brazil, and West Africa, 1780–1945*. New York: Cambridge University Press.

Stonequist, Everett W. 1937. *The marginal man*. New York: Russell and Russell.

Trípoli, Mailde Jerônimo. 2006. *Imagens, mascaras, e mitos: O negro na obra de Machado de Assis*. Campinas: Editora Unicamp.

Turner, Victor Witter. 1969. *The ritual process: Structure and anti-structure*. Ithaca: Cornell University Press.

Virgillo, Carmelo. 1966. Love and the 'Causa Secreta' in the tales of Machado de Assis. *Hispania* 49(4): 778–786.

Wasserman, Renata R. Mautner. 2008. Race, nation, representation: Machado de Assis and Lima Barreto. *Luso-Brazilian Review* 45(2): 84–106.

Whalen, T. 2004. Introduction: Rhetoric as Liminal Practice. RHETOR I. http://ourspace.uregina.ca/bitstream/handle/10294/664/Rhetor_Vol_1_2004.pdf?sequence=1

Yoshino, Kenji. 2006. *Covering: The hidden assault on our civil rights*. New York: Random House.

Young, John K. 2006. *Black writers, white publishers: Marketplace politics in twentieth-century African American literature*. Jackson: University Press of Mississippi.

CHAPTER 7

"Father versus Mother": Slavery and Its Apparatuses

Fernando Sousa de Rocha

In 2011, a TV commercial in celebration of Caixa Econômica Federal's (CEF) 150th anniversary stirred a commotion. To prove the bank's effectiveness in helping Brazilians with their finances and the faith that Brazilian celebrities placed in the bank, CEF's commercials used the images of the famous individuals who once had accounts with it. In their commercial portraying Machado de Assis, the world-renowned mulatto writer was played by a white actor. Assis had been whitened. Although it was supposed to remain unnoticed, given that whitening permeated even the notion of racial democracy, complaints against CEF's white Machado resulted in a second commercial, this time with a mulatto actor. Such reblackening of Assis is certainly part of a wider movement, also noticeable in the criticism of Assis's literary works, the most important of which being *Machado de Assis Afro-descendente*, by Eduardo de Assis Duarte (2009).[1] Rather than seeing Assis as a writer who rarely commented on matters related to the experiences of Afro-descendants, critics have collected the instances in which he does so and proposed new readings of his works. This chapter aims to contribute to such readings, focusing on the short story "Father versus Mother" as a text that depicts a microcommunity of Africans and Afro-descendants—free, freed, or enslaved—that

F.S. de Rocha (✉)
Department of Spanish and Portuguese, Middlebury College,
Middlebury, VT, USA

© The Editor(s) (if applicable) and The Author(s) 2016
L. Aidoo, D.F. Silva (eds.), *Emerging Dialogues on Machado de Assis*, DOI 10.1057/978-1-137-54174-1_7

91

is defined by a sociability stemming from the experience of enslavement. Assis's story begins with an initial postulate that slavery implied, in its practice, "trades and tools" (1966, 101), such as slave catching—the protagonist's main occupation—as well as masks, iron collars, and anklets used to punish slaves. This chapter will examine these trades and tools, delineating slavery in order to explore how they delimit the microcommunity that Assis represents in his story.

In "Father versus Mother," the narrator makes it clear from the very start that there is a connection between trades and tools, affirming, "If I mention certain tools it is only because they are linked to a certain trade" (101). In fact, one of the apparatuses cited is the iron collar, which, as the narrator notes, "was used for runaway slaves" (101), thus being directly related to the protagonist's occupation. Also, according to the narrator, the iron collar functioned as an index of a slave's repeated crime of running away, therefore aiding in recapturing them. The same might not be said, however, in relation to another apparatus the narrator mentions, the tin mask—since it bears no relation to the occupation of catching runaway slaves. The narrator himself appears to realize the impropriety of his own choice of example, for he concludes his not-so-short description of the mask with a negative exhortation to the reader: neither the reader nor the narrator should concern themselves with masks. If this is the case, however, why should the narrator mention them? Only to invite the reader to not mind this aspect of the culture that slavery engendered? And, above all, why should we readers put aside the concise, insightful analysis that the text provides us in portraying the mask? Is it simply the case that in a freer style, the writer went off topic but, acknowledging he went astray, redirects the narrative back to a real relation between a trade and the tools of the trade? Or did the discussion about the mask serve only to set the stage for the story that is later told about Candinho, the slave catcher? To my mind, what this link between trade and tool—occupation and apparatus—reveals is a much more fundamental relation, one that is also more malleable and insidious. It is not only a matter of how certain apparatuses were used in the practice of certain occupations, but also how these apparatuses, be they directly employed in the occupation portrayed in the story or not, partook in the constitution of the very possibility of construction of subjectivities and sociabilities.[2]

Therefore, it behooves readers, contrary to the narrator's indication, to concern themselves with tin masks, iron collars, and iron anklets, taking the narrator's contradictory negative exhortation as an awry recuperation of what is socially repressed. In doing so, we may start recomposing, even if partially, the apparatus—in the broader sense of the term—of which the mentioned punishing tools are a part. Within this context, the narrator's excuse, his logical construction "If I mention..., it is only because..." begins to operate as a positive invitation that, as such, turns out to be broadly encompassing and punctual, just like the apparatuses out of which it is born. The tin mask, for example, responds to a specific vice—drunkenness—and focuses on one part of the enslaved body, the mouth. In this specialization of the vices and particularization of the body, what is at play is a technicization of punitive practices, in such a manner that each vice and its corresponding body parts are equivalent to a certain punishing device. Apparently quite simple, such a device is, in fact, rather elaborate regarding the relationship between vice, device, punishment, and correction.

In this production of docile bodies—bodies that, in an inversion of the narrator's sarcastic remarks, conform to slavery and blows—there too is a technicization in terms of not only the manufacturing of the apparatus, but also of its use.[3] This is evident, for instance, in Jean-Baptiste Debret's description of the punisher who carries out the act of whipping, being careful enough to manufacture his own tool in order to make his task easier (1978, 356). Having in his possession an improved device to accompany his perfected technique, the punisher may then carry out the punishment more effectively. In his *Voyage pittoresque et historique au Brésil*, Debret tells us, "People admire the ability of the punisher who, in raising his arm to strike a blow, slightly scratches the epidermis, leaving it in open flesh after the third whip" (356). Apparatus and technique combined, one responding to the needs of the other and thereby leading to their improvement, enable the proper duration and depth necessary for an exemplar punishment, as well as the possibility of saving enough strength to finalize the punishment (356). In this need to moderate one's actions, there lies the implied possibility that such an action can become immoderate, excessive in the technicized relation that ought to exist between indocility and punishment. In this sense, punishment represents a dangerous continuity between the production of the enslaved body and its destruction and unproductive dismemberment.

It is this tearing into pieces of the unproductive enslaved body that is at the root of the cruelty that the narrator of "Father versus Mother" notices: "It was grotesque, this [tin] mask! But a humane social order is not always achieved without the grotesque, and sometimes not without the cruel" (101). From the grotesque to the cruel, we witness the shift from a punishment that favors production, such as the tin mask itself, to one that may threaten it, causing a waste of property with nothing being produced. As the narrator notes, "The feeling of ownership moderated [the owner's] actions, because money hurts too" (101–102). No slave should be punished to the point of rendering him or her useless.

Beyond its punitive function—controlling and restraining slaves' capacity to ingest food and liquids, limiting their vision and constraining respiration—the tin mask constitutes a specialized imprisonment, for it allows the slave to continue working, nevertheless coupling the body with a mobile form of imprisonment. The grotesque, therefore, would reside in this manufacture of a prison-body, a mode of imprisonment that aspires to be the enslaved body itself.[4] It is not difficult to take the narrator's observations about this coupling of bodies and prisons a few steps further, to their logical conclusions. According to the narrator, iron collars were obviously heavy (Assis 2007, 466); (if we then imagine prolonged use of the collar or the mask), we can also understand their subsequent damage to the body. Debret offers a more in-depth description of the iron collar than does Assis's narrator. It is not merely, as in the short story, a device that was "less a punishment than an identification" (Assis 1966, 101), but in fact a device that had been conceived with the efficiency of catching runaway slaves in mind. It not only made the escape more difficult and aided in the catching, particularly when it came with "a projecting iron shaft on the right or left" (Assis 1966, 101), as we see in Debret's illustration (345). The iron collar effectively blurred the boundary between punishment and mutilation. As Debret points out, at the moment the slave catcher holds onto the shaft and leans on it with all his weight, "the inverse pressure is produced at the other end of the collar, forcefully lifting the slave's jaw; the pain is terrible and ends any resistance, mainly when the pressure is renewed with jolts" (343). Captured, the enslaved has two options: to either become docile and accept subjugation or resist and risk severe injury.

Of all the devices cited by the narrator, none seems to push the limits of punishment as far as the thumbscrews (ironically called in Portuguese *anjinhos*, literally meaning little angels). These consisted of one or two rings that were placed around the tip of the thumb or finger. The rings were "gradually tightened, by means of a screw that diminished [their] diameter…, inflicting atrocious pain on the victim and often the breaking of the bone and resulting in permanent mutilation" (Moura 2013, 44). Thus, in the case of the thumbscrews, the enslaved body could be quickly torn to pieces, although this did not necessarily imply utter unproductivity, since—not having the entire finger smashed or amputated—the slave would still be able to grip and hold objects.[5]

Alongside this continuity between the production of the enslaved body and its destruction, there emerges another continuity in the very formation of an identity for the enslaved body. If we focus on the description of the different apparatuses in the production of the slave body, we notice that there is a shift from actions and their results (drunkenness and theft, related to the tin mask) to the identification of a specific agent (runaways, related to the iron collar). From drunkenness and theft to runaways, what is at stake is an ideological continuum in which enslaved bodies may be the means for realizing certain actions (in the same manner that they are a means for production) but are also agents subject to a certain identity within the slavocratic society. In this sense, the runaway slaves of Nova Friburgo, a city in the state of Rio de Janeiro, are quite illustrative, insofar as the slaves were iron branded with the letter *F* for *fujões* (runaways; Botelho 2010). An identity for a specific group among enslaved Africans and Afro-descendants was thus created and furthermore made easily recognizable, being inscribed on the enslaved body, so that identity and subjected body were fused as a body identity. As an example, the case of the runaways from Nova Friburgo evinces the extent to which the joining of apparatuses and enslaved bodies could potentially engender a subaltern identity. In other words, within the slavocratic order, every enslaved body is forcefully placed into a certain identity—a place in the spectrum of power and social reality.

In as much as the delimitations between enslaved, free, and freed Africans and Afro-descendants were not always clear-cut, visible forms of identification and categorization of nonwhite bodies could also produce anguishing ambiguities. Visible signs of slavery would separate the enslaved from the free or freed. But what would happen if, for whatever reason, such signs remained unseen? What if they were erased? What if the slave did not bear them?[6] Any nonwhite, as Hebe Maria Mattos observes, "continued to have even his or her right to come and go dramatically dependent on the usual recognition of his or her condition of being free." If mistaken for a slave, free or freed blacks "would automatically be suspected of being runaway slaves—therefore subject to all types of arbitrary acts" (Mattos 2000, 21). In fact, in Assis's story, the protagonist Candinho, eager to catch a slave, ends up detaining a freed black by mistake. The slave catcher "melted into a thousand apologies, but did not escape a pummeling at the hands of the man's relatives" (106). The violence with which the free man's relatives respond to Candinho's mistake constitutes a reaction—in the same degree—to the violence exerted during the act of capturing the runaway slave, not to mention the distress stemming from the difficulty of proving one's condition as a free person. The reaction of the free man's family reflects the desperation when faced with the possibility of being thrown into a social class characterized by subjugation and, to a great extent, dispossession.

In truth, being a slave catcher was not an occupation that could clearly distinguish an enslaved African or Afro-descendant from a free or freed one. As Lara notes regarding the colonial period, there were cases in which slave catchers (or their soldiers) were arrested under the suspicion of being themselves runaway slaves (1988, 314–16). To be a slave catcher was not a noble occupation, as Assis's narrator states, precisely because of its social proximity to slavery. Nobody chose this occupation "out of a liking for it, or because he had been trained to it. Poverty, the need for a little extra cash, unfitness for other work, chance, and, occasionally, a natural taste for serving" (102)—these were the reasons that would lead someone to become a slave catcher. Candinho himself "yielded to poverty when he took up the trade of catching slaves" (102). As a worker, Candinho almost occupies a social nonplace, inasmuch as "he could not stick to a job or trade" and "lacked stability" (102). Candinho did not possess the *habitus*—in Bourdieu's (1985) sense of the term—to really invest in any occupation that required a considerable learning process, which obviously limited his employment options.

Candinho thus ends up a slave catcher, since this occupation "did not oblige him to remain seated for long hours together. All it required was strength, a quick eye, patience, daring, and a piece of rope" (105). As a slave catcher, Candinho "lost little time" (105) and "with one leap the reward was in his hands" (106). Without the habitus for long-term investments in an occupation, Candinho turns to one that depended solely on psychophysical characteristics resulting more from personal dispositions than from a process of apprenticeship. Accordingly, being a slave catcher required the basic use of one single, simple object and the minimization of time between the job done and its monetary compensation, which for Candinho should take place in a leap. Precisely because it was not based on apprenticeship and specialization, slave catching began to attract other individuals in need. "As the business grew," the narrator states, "more than one unemployed fellow upped and got himself a rope, went to the newspaper offices, copied down the advertisements, and joined the hunt" (106). Facing new competition in an occupation that was already so dependent on an uncertain object—runaway slaves—Candinho finds himself in a very delicate economic situation, without money to support his family and the son who would soon be born. Aunt Mônica's view on his occupation is thus justified: "I don't say you are a loafer, but the occupation you have chosen...it's not steady" (105).[7] Beyond economic instability, slave catching is an *ocupação vaga*—an occupation for vagrants—given the constant spatial dislocation that it entails. Due to this incessant vagrancy, uprooting individuals from a fixed space in the urban cartography, slave catchers would be socially closer to the mass of slaves who, circulating in the streets of Rio de Janeiro, either ran errands or as the story's narrator notes, "asked the master to set a price on their daily service, and went out and earned it peddling in the streets" (102). Aunt Mônica's tact and above all her assurance that it was not a matter of Candinho's subjectivity but rather a characteristic inherent to the occupation aim at appeasing Candinho; they constitute attempts to avoid hurting his feelings. But, most importantly, it was necessary to avert mistaking him for one of the many other vagrants in the city.

These imprecise distinctions between slave catcher and slave are further complicated when the former, as in Candinho's case, is African or Afro-descendant. Although Assis's text never explicitly states Candinho's race, it is suggested that both Candinho and his wife Clara are not white. Pointing out the couple's propensity for laughter, the narrator says that "the newlyweds laughed at everything" and that "even their names were the objects of puns: Clara (bright), Neves (snow), Candido (white)" (104). Their names were laughable precisely because they were paradoxical given the true color of their complexions. Due to his race and occupation, Candinho was closer to the Africans and Afro-descendants he wished to capture than was probably desirable. In fact, that an African or Afro-descendant should participate in the production of the enslaved body not as the one who is subjugated but as the one who seeks to subjugate was not exceptional. In Rugendas's words, slave catchers are "free blacks who enjoy a fixed salary and are in charge of roaming the neighboring districts every once in a while in order to capture runaway slaves and take them back to their owners or, if these were unknown, to the nearest jail" (1949, 256). Positions of power, such as that of a slave catcher, were not exclusive to free blacks. Rugendas, for instance, mentions the case of foremen who were themselves enslaved (239). Debret, when describing whipping as a form of punishment, portrays the punisher (1978, illustration, 45) as another black man with an iron around his waist (357), which, as Debret himself indicates, is a way of augmenting punishment to runaway slaves (344). Thus, in Debret's portrayal, a slave who had previously run away now acted as a punisher of other undisciplined slaves who were "guilty of serious faults: desertion, theft, injuries resulting from fights, etc." (355). In the end, the moment he took the undisciplined slaves back to jail, the punisher would receive his "right to a *pataca* for each 100 whippings accomplished" (355), just like slave catchers received "the usual compensation of four thousand *réis*" (343) and Cândido, in Assis's story, would receive his, of one hundred thousand *réis*.[8]

The complex relationships between Africans and Afro-descendants belonging to different groups and social classes allowed thus for different loci for social agency, which in turn might lead to an entanglement of power relations and social identities. The very act of capturing a runaway slave in this sense constituted a performance, a close fight that placed runaways and catchers in such physical contiguity that they might potentially become indistinct. In fact, the titular fight that takes place between Candinho and Arminda, the runaway slave, constitutes a corporeal investment in a conflict that draws Candinho and Arminda: one, Afro-descendant and the other, simultaneously closer and farther apart. What Assis's story gradually develops is the intersecting relationship between an Afro-descendant father and an Afro-descendant mother, both on the verge of losing their children, given their subaltern positions in the social structure.

Arminda, as a slave, was always on the verge of losing her offspring, given that her children, property of the same individual who owned her, could be sold at any time. In Assis's story, there is a subtle indication that the story takes place before the Law of the Free Womb, stipulating that every child born in captivity after 1871 would be free. In reiterating the abortion that Arminda suffered, the narrator notes, "The fruit of some months came into this world without life, between the groans of its mother and the despairing gestures of its owner" (112). As for Candinho, almost a member of a *Lumpenproletariat* due to the vagrancy of his occupation, he can at any moment lose his son because of his lack of financial means. Socially, the offspring of one and the other Afro-descendant are tragically living on the brink of death. Regarding the slave catcher's son, Aunt Mônica states that the baby "is certain to die, living on next to nothing" (107). Such dramatic force in her speech is not only rhetorical, being anchored in the reality of a great number of children in eighteenth- and nineteenth-century Rio de Janeiro. There is a great degree of probability that Candinho and Clara's son, like so many other children from poor families, might indeed end up dying.[9] As for the son of the enslaved mulatto woman, he does encounter death. However, this encounter is the result of that other one, which could only take place within the slavocratic order, between one free (or freed) Afro-descendant, the slave catcher, and one enslaved Afro-descendant, who miscarries her child "driven by fear and pain, and after some struggle" (112). In other words, Arminda suffers a miscarriage due to the emotional and physical torture of her fight whereby her body struggles for freedom in its contact with another black body that wishes to impose subjugation on her. This fight between the slave catcher and the runaway slave is, therefore, the performance of two Afro-descendants who exist in close proximity to subjugation, dependency, and freedom.

While placing a physical body into a social conflict, such performance dislocates and complicates the mother–child and father–child relations, insofar as it is necessary to reinsert the father in the scene between mother and child and, inversely, to reinsert the mother in the scene between father and child. "There was a struggle then," the narrator tells us, "because the slave pulled back, moaning, dragging herself and her unborn child" (111). In the close fight fostered by the slavocratic order, the black woman, enslaved, uses her own body and her child's body, as masses and weights, in order to defend herself against the act that would ultimately restitute her former social locus, from which she attempted to escape. Arminda dragged herself and dragged her child as a form of resistance to this social locus where her body takes form structurally as a punishable body. For this same reason, her allegation that her master "probably would have her beaten with whips" (111) easily becomes, in the narrator's discourse, a certainty, reproducing in indirect speech not only of the slave catcher's train of thought, but also of slavocratic ideology as a whole. In her physical struggle with the slave catcher—a temporary, substitute embodiment of the master's power—Arminda "suddenly realized no one would come to set her free, but quite the contrary" (111). Everyone—I must here make explicit what Assis's narrative leaves implicit—was already shackling her, not necessarily because they acted like slave catchers or slave owners, but because whoever witnessed the scene "understood what it was and naturally did not come to the rescue" (111). To act within a social order implies practices that, precisely because of their unintentional nature, carry out a naturalization of a social construct. As evinced in Assis's narrative, the logical consequence of collectively understanding social roles is formed naturally when the acting meets the nonacting. By means of this naturalization, Candinho can justify making use of the same action as

Arminda—dragging one's body—reconducting the runaway to the social locus of the enslaved and punishable black body. Candinho, the narrator describes, "kept on pulling the slave woman down the Rua dos Ourives toward the Rua da Alfândega, where her master's house was" (111). Since both of them are engaged in the same act, the dragging of the body functions as a performatic, embodied discourse, which operates in opposite directions, so that two contiguous social loci are negotiated.

This same contradiction, which is established within an embodied discourse shared by two close but antagonistic social agents, is also to be found in the father–child relationship, mediated by the mother. During his struggle with the runaway slave, Candinho "was in no joking mood, because of his baby that was back there in the pharmacy, waiting for him" (111). To say that a newborn awaits his father is obviously an absurdity, understandable only because of a projection of the father's desire. It is Candinho, the father, who expected to regain his son, left at the spur of the moment with the pharmacist, in the same manner that Arminda truly expected a baby. It was also Arminda who could prolong the son's wait for his father—even indefinitely, given that, if Cândido did not capture any runaway slave, he would be forced to abandon him at the "wheel" of the foundling hospital.[10] She could also shorten it and promote the rejoining of the ties between father and son. Thus, in both cases, in relation the acts of both dragging and waiting, there emerges a bodily negotiation between agents who, although very close in their fields of social insertion, move toward the resolution of a conflict that can only favor one or the other, which is finally realized with the death of the child that Arminda carried in her womb.

"Father versus Mother," the expression that serves as title to Assis's story, functions as a writing strategy inasmuch as it captures the essential conflict in the story without revealing its ending. However, due to its ambiguity, it points to another possible contradiction, which would arise between the white father, himself a slave owner, and the black mother, his slave. The black mother's cry and the white father's despair coincide in the stillborn baby, at the same time offspring and property. Although Assis's text bears no indications regarding the father of Arminda's baby, it is not far-fetched to think that her owner might very well be the father, since it was not uncommon for slave owners to sexually abuse enslaved women. If this is the case, Assis's story opposes not only a free (or freed) Afro-descendant father to an enslaved Afro-descendant mother, but also an enslaved Afro-descendant mother to a free Euro-descendant father. In this regard, a further opposition can also exist between the free (or freed) Afro-descendant father to a free Euro-descendant father. In this field of oppositions, there remains, potentially, the possibility of inverting the dominant/dominated hierarchy wherein the slave catcher remained "an instrument of the force by which law and property rights [were] maintained" (Assis 1966, 102). In the long run, the slave catcher's son, "the blessed fruit that would bring the couple their longed-for fortune" (104), survives while the slave owner's offspring and property, "the fruit of some months" that Arminda carries with her, comes "into this world without life" (112). With the fetus lying on the ground next to its mother, Candinho runs to the Rua da Ajuda to regain his son, "without caring to know" the consequences of the disaster" (112). But what consequences could there be? A whipping? An invaluable loss of property, bearing in mind that the slave trade had been banned since 1831, at least officially?

Whichever the consequences of the disaster for either the runaway slave or her owner, such disaster takes root within a slavocratic order for which an Afro-descendant child must die so that another may live. Despite his ideological explanation, Candinho, himself an Afro-descendant, induces the death of another Afro-descendant so that a third one may have a chance of having a life, even if miserable or subaltern. His occupation is therefore not limited to capturing enslaved Africans and Afro-descendants, but also involves control over the black population in Brazil and the resources (such as one's offspring) that will be available to it. As a slave catcher, Candinho is also the one to punish Arminda and her baby, transforming an apparently simple and rudimentary tool—the rope with which he captures Arminda—into an efficient apparatus to control black bodies, including the distribution of lives and deaths. Trades and tools, as Assis indicates at the beginning of his story, are not to be disregarded, for they produced punishable productive black bodies as well as subjectivities placed in the realm of power. Taking Assis's story to its logical paroxysm, the most severe result of our refusal to face the consequences of the slavocratic disaster is a microcommunity of Afro-descendants who control, punish, and annihilate each other for the benefit of white elites.

NOTES

1. As Dixon points out, the critical interest in Assis's racial identity "coincides with the deterioration of 'racial democracy' as the primary ideology for explaining color in Brazil" and with the critique of racial democracy's racism (2010, 39).

2. I have opted to translate *aparelhos* as "apparatuses" in order to maintain the connotations that the word has in Portuguese, given that it can mean "tools" and "machines," but can also have the broader meaning of an operating organization or system, as in the expression *aparelho de Estado*. In this sense, *aparelhos* is closer to "apparatuses" rather than simply "tools," the word that Helen Caldwell opts for in her translation of Assis's story.

3. The notion of "docile bodies" is elaborated by Michel Foucault in a chapter in *Discipline and Punish* [*Vigiar e punir*] (1987), titled precisely "Docile Bodies," in which the author also proposes the concept of a technicization of the practices of punishing and disciplining.

4. This prison-body is an example of what Foucault perceives as the connection body-object (1987, 130).

5. As Moura notes, slave catchers in Brazil often used thumbscrews to force runaway slaves to reveal their owners' names, without which catchers could not receive their compensation (2013, 44). One must also observe that the gradation the thumbscrews allowed for, with more or less compression of the tips of the thumbs or fingers, responds again to the need for a technique that balances out, in the most efficient manner possible, the punishment and mutilation of the enslaved body.

6. As far as Colonial Brazil is concerned, Lara notes her inability to find any document that would prove that the 1741 Alvará (order), which determined a bodily mark for captured runaway slaves, had been put in place (1988, 296).

7. The original Portuguese reads, "Não digo que você seja vadio, mas a ocupação que escolheu, é vaga" (2007, 469). The English translation of *vaga* as "not steady" does not accurately render the connotative meanings of "vago," which also means someone who wanders (related to the words "vagrant" and "vagrancy" in English).

8. A *pataca* was a silver coin worth 320 *réis*, currency used in Brazil until 1942.

9. For analyses of child abandonment and mortality, see Trindade (1999) and Venâncio (1999).

10. As Caldwell notes in her translation of Assis's story, the Wheel was a "turn box in the wall of a foundling hospital in which an infant was placed" (1966, 107).

References

Assis, Machado de. 1966. Father versus mother. In *The psychiatrist and other stories*. Trans. Helen Caldwell, 101–112. Berkeley: University of California Press.

Assis, Machado de. 2007. Pai contra mãe. In *50 contos*, ed. John Gledson, 466–475. São Paulo: Companhia das Letras.

Assis Duarte, Eduardo de. 2009. Estratégias de caramujo. In *Machado de Assis afro-descendente: Escritos de caramujo*, ed. Eduardo de Assis Duarte. Rio de Janeiro: Pallas.

Botelho, Janaína. 2010. Os pretos do libambo. *História e memória de Nova Friburgo*, http://historiadefriburgo.blogspot.com/2010/03/os-pretos-do-libambo.html

Bourdieu, Pierre. 1985. The genesis of the concepts of *habitus* and *field*. Trans. Channa Newman. *Sociocriticism* 2(2): 11–24.

Debret, Jean-Baptiste. 1978. *Viagem pitoresca e histórica ao Brasil*, vol. 1. Trans. Sérgio Milliet. Belo Horizonte: Itatiaia.

Dixon, Paul. 2010. Machado de Assis's early 'mulato' narratives. *Afro-Hispanic Review* 29(2): 39–54.

Foucault, Michel. 1987. *Vigiar e punir: Nascimento da prisão*. Trans. Raquel Ramalhete. Petrópolis: Vozes.

Lara, Silvia Hunold. 1988. Capitães-do-mato. In *Campos da violência: Escravos e senhores na Capitania do Rio de Janeiro, 1750–1808*, 295–322. Rio de Janeiro: Paz e Terra.

Mattos, Hebe Maria. 2000. *Escravidão e cidadania no Brasil monárquico*. Rio de Janeiro: Jorge Zahar.

Moura, Clóvis. 2013. *Dicionário da escravidão negra no Brasil*. São Paulo: Edusp.

Rugendas, Johann Moritz. 1949. *Viagem pitoresca ao Brasil*. São Paulo: Círculo do Livro.

Trindade, Judite Maria Barboza. 1999. O abandono de crianças ou a negação do óbvio. *Revista Brasileira de História* 19(37): 35–58.

Venâncio, Renato Pinto. 1999. *Famílias abandonadas: Assistência à criança de camadas populares no Rio de Janeiro e em Salvador—séculos XVIII e XIX*. Campinas: Papirus.

CHAPTER 8

The "Chinese Question" in Machado's Journalism

Sonia Roncador

You, my Brazilian friends, seem to want the Chinese to grow and harvest your coffee. Your country will be overpopulated. One hundred Chinese will arrive, and soon after there will be another hundred thousand. In 10 years both São Paulo and Rio will have their own Chinatown, full of signs painted in red and black, paper lanterns, seedy pubs infected with opium, all sorts of secret associations, an incessant profusion of silk tunics and queues.... All other colonies, Portuguese, Italian, and German, will gradually be pushed back to their original countries—and within 20 years the entire Brazil will become China.

—**José Maria de** (Eça de Queirós, "Chineses e Japoneses," *Gazeta de Notícias*, 1894, 70).[1]

I

A nacionalização ou grande naturalização e naturalização tácita [*Nationalization or Grand and Tacit Naturalization,*] (1886), a booklength pamphlet on the highly debated topic of naturalization at the peak of the Brazilian Great Immigration period (circa 1870s to 1920s), constitutes an illuminating entry into the racially motivated premises of citizenship in late imperial and early republican Brazil. Its author, Brazilian writer and

S. Roncador (✉)
University of Texas, Austin, Austin, Texas, USA

© The Editor(s) (if applicable) and The Author(s) 2016
L. Aidoo, D.F. Silva (eds.), *Emerging Dialogues on Machado de Assis*, DOI 10.1057/978-1-137-54174-1_8

politician Alfredo d'Escragnolle Taunay (1843–1899), had systematically been advocating the enhancement of naturalized immigrants' political privileges, in particular, their entitlement to intervene in the national political arena as both voters and legislators.[2] Drawing extensively from other nations' "more benevolent" legislations, as well as appealing to his peers' embarrassment in the face of the political disenfranchisement of a number of "heroic aliens" in the country, Taunay's pamphlet promoted the implementation of a massive naturalization, or, as he puts it, a "nationalization" of all immigrants who satisfied certain requirements of residency and moral propriety. In reality, the so-called grand naturalization, which granted electoral and/or legislative power to all *naturalizados*, had just been added to the constitution's immigration code.[3] "What should be done next," Taunay believed, "[was] to complete the *grand naturalization* by decreeing the *tacit naturalization*—we call 'nationalization' the consolidation of these two types of naturalization" (1886, 91; original italics; 91).

However, in the context of the imminent abolition of black slavery and concomitant formation of a multiethnic low-paid working class, Taunay's public plea for a nationalization (or tacit grand naturalization) held, at the very least, ambiguous implications: it proposed massive automatic access to nationality in Brazil, where legal citizenship did not entail sociopolitical empowerment for the majority of its population (Vieira 2005, "Novos cidadãos" 196). As Octavio Ianni has argued, for instance, within the *paulista* pro-republican ideological discourse, massive access to national citizenship simply functioned as a strategy to expand the work market so as to absorb an abundant cohort of labor immigrants en route to São Paulo's coffee plantations (Vieira 2005, 196). Besides, according to Taunay's vision of Brazil's path toward modernization, extensive naturalization would primarily appeal to European ("preferably German") immigrants, whose "exemplary diligen[ce]" would strengthen the national battle against the "deleterious flood of indolence" contaminating the Brazilian population (Taunay 1884, 3).

Before the tacit grand naturalization was finally signed into law in 1889, it thus had already been debated in a number of political and intellectual public venues. As we learn from one of Machado de Assis's *crônicas* (1839–1908), which appeared in his widely read "Bons Dias!" (Good Morning!) newspaper column on October 28, 1888, his old "illustrious friend" Taunay had recently resubmitted his nationalization proposal to his Senate peers. Although a supporter himself of politically empowering the country's naturalized citizens, Machado was nonetheless skeptical about the ethics as well as the instrumentality of the tacit naturalization type. According to him, the very compulsory aspect of an automatic naturalization process, one that he critically defined as "forced (Brazilian) nationality," might discourage prospective immigrants from moving to Brazil: "When a person is about to leave his home country, he doesn't think of changing his original nationality for another." In addition, for Machado, this type of forced naturalization might produce other "inconveniences" as well. One of them, in particular, leads us to this paper's thematic focus on the late nineteenth-century intellectual debate about the racial and cultural pros and cons of massive Chinese emigration to Brazil. As Machado ironically argued, Taunay's bill might actually attract some controversial groups of migrants, especially the Chinese, whom Taunay himself considered a "threat" to national prosperity, "like a tenebrous cloud prone to all kinds of atrocities" (1886, 3). However, given that Brazilian immigration authorities could not prevent *Chins* (as Chinese immigrants were then disdainfully called) from entering the country, "by the end of two years or even one, we would have thousands of Chins turned into Brazilian citizens. It would be impossible to exclude them from the law" (Assis 1888).[4]

It was within such political circumstances that Machado addressed the Chinese transnational migration issue, thus demonstrating, albeit from a different angle, his recently acknowledged interest in the overlapping questions of race/ethnicity and citizenship.[5] Yet, as with other thematic concerns in his writings, deciphering Machado's thoughts about Asian immigration is anything but straightforward. Did Machado share with a number of intellectuals of his generation an aversion to Asians? Or did he use the diasporic Chinese referent as a rhetorical strategy to challenge Taunay's nationalization project, by way of revealing the project's false promises of undiscriminated immigration entry and integration policies? Additionally, by juxtaposing Machado's *crónicas* about Chinese immigration, critics have noticed the writer's ambivalent and often contradictory positions. For example, as Osmar Pereira Oliva has observed regarding Machado's "A semana" (The Week) column in the newspaper *Gazeta de Notícias* (1892–1900), Machado would portray the emblematic Chin as a compliant and assiduous worker, only to, in a subsequent *crónica*, challenge his readers' belief in his pro-Chinese convictions, expressing fear of a massive departure of European immigrants in the face of a "yellow invasion" (Oliva 2008, 82).

Instead of attempting to resolve Machado's dubious assumptions regarding the question of Asians in Brazil (as Oliva has done), my goal here is to explore the functionality of what I consider the writer's intentionally inconsistent viewpoint. By way of such an elusive positionality, Machado de Assis managed to engage with Brazilian elites' diverse and divisive economic and political inclinations, as well as their self-interested interpretations of the problem of the so-called "coolie trade" to the Americas. By ambivalently embracing the anti-Chinese xenophobic vogue of his generation, Machado ended up addressing the contentious overlap of nonwhite immigrant servitude and black slavery in Brazil. As my analysis of a few *crônicas* demonstrates, Machado was interested in the "Chinese question" as a way to explore connections between European imperialism and new forms of transnational human trafficking following the demise of black slavery in the Americas. At the same time, he engaged with the divisive public debate about the desirability of "Chins" in order to ultimately denounce the whitening ideology that would soon give rise to the republican regime. As other scholars have already argued, late nineteenth-century literature about Chinese immigration (namely, pamphlets, reports, newspaper *crônicas*, and proceedings of political events) constituted one of the most productive forums through which to expose Brazilian elites' overlapping concerns about the future of the nation. Placed by the imperial racial system somewhere between whites and blacks, Asians, especially the Chinese, were perceived as the ideal laboring population to function within the ideological framework of racialized servitude—a regime that elite Brazilians wanted to preserve at all costs. On the other hand, Asians were nonetheless seen as potential "ant-like" invaders (i.e., silent and abundant), and, by implication, as a dangerous means of Mongolization of the racial and cultural patrimony. My current inquiry into Machado's stance on Chinese immigration and his engagement with his peers' racially inflicted renderings of diasporic Chinese thus emerges along with other scholarly work that has challenged traditional assumptions about the writer's indifference toward slavery and other pressing racial questions of his time.

II

Brazilian elites turned their eyes to China and the influx of Chinese immigrants to the Americas in particular, as soon as they realized the mismatch between European labor immigration and the plantation work regime they tried to force on their immigrant laborers.[6] In the Brazilian narratives of European insubordination and failed acclimatization, the Chinese emerged as docile and resilient workers, rigorously disciplined by an overruled and punitive regime of pitiless emperors. However, because of influential sinophobic discourses by public figures, such as d'Escragnolle Taunay and, previously, planter and intellectual Luis Peixoto de Lacerda Werneck, there never emerged a numerically relevant community of Chinese during the Brazilian Great Immigration period or beyond. Yet, as Jeffrey Lesser argues, "The physical presence of Asians was never necessary for images of Chinese to float like an omnipresent specter through discussions of ethnicity in Brazil" (1999, 14). In a way, the very absence of this collective ethnic Other favored the emergence of a "complex and divisive" public debate comprising a wide variety of ideological viewpoints from liberal to conservative politicians, proto-industrialists and commercial entrepreneurs to plantation owners and abolitionist intellectuals (Lesser 1999, 15). Due to a lack of solid knowledge about the Far East, low conviviality with diasporic Asians, and certainly the influx of a number of overseas studies, consular reports, and travelers' accounts of the Chinese diasporas in other countries, elite Brazilians for the most part had to rely on the contentious renderings of the Asian migrant that they found in these well-circulated writings.[7] As already argued by other scholars, late nineteenth-century Brazilians' portrayals of the Chinese immigrant and immigration constituted important venues for identifying and tackling several pressing socioeconomic and related cultural and racial issues concerning that especially fast-shifting period. Given national leaders' goal of "de-Africanizing" Brazilian society in the face of the deep transformations of the time, the Asian immigration debate provided a means for several authorities to set the parameters for the formation of "modern" non-black peasantry and urban working classes and strategic settlements in the Brazilian hinterlands, as well as for defining new immigration policies vis-à-vis the desired national racial stock. On the other hand, in dealing with a constituency of migrants perceived not only as nonblacks but also as non-whites, Brazilians were clearly divided between those who believed that the Chinese were racially akin to the native indigenous ethnic groups and would therefore gradually disappear by way of miscegenation and those like Werneck Lacerda who believed that "Brazil's race-in-formation was not powerful enough to overcome millions of inferior Asians" (quoted in Lesser 1999, 19). This led to fears of a hyper-Mongolization of the national culture, "which had already suffered 'the deformity of the indigenous and the African'" (quoted in Lesser 1999, 19).

As suggested in Lesser's analysis of the conflicting agendas comprising the public debate around Asian immigration, the symbolic centrality of overseas Chinese had to do with their nebulous racial status, placed hierarchically somewhere above blacks and below whites. Relying on the histories of indentured and low-wage contracted Chinese workers in other American contexts,[8] several Brazilian intellectuals and politicians argued that diasporic Chinese labor hovered between the subservience of black slaves and white discipline and diligence, thus potentially functioning as a smooth "step forward on the path to full wage labor" (Lesser 1999, 15). Additionally, the stereotypical docile and hardworking Chinese came to emblematize, in some conservative circles, the idealized free worker model that would preserve Brazil's culture of servitude in the post-abolition era. Conversely, detractors of Chinese immigration saw the contractual arrangements associated with Chinese labor terms as catastrophic models to be transplanted to Brazil. While some anti-Chinese interlocutors denounced the evil of such slave-like arrangements, others perceived these work terms as menacing their aspirations for national social order and moral and economic progress and the growth of a working class that they envisioned as primarily composed of European immigrants. Drawing mainly from US-based xenophobic narratives about Chinese labor, blaming it for local salary compression and massive layoffs, these Brazilians imagined similar risks of popular unhappiness and turmoil, or even the general flight of white immigrants back to Europe. Indeed, according to Portuguese Eça de Queirós's influential *crónica* "Chineses e Japoneses" (published in Rio's *Gazeta de Notícias* on December 1–6, 1894), white European people, "who have invented the most noble theories about work freedom" (65), would never accept the same labor terms that employers managed to impose on Chinese immigrants in the United States or Cuba; therefore, Brazil's "worthy" immigrants would "gradually be pushed back to their original countries—and within 20 years the entire Brazil [would] become China" (70).

Eça de Queirós's paranoid anticipation of Brazil's cultural Mongolization reflected the anti-Chinese sentiment, or sinophobia, that came to distinguish the presence of these immigrants in the Americas, in particular, during the second half of the nineteenth century.[9] Besides accusations of encouraging general salary compression and unemployment, the mainstream narrative of Chinese immigration was built on fear of a massive yellow invasion (in Queirós's terms, a "silent ant-like invasion") and the perception that Asians were unwilling or unable to assimilate. This assumed "inherent inassimilability," in Evelyn Hu-DeHart's words, "meant they would never integrate into local society, thus constituting a troubling, permanent alien presence" (2009, 56). On the other hand, it is worth mentioning the fears, prevalent even among sinophobic intellectuals, of the negative repercussions of the slave-like living and working conditions imposed on these immigrants. To be sure, as the British aggressively strengthened their commercial relations with China in the aftermath of the Opium Wars (1840–1842; 1856–1860) and enforced a ban over the trans-Atlantic African slave trade, a "yellow trade" emerged between British traders in the Southern Chinese treaty port of Amoy and wealthy farmers or entrepreneurs in several New World nations (namely, the USA, Peru, and the British and Spanish Caribbean). According to Hu-DeHart, British traders (and later the Macao-based Portuguese) were generally known in Cuba as *negreros*, or slave traders. This was in part because such traders systematically employed the services of surviving African slave ships. But it was also due to their complicity with an ongoing system of indentured servitude, involving coercive methods of labor recruitment in China as well as other humiliating practices, such as public auctions of these workers' contracts in the Havana central slave market (Hu-Dehart 2009, 85). As Avtar Bhrar argues, the way diasporic communities "[came] to be relationally positioned in a given context" would prove crucial to their identity negotiations and future opportunities in that specific context (1996, 183). In the case of the nineteenth-century Chinese in Cuba (as well as in other slavery-based societies in the Americas), these diasporic subjects "were regarded and treated no differently from the slaves," regardless of their sense of racial superiority in relation to the Afro-Cubans; "the *esclavista* (slave owner) mentality…was simply extended to cover the coolies as well" (Hu-Dehart 2009, 85).

Perhaps due to the diplomatic crises generated by this cruel business of human trafficking, by the time Machado de Assis wrote most of his *crônicas* about Chinese immigration, the "coolie trade" had already entered into steep decline.[10] However, news about the historic crosscurrents of the African and the Chinese diasporas continued to resonate in other international contexts, as revealed by the Brazilian political debate surrounding the Chinese question. The diasporic Asians' slave-like realities may also have played into Machado's concealed ways of condemning Brazil's own long-enduring slavery within the politically constrained space of his columns. As Eduardo de Assis Duarte (2007) argues, thanks to editorial censorship, not to mention the pact of complacency between writers and their mostly white readership, Machado's interest in the question of Afro-Brazilianness either was relegated to the margins of his work (for the most part, addressed in his journalistic writings, considered less prestigious) or else shielded by recurrent "strategies of dissimulation." Such strategies included the use of unreliable narrators, the attenuating effects of irony and humor, and a variety of pseudonyms whose real identity, in some cases, would be discovered only after the writer's death. By creating different personae for his columns, Machado thus managed to speak from a plural ideological standpoint and to explore the multifaceted aspects of several divisive issues of his politically shifting times (Gledson 2006, 135). The remaining sections of this chapter address *crônicas* in which Machado referred to the plight of ethnically marked labor immigrants in the age of late nineteenth-century imperialism, the conflation of nonwhite immigration and slavery, and the elite Brazilians' whitening ideology framing their politics of manual labor employment in the postslavery era.

III

If, at the outset of his journalistic career in the mid-1850s, a "fearless and aggressive" young Machado would praise the newspaper medium as a true "symptom" and "expression" of democracy (2011), in the course of the following decades, his judgment would certainly be challenged by his own experience as a *cronista* in continuous negotiations to build and secure public esteem in the then growingly competitive business of signed columns. Further job-related circumstances in his life, specifically his chief position at the secretary of agriculture in the 1880s, would also dissuade him from openly addressing the controversial political issues of the period. Under the pseudonym Dr. Semana (Dr. Week) in the renowned magazine *Semana Ilustrada*, Machado wrote a *crônica*, "Carta do Dr. Semana ao Imperador da China" (Dr. Week's Letter to the Emperor of China) that tackled some of these contentious issues.[11] The *crônica* in question consisted of a fictitious open letter addressed to the Chinese supreme authority (probably Emperor Tongzhi or his father Xianfeng, of the late Ch'ing dynasty) for the sake of denouncing the few Chinese immigrants settled in Rio, who were, according to the cronista, dishonoring their "virtuous race," "the political importance of their nationality," and their noble Confucian language with the self-ridiculing job of street-vending "camalô e sadinha" (a poorly pronounced version of "shrimp and sardines"). Lest he be wrongly accused of xenophobia or nativism, the cronista went on to promote himself as an "ethically cosmopolitan" intellectual, not to be confused with those "optimistic" advocates of indigenous labor as a more viable solution to the workforce shortage problem subsequent to the British ban on the African slave trade. However, his message to the emperor—whom he jocularly calls "Your Obesity"—could not be clearer: "Sail your degenerated Mandarins back to their celestial homes, and force them to return to the delights of cangue[12] and impalement…. Don't let your deserted noblemen rot in the slums of Rio de Janeiro."

Consistent with history, this early *crônica* is one of the few nineteenth-century records of the small group of Chinese immigrants, who were poorly settled in Rio de Janeiro's slums and mostly devoted to selling raw fish in the streets. The first attempts to establish a community of Chinese workers in Brazil date back to Portuguese king Dom João VI's failed project to grow tea on the imperial estate, now Rio's Botanical Garden. According to Lesser, in 1854 the London-housed Brazilian diplomatic delegation received imperial orders to negotiate the trade of a few thousand Chinese to work on Brazil's laborer-deprived coffee plantations. However, strong opposition to this pending negotiation, as well as the already mentioned international legal disputes surrounding the "coolie trade," discouraged the government from pursuing this plan (Lesser 1999, 19). As a result, by the time Machado published his *crônica* (on April 17, 1864), there were a very limited number of Chinese in Brazil. And yet, in Lesser's words, "even this small number caused an outcry" (19).

Rio elites' loud protest—or, in Daphne Patai's fine expression, their "surplus visibility" (1991, A52)—against the city's small Chinese community reflected the maligning of Asian immigration and immigrants in other nations, especially the United States and Cuba. According to Yen Ching-Hwang, diasporic Chinese did not enjoy a good reputation in their own nation either, where they were often accused of betrayal and desertion vis-à-vis the Ch'ing government policy prohibiting emigration (1985, 22). In addition, as I infer from Machado's *crônica*, elite Brazilians' outcry may also have emerged from their conflation of Chinese immigration with slum-dwelling and street-vending. Nineteenth-century Brazilian society generally saw urban poverty as racially marked, vicious, dangerous, and contagious (Chalhoub 1996, 20–35). Indeed, besides the impact of European racialist theories representing the Mongoloid race as inferior to the Caucasoid—and, among the Asians, the Chinese as inferior to the Japanese—social factors such as economic poverty and subemployment in slave-associated servile occupations affected the cultural imaginary of

Chinese immigrants.[13] In this context, according to Lesser, both detractors and advocates of Asian immigration held diasporic Chinese culture in low esteem, and several relied on the opium-addicted and criminal Asian stereotype in order to morally equate this immigrant group with Afro-Brazilians. As a case in point, the pro-Chinese immigration Tavares Bastos, himself a founding member of Brazil's International Society of Immigration (1866), endorsed the general perception of the "Chins" as "disgusting spiritually" and "repugnant physically" (including an aversion to the male Chinese "cross-dressing" codes—a misreading of their silk tunics and queues). Another apt example is Machado's longtime friend Quintino Bocayuva, who wrote a popular pamphlet, *A crise da lavoura* (The Agricultural Crisis, 1868), in which he introduced the same humiliating stereotypes, only to defend Chinese immigration as economically profitable and harmless to the mainstream whitening project: "Their soul is permanently [in China] and they work for the money to return to their country" (quoted in Lesser 1999, 21).

Published just a few years before Bocayuva's political thesis, Machado's portrayal of the plight of real-life Chinese "rotting in Rio's slums" would at least complicate the spectrum of socioracially biased stereotypes of these immigrants. Besides producing comic relief, the cronista's reliance on excessively caricaturesque Chinese types (the "camalô, sadinha, pesse" street vendor and the cartoon-like obese emperor) was also perhaps meant to mockingly mirror his peers' (and readers') own cross-cultural misperceptions. On the other hand, Machado's interest in the Chinese immigration issue had an international resonance. Toward the end of his missive to the Chinese emperor, the cronista actually made a point in associating the main focus of his plea (the plight of Chinese immigrants in Brazil) with the opium and (Lipton) tea trade "indulging [the emperor's] allies in Sir James's office." As indicated by this ironic reference to the British-Chinese "alliance" or commercial partnership, Machado was critically aware of the global power dynamics then generating and sustaining the "coolie trade." Strictly speaking, the victimizing transnational trafficking of Chinese workers comprised one among other unpopular commercial operations involving British imperialist advances into Asia in the years following the Opium Wars. In this sense, therefore, the cronista's missive about real-life degenerative living conditions of the Asian diaspora in Brazil could be read as resulting from his desire to see emerge a mobilized Chinese government, militarily capable of rescuing its "deserters" back into a more dignifying life, even if under the government's strict and punitive emigration laws ("Sail your degenerated Mandarins back to their celestial homes, and force them to return to the delights of cangue and impalement"). And yet, Machado's eccentric portrayal of China's rescuing technology—"an invincible army of [medieval] junks"—leaves us no doubt about his cynicism and sardonic sense of humor in the face of Europe's rising imperialism in the Far East.

In the early 1880s, the cronista Machado would return to the topic of Asian immigration inspired by the eventful and highly reported business trip to Brazil by a Chinese entrepreneur, T'ang T'ing-shu (whom the Brazilians called "first-class Mandarin Tong King Sing"), and his assistant, G. C. Butler, both representing the Chinese Steam Navigation Company. According to Lesser, this visit reflected the transfer in the mid-1870s of Chinese immigration control and interests from the private domain of British or Portuguese *negreros* into the realm of state-sponsored agencies and diplomacy. In addition, despite persistent anti-Chinese xenophobia, many Brazilians supported building up economic relations with China by means of large-scale ventures, such as launching a regular maritime line between the two nations. However, as revealed by several journalistic *crônicas* and cartoons, and by popular plays like Arthur Azevedo's *O mandarim* (The Mandarin [1884] 1985), what rendered T'ing-shu and Butler's visit symbolically appealing was less the economic and diplomatic relevance of their trip than its racial and cultural idiosyncrasies—namely, the "disturbing" fact of two nonwhite males (the Mandarin's assistant was African American) occupying positions of institutional authority and white privilege. Elite Brazilians thus reacted as if they were forced to review their own racial stereotypes: "While Tong was remade into an acceptable quasi-European, G. C. Butler...seemed to shock observers by being 'intelligent' and having 'all the refinement of Parisian elegance'" (Lesser 1999, 32). It was therefore in response to such cross-cultural and racial misencounters that Machado commented on T'ing-shu's visit to Brazil and readdressed the issue of Asian immigration.

Under the pseudonym Lélio, Machado wrote an ingenious *crônica* in the *Gazeta de Notícias* multiauthored column "Balas de estalo" ["Shattering Bullets"] (October 16, 1883) aimed at divulging T'ing-shu's "modest impressions" about Brazilian society. The *crônica* in question was presented as a verbatim reproduction of a fictitious letter by "our illustrious guest," written in no less fictitious Cantonese which, according to the cronista, was preserved intact so as to leave unintelligible the Mandarin's "excessively raw verdicts" about "our" country. To the assiduous readers of his "Balas de estalo" *crônicas*, however, the cronista's refusal to translate an otherwise potentially insulting letter may have sounded like another of his typically ironic jokes. In fact, as he suspiciously went on to explain, the Mandarin had decided to insert in different sections of his text a few words in Portuguese "for not finding an equivalent term in his native language, or (it seems to me) for the sake of proving to be a somewhat connoisseur of the Portuguese language." The resulting *crônica* was therefore a combination of nonsensical "Cantonese" phrases, overly critical Portuguese expressions, and even some English expressions, as indicated by the following passage:

> Upa Costa Braga relá minag katu Integridade abaxung kapi a ver navios. Lamarika ana bapa bung? Gogó xupitô? Nepa in pavé. Brasil desfalques latecatu. Inglese poeta, Shakespeare, kará: make money; upa lamaré in língua Brasil: — mete dinheiro no bolso. Vaia, Vaia, gapaling capita passa a unha simá teka laparika. Eting põe-se a panos; etang merú xilindró.

As in other passages, this paragraph shows Machado's Mandarin horrified by both the intense political corruption and also the lack of criminal law enforcement in Brazil. Given T'ing-shu's well-publicized "liberalism" as one of his signs of "quasi-Europeanness," the cronista certainly knew about the Mandarin's moral conflicts with the super-empowered Brazilian elites. In fact, such ideological divergences most likely determined the Mandarin's impromptu departure from Brazil, as well as his refusal to act as a sort of facilitator of Chinese labor emigration on behalf of Brazilian plantation owners. Perhaps another reason for T'ing-shu's "sudden disappearance" (as newspapers described his unannounced departure) was Brazilians' "excessive animosity" and use of "too many ugly epithets" against the Chinese. This was suggested by Machado himself in his *crônica* (published September 18, 1892), in which he ironically proclaimed expertise in all things Chinese.

In a *crônica* published in the same "Balas de estalo" column only one week after the Mandarin's fictitious letter, Lélio (alias Machado) addressed the maligning of Asian labor emigrants. The *crônica* in question corresponded to another invented missive, "contain[ing] highly valuable information in regard to the issue of Asian immigrant laborers." Perhaps in mocking the attitude toward the truth value ascribed to officially accredited reports, Machado was quick to inform his readers that the missive in question—from a certain Mr. Webster, Viceroy of India, to the British Colonial

Secretary, Lord Granville—had been first published in the *London Gazette* and later translated into Portuguese, precisely because of its "appeal" in a country such as Brazil, where "there [was] too much horror against the coolies." Written in a jocular fashion and relying heavily on grotesque stereotypes of Chinese workers, the allegedly official report aimed at offering the British governors news about an "alternative labor source solution" that might be considered for those American countries "that had been employing the coolie work, or were about to." According to the viceroy, the services by the "ordinary coolie" (*Chim comum*) had long been replaced across Asia by a "much superior coolie species": the chimpanzee. Besides their improved work quality and production, chimpanzees supposedly represented a low-maintenance cohort of workers: (1) their daily diet (coconuts and walnuts) was far more frugal than the costly poultry common in the Chins' food regime (Chinese immigrants were actually known in Brazil as "chicken thieves"); (2) they wore no clothes, shoes, or hats; and (3) they did not have their minds fixated on their home country. In this particular regard, according to the missive's author, chimpanzees lacked any national sentiment and therefore were the least likely workers to pursue a "consular complaint" or to organize a rebellion: "Every ordinary coolie's insurgence [was] proven to result from his notion of a national government, an emperor and several Mandarins."

Needless to say, the missive's nonsensical data, and even its comical aspects (including the grotesque Portuguese pun *chim/chimpanzé*) did not hide its anti-Chinese xenophobia, even though, in typical Machadoesque fashion, it did not openly denounce racism either. On the other hand, some of the passages, especially the final ironic comments about the advantageous chimpanzee labor, may have shaken Machado's readers' racialist premises. For example, one of the text's highlights involved the juxtaposition of quadrupeds and bipeds in an attempt to prove the intellectual parity between chimpanzees and human beings, regardless of race or nationality. As the cronista argued, body posture should not be seen as a natural sign of virtue, given that "in Europe or other regions, several human beings [were] bipeds out of sheer habit, upbringing, family usage, emulation, and other causes, which did not necessarily imply the possession of intellectual faculties." In addition to their intellectual equivalence to human beings and, sometimes, even superiority, according to Machado's conclusions, chimpanzees might also represent a consensual labor crisis solution for elite Brazilians. In other words, Brazilians who were usually supportive of Asian labor might instead lean toward the monetary advantages of hiring chimpanzees, whereas those normally fearful of the Mongolization of the national race might celebrate the fact that "the chimpanzee would never mix with the countries' existing races."

As indicated by his ironical rationale ostensibly favoring the importation of chimpanzee labor, Machado actively participated in the overlapping debates of slavery, immigration, and national race in less than conventional ways, thus rendering particularly challenging the task of decoding the nuances of his stance on such divisive issues. By seemingly siding with his peers' as well as readers' sinophobic presumptions, he explored new ways of exposing the multiracial and ethnic victimization pattern defining Brazilian cross-social relations—in other words, the perverse conflation of nonwhite immigrant servitude with black slavery in Brazil, amounting to the preservation of the country's long-established culture of servitude in the postslavery era. As previously stated, Chinese immigrants actually emblematized the elite's idealized standards of servitude, especially for those who perceived them as combining white diligence and black docility. On the other hand, as ironically suggested in Machado's *crônica*, "ordinary Chins" were feared to potentially jeopardize elite Brazilians' whitening aspirations, and therefore should be discarded as an alternative source of labor. To be sure, the author of several of the greatest "Balas de estalo" *crônicas* would not have evoked the national whitening ideologues if he had not had a labor solution (however, tongue-in-cheek) to share with them: to populate Brazilian plantations, and perhaps even some cities, with laboring chimpanzees.

IV

Machado very likely saw the "Chinese question" as an appealing opportunity to denounce the whitening immigration policies of his time. The above-quoted passage on chimpanzees is paradigmatic of his ironical response to mainstream apprehension of Chinese immigration as a potential means to Mongolize Brazilian culture. Another good example of Machado's perception of the racially charged premises of citizenship is his *crônica* about Taunay's controversial proposal of compulsory naturalization, also published in Rio's *Gazeta de Notícias*, at the verge of slavery abolition. Machado may have received Taunay's proposal as deceptive assurance of the indiscriminatory political empowerment of the country's immigrant communities. As a frequent spectator at congressional hearings and public meetings, Machado was aware of Taunay's long campaign in favor of increasing the number of naturalized immigrants in Brazil, as well as enhancing such *naturalizados*' political citizenship through electoral legislation.

On the other hand, Machado was also well aware of Taunay's intention to legally establish whiteness as a condition for naturalization and citizenship in Brazil. As a founding member and vice president of the Rio-based Central Immigration Society (1883–1991), Taunay and his fellow members (several with a German "pedigree") unanimously promoted European labor immigration over any other nationality (Jobim 2005, 16). They enthusiastically promoted the country's economically successful German colonies in southern Brazil and proactively advertised a Brazilian "promised land" in German newspapers. Not surprisingly, their pro-European immigration propaganda was predicated on anti-Asian xenophobia, as is clear from the following passage from a document written by Taunay in the society's official newspaper, *A immigração* (Immigration) in the December 1883–August 1884 edition: "The Chinese element is an obstacle against the only sought-after immigration: European," he argued, alluding to the common paranoid narrative that invasive and cheap Chinese laborers would scare away European immigrants. His national and racial biases became more obvious as he went on to say, "We need to ask the civilized nations for energy and strength, be it intellectual or physical.... Degenerated races, weak, impregnated with the most offensive vices, and inferior to our own ethnic elements, cannot help us achieve our goals" (2).

Given Taunay's calculated rendering of the Chinese element as an obstacle to the local elite's whitening goals, it should not come as a surprise that he not only verbally approved of the U.S. Chinese Exclusion Act of 1882, but also came out in favor of excluding the Chinese from his own naturalization proposal.[14] Although the newly born republican government only temporarily succeeded in passing an exclusion act against immigration from Asia and Africa, between 1890 and 1892, national leaders in years to come would find other ways of establishing and enforcing racial prerequisites for legal citizenship in Brazil. A better understanding of Machado's stance on Asian immigration reveals a writer keenly aware of the dominant attitude toward race and citizenship. His strategy to ambiguously engage with prevailing renderings of Chinese immigrants added to his repertoire of concealed ways of ridiculing the national culture of nonwhite servitude. Additionally, his Chinese immigration *crónicas* challenged then-emerging national myths of exceptional hospitality and miscegenation, as such writings also pointed toward the elite's own deceptive ways of enforcing whiteness as a sine qua non condition for full citizenship in Brazil.

NOTES

1. All translated quotations throughout this paper are mine. Note also that the columns in the *Gazeta de Notícias* have no page numbers.
2. According to Martha Victor Vieira, until 1860, naturalization petitions were analyzed case by case by Brazilian congressmen. Petitioners "had to meet all the legal requirements, as well as socially network with members of the ruling class" in order to qualify for legal citizenship (2005, 191).
3. The 3.140 law, also known as the Saraiva Bill, was passed on January 9, 1881. Although this election law increased the political power of naturalized citizens, overall, it negatively impacted the number of eligible voters by increasing the socioeconomic bar as well as institutionalizing the "alphabetized [voter] rule" (Vieira 2005, 194).
4. Despite such an argument, Machado was certainly aware of legal maneuvers, such as the U.S. Chinese Exclusion Act of 1882, to institutionalize entry bans against specific groups of immigrants. Brazil also had a temporary prohibition act against Asians and Africans from 1890 to 1892.
5. To my knowledge, the theme of Chinese immigration first appeared in Machado de Assis's journalism on April 17, 1864, in his "Dr. Semana" (Dr. Week) signed column in the magazine *Revista Ilustrada*. Machado later published several other *crónicas* about the same topic in the *Gazeta de Notícias*: two in the multiauthored "Balas de estalo" (Shattering Bullets) column (October 16 and 23, 1883); one in his "Bons Dias!" column (October 28, 1888); and finally, seven crónicas in his "A semana" ("The Week") column (August 14, 1892; September 11, 18, 25, and 28, 1892; May 28, 1894; October 18, 1896).
6. For those interested in mid-nineteenth-century European immigrants' organized rebellions, I recommend the interesting testimony by Swiss immigrant Thomas Davatz, *Memórias de um colono no Brasil* (Memoirs of a Colonist in Brazil, 1850), as well as Luiz Felipe de Alencastro and Maria Luiza Renaux's "Caras e modos dos migrantes e imigrantes" (*História da vida privada no Brasil*, vol. 2).
7. Jeffrey Lesser's (1999, 23) chapter, "Chinese Labor and the Debate over Ethnic Integration" mentions the impact of two widely circulated books in particular: Alfred Legoyt's *L'émigration européenne, son importance, ses causes, ses effets, avec un appendice sur l' émigration africaine, hindoue et chinoise* (1861) and Leonard Wray's *The Practical Sugar Planter* (1848).

8. For more on the nineteenth-century Chinese diaspora in other American countries (namely, the United States, the British and Hispanic Caribbean, Mexico, and Peru) consult Madeline Hsu's *Dreaming of Gold, Dreaming of Home: Transnationalism and Migration between the United States and South China, 1882–1943*; Elliot Young's *Alien Nation: Chinese Migrations in the Americas from the Coolie Era through World War II*; Moon-ho Jung's *Coolies and Cane: Race, Labor and Sugar in the Age of Emancipation*; Lisa Yun's *The Coolie Speaks: Chinese Indentured Laborers and African Slaves in Cuba*; Kathleen Lopez's *Chinese Cubans: A Transnational History*; Grace Peña Delgado's *Making the Chinese Mexican: Global Migration, Exclusion, and Localism in the U.S.-Mexico Borderlands*; Robert Chao Romero's *The Chinese in Mexico, 1882–1940*; and Walton Look Lai's *Indentured Labor, Caribbean Sugar: Chinese and Indian Migrants to the British West Indies, 1838–1918*.

9. Eça de Queirós himself served as general consul in Havana from 1872 to 1874, that is, during the demise of the China-Cuba "coolie trade," finally suspended in 1874. As his critics have argued, his consular experience in Cuba gave him the authority to write *crónicas* on the subjects of China international relations and immigration policies, as well as inspired him to write one of his most acknowledged stories, *O mandarin* (1880). On the other hand, in these frequent anti-Chinese immigration narratives, including abject depictions of overseas Chinese in filthy and promiscuous neighborhoods in Havana, he deliberately avoided addressing the lucrative Macao-based Portuguese participation in the "coolie trade."

10. For a thorough study of such diplomatic tensions between China and the overseas Chinese host nations, see Yen Ching-Hwang's *Coolies and Mandarins: China's Protection of Overseas Chinese During the Late Ch'ing Period (1851–1911)*.

11. "Dr. Semana" was actually a sort of collective penname long used by a number of cronistas in Henrique Fleuiss's *Semana Ilustrada* (1860–1876).

12. A cangue was a punishment device similar to the Western pillory.

13. The Japanese emerged in the West as militarily superior to other eastern countries (China and Russia in particular).

14. The following quotation was taken from Taunay's speech to his fellow senators in late 1888: "I agree with the U.S. Americans who denied [Chinese naturalization] through Congress's special act; I think it was in 1878. All descendants of blacks or whites are eligible for acquiring the grand naturalization, but not the ones belonging to the yellow race—this is the law of the American Congress" (*Proceeding* 1888, 316).

122   S. RONCADOR

REFERENCES

Assis, Machado de. 1888. Bons Dias! *Gazeta de Notícias*, October 28.
Assis, Machado de. 2011. *O Jornal e o livro*. São Paulo: Companhia das Letras.
Azevedo, Arthur. (1884) 1985. O mandarim. In *Teatro de Artur Azevedo*, vol. 2. Rio de Janeiro: Instituto Nacional de Artes Cênicas.
Bhrar, Avtar. 1996. *Cartographies of diaspora: Contesting identities*. New York: Routledge.
Chalhoub, Sidney. 1996. *Cidade febril: Cortiços e epidemias na corte imperial*. São Paulo: Companhia das Letras.
Ching-Hwang, Yen. 1985. *Coolies and mandarins: China's protection of overseas Chinese during the late Ch'ing period (1851–1911)*. Singapore: Singapore University Press.
Duarte, Eduardo de Assis. 2007. *Machado Afro-descendente: Escritos de caramujo*. Rio de Janeiro: Pallas.
Gledson, John. 2006. Bons Dias! In *Por um novo Machado de Assis: Ensaios*, 134–187. São Paulo: Companhia das Letras.
Hu-DeHart, Evelyn. 2009. Indispensable enemy or convenient scapegoat? A critical examination of Sinophobia in Latin America and the Caribbean, 1870s to 1930s. *Journal of Chinese Overseas* 5(1): 55–90.
Jobim, José Luis. 2005. 'Quem deve ser brasileiro?': As opiniões de Taunay e Machado de Assis sobre a nacionalização. *Matraga- Revista do Programa de Pós-Graduação em Letras da UERJ* 17: 13–23.
Lesser, Jeffrey. 1999. *Negotiating national identity: Immigrants, minorities and the struggle for ethnicity in Brazil*. Durham: Duke University Press.
Oliva, Osmar Pereira. 2008. Machado de Assis, Joaquim Nabuco, Eça de Queirós e a imigração chinesa—qual medo?. In *Proceedings to XXI ABRAPLIP Conference*, 66–84. São Paulo.
Patai, Daphne. 1991. Minority status and the stigma of surplus visibility. *Chronicle of Higher Education* 38(10): A52.
Proceedings of the Imperial Senate of Brazil. 1888. Vol 6. Rio de Janeiro: Imprensa Nacional.
Queirós, José Maria Eça de. 1894. Chineses e Japoneses. *Gazeta de Notícias* (December 1 and 6), 70.
Taunay, Alfredo d'Escragnolle. 1884. Acta da 1a sessão preparatória. *A Immigração: Órgão da Sociedade Central de Immigração* (December1883–August): 2–5.
Taunay, Alfredo d'Escragnolle. 1886. *A nacionalização ou grande naturalização e naturalização tácita*. Rio de Janeiro: Imprensa Nacional.
Vieira, Martha Victor. 2005. Os novos cidadãos brasileiros: Naturalização e razão de estado, 1882–1891. *Estudos de História* 12(1): 191–210.

PART III

Women in Machado's Work

CHAPTER 9

Writing Womanhood in the New Brazil: Machado's *Lição de Botânica*

Earl E. Fitz

Written two years before his death, *Lição de Botânica*, Machado's final play, stands as a singular achievement in his oeuvre—one that merits more critical attention than it has received. It constitutes a much greater social, political, and artistic achievement than the mere *divertissement* Bosi takes it to be (1970, 273). Other commentators have shown a similar lack of interest in this text. Lisboa, for example, does not discuss it, nor do Stein or Xavier. And while it purports to open new discussions concerning Machado de Assis, the often cited and corporately authored study, *Machado de Assis*, does not include a section devoted to Machado's theater.[1] Though I agree with Magaldi, one of the relatively few critics who does concern himself with this neglected aspect of Machado's work, that the play's protagonist—a young woman named Helena—"represents an advanced phase of female psychology" (121) [my translation],[2] I do not believe that her characterization rests on a "pernicious coquetry" that, for her, marriage is necessarily the "supreme good to which to aspire," or that, after marrying, she will give up all her interests and ambitions (122). When, in 1863, Machado's friend and republican confidant, Quintino Bocaiúva, wrote that his plays (to that point) were "to be read and not staged" (Alencar 1962, 1137), that is, for reading and not for presentation, he was saying some-

E.E. Fitz (✉)
Vanderbilt University, Nashville, TN, USA

thing incisive about the theatricality of Machado's efforts for the stage, not about the Brazilian master's development of the theme of feminine agency, which, in my reading of it, drives this late one-act comedy.

Yet, what we might call the sociopolitical importance of Machado's female characters to his plays has not gone altogether unnoticed (Loyola 1997, 58–71). And though he does not elaborate on this intriguing comment, Pontes, too, writing in 1962, notes that it is Machado's treatment of his *senhoras* that separates his early theater from his later efforts—the outstanding example of which is *Lição de Botânica* (81; 77). More to the point in terms of the issue taken up here, Pontes also counts *Lição de Botânica* as ranking among Machado's best plays (82), one that I feel offers us a useful insight into the intellectual, artistic, and political thinking of Machado de Assis as he neared the end of his life. Consistent with Machado's later novels in that it features a determined female protagonist who insists on her own chance at self-realization, *Lição de Botânica* is built around the issues of "sexual politics, of gender and discourse, of love and marriage as institutions, and of the shifting situation of women in an ideological arena just then beginning to be problematized" (Lisboa 1996, 6, 19). With respect to this theme, the play is cut from the same cloth as the author's narratives. The main character, Dona Helena—who can be thought of as an updated and more sharply focused version of the character Helena from Machado's 1876 novel of the same name—is presented as being very much her own person, a point that comes through clearly in this 1906 comedy. In my view, the Helena of 1906 is the embodiment of what Machado de Assis appears to have felt the new, post-Republic Brazilian woman would be like. In this sense, *Lição de Botânica* is best read as the theatrical counterpart to a major theme (the emancipation of Brazilian women) that Machado had been developing more and more in his novels (see Fitz 2014).

The play is built around five interlocking motifs: botany (especially gramineous plants, or grasses), doors, keys, flowers (especially the perianth), and books. These recurrent objects lend unity and coherence to this fast-moving comedy and allow for a more concise and ironic dialogue to take place between the four players (three women and one man, a distribution not lacking in its own gender-sensitive implications). The relationship between science and society might be said to constitute another basic motif of this play since a great deal is made of the importance of science to a progressive, enlightened society (envisioned here as a beautiful, healthy plant; hence the significance of botany to the play) and its ability to learn and evolve, to adjust its attitudes and beliefs as new knowledge is discovered.[3] The play's structure also reflects a fundamental reversal of action in that what seems to be the basic conflict in the first scene (we are led to think that the main relationship will involve Dona Leonor's niece, Dona Cecília, and the Baron Segismundo de Kernoberg's nephew) turns out to be a very different one by the final scene (where we have learned that the play's primary focus is on the unconventional, and, at the end of the play, still undecided relationship between Dona Helena and the baron himself; see Loyola 1997, 65–66, 71). That the key question (whether the female protagonist will accept the baron's proposal of marriage or not) remains so pointedly undecided at the end strongly suggests that this long-overlooked play asks us to think about something else.

A corollary to this first, structural inversion is a second, and much more important, one involving an unexpected inversion of power. In his first appearance on the stage, the baron is the epitome of power, arrogance, and domination; not only is he a man of means and a baron, he is also a scientist—a profession he feels is superior to all others. Though, for the most part, presented as a comic figure (which allows the audience/reader to laugh at the silliness of patriarchy, its vain values, and self-aggrandizing modes of being), his potential for change also makes him a very serious character. In the end, however, his power (or, apropos of patriarchy, what he has naively assumed was his "natural" power) has been shown to be artificial and he is no longer dictating the terms of the situation; a young woman, Dona Helena, is. Given the complexity of the baron's characterization, we can surmise that he is far from exemplifying the dull-minded and vulgar *tolo* (fool) that preoccupied Machado in his first published work, "Queda que as mulheres têm para os tolos" (1861), a translation and rather strategic adaptation of Victor Hénaux's "De l'amour des femmes pour les sots," itself an adaptation of Louis Champcenetz's "Petit traité de l'amour des femmes pour les sots."[4] The importance of these two works to Machado de Assis's intellectually formative years, and especially, to his understanding of both gender and civic responsibility, cannot be minimized.

Even more importantly, the character of Helena, who clearly has no interest in *tolos*, is that of a *woman de espírito* (of great spirit), the implication being that, in the modern and progressive republic that Brazil sought to be, neither *tolos* nor *tolas* could be tolerated (see Maia Neto 1994, 21–38). Finally, *Lição de Botânica* also provides its audience a strong sense of social progress already made as far as the status of women is concerned. The first of the three female characters that the audience encounters is the witty and sharp, if not always comprehending, Dona Leonor—an older, more experienced woman and the aunt of the two younger women, Dona

Cecília and Dona Helena, the latter a young widow (a character type in which Machado the narrativist had long been interested). Dona Leonor and her ideas about gender and social propriety can be taken as representing the outlooks and mores of an earlier generation of Brazilian women while the attitudes and desires of the two younger female characters can be seen as representing those of Brazil's present and future. And, of course, of these two younger women, it is Helena who carries the flag of the more independent and increasingly empowered Brazilian woman.

That the demonstration of this is Machado's thematic goal here is not as surprising or as unexpected as it might at first seem. For one thing, Machado would have been well aware of his compatriot Aluísio Azevedo's belief that women were inherently superior to men. "Azevedo's Naturalist aesthetics," in the words of Affonso Romano de Sant'Anna, "stress the supremacy of the feminine over the masculine, of the female over the male in a pattern which can be summed up in this way: Sovereignty is to slavery as the feminine is to the masculine. That is, the feminine rules where the masculine submits" (2000, 216). While it is doubtful that Machado saw the issue in terms quite this stark, it seems very likely that, as a creative and socially conscious man of his time and place, he would have regarded the emancipation of women as being at least as important to the future of Brazil as the abolition of slavery had been. One likely reason he would have understood the connection between these two burning issues is that the well-known Brazilian abolitionist writer Nísea Floresta (the pseudonym of Dionísia Gonçalves) had translated Mary Wollstonecraft's *A Vindication of the Rights of Women* into Portuguese and arranged for its 1832 publication in Brazil, where it was widely read and discussed among the intelligentsia. And he surely would have known about the convincing arguments of feminist leader Francisca Senhorinha da Motta Diniz, who, writing in 1890, had this to say about women and women's rights in late nineteenth-century Brazil: "We want to regain our lost rights; we want true education, which has not been granted us, so that we can educate our children; we want pure instruction" (a line that echoes in Helena's desire for an education in *Lição de Botânica*) "so we can know our rights and use them appropriately; …" and, finally, "we want to be our husbands' companions, not their slaves"[5] (Burns 1980, 371–72). As I argue in *Machado de Assis and Female Characterization: the Novels* (2014), Machado's novels—from *Helena* to *Memorial de Aires*—bear out his support of this position. In addition, there is also the likelihood that Machado would have been aware of a similar struggle going on in the USA, where the effort to emancipate both African slaves and women predates the American Civil War, reaching its climax in the great Civil Rights movement of the 1960s. As Louis Menand writes, with reference to Brazil's northern neighbor, "Tension between advocates of women's rights and advocates of rights for African-Americans goes back to the days of the abolitionists, and it continued after the Civil War. The view of the African-Americans in these disputes was that blacks came first.... The view of the women was that a law protecting all African-Americans from discrimination as a class would leave one group legally unprotected: white women" (2014, 79). It strains credulity to believe that Machado would not have been fully informed about this struggle in the USA, or to think that he would have missed its parallel importance for Brazil.

Then, too, Machado would surely have been cognizant of the progressive positivist agenda which, in addition to its struggle "to codify the diverse yearnings for progress expressed in many sectors of Brazilian society," also viewed women as beings who were "superior to men" (Burns 1980, 254, 255). While Machado's attitudes with respect to positivism were tangled, to say the least, there is no reason to believe that he would have disagreed with the positivists on this particular point. Indeed, as we shall see, characters from his final two novels address this very point in no uncertain terms. For all the reservations Machado had about it, positivism exerted a very powerful and progressive force in late nineteenth- and early twentieth-century Brazil and he would have been fully attuned to this. Positivist ideas about the need for racial equality in Brazil were closely entwined with an equally revolutionary belief in the emancipation of women. In short, it would have been very odd indeed if Machado had not been supportive of these new and clearly needed reforms. Brazil, moreover, is notable for the strength and vitality of its women's movement during the late nineteenth- and early twentieth-century period (see Burns 1980, 371–72; Callahan 2011, 110, 159n12), and it is all but inconceivable to think that Machado would not have been aware of the stupidities and injustices involved in the subjugation of women and of the potential benefits that would accrue to Brazil if women—the other 50 % of the population—were unshackled and encouraged to engage with the progress of the Brazilian Republic.

Finally, there are Machado's own female novelistic characters, from the well-intended but still too passive Lívia (the first of Machado's young widows to play a major role in one of his novels) in *Ressurreição* (1872) to the strong-willed and determined Fidélia[6] (another young widow) in

Memorial de Aires (1908), who show a steady and sustained development in the direction of agency (see, e.g., the entries in *Memorial de Aires* for October 6, 1888, and October 10, 1888, among several others). Already in the Brazilian master's second novel (*A Mão e a Luva*, 1874), for example, it is the proud and strong-willed main female character, Guiomar, who controls the action. And in his third novel, *Helena* (1876), he presents his readers with a full-fledged female protagonist who, at several different points in the narrative, establishes herself as a powerful force for positive change and as the character whose vision of her own future lends itself to being read as a blueprint for a new and better Brazil—one that is stronger and more just and in which power is equally shared between men and women (with the humbly born Helena herself laying out this vision). This singular interest in strong, forward-looking female characters continues in Machado's subsequent novels as well. Indeed, it grows less symbolic and oblique and more overt, becoming, finally, a striking part of his overall work (Santiago 1978, 29). In the 1904 *Esaú e Jacó* [Esau and Jacob], for example, the wise and sagacious character, Aires (commonly thought to be a portrait of Machado himself), actually declares that he prefers the conversation of women to that of men, whose gendering, in his learned opinion, tends to aggravate banality, whereas that of women tends to correct it (see Chap. 31). And in Machado's final novel, *Memorial de Aires* (1908), this same Aires, now a diarist, writes quite unambiguously that women are stronger than men, more patient, and better able to endure pain and adversity (see the entry for August 24, 1888). It is not impossible to read this unabashed declaration about the strength of women in the 1908 novel as a considerably more explicit version of what Machado is showing us about Helena in the 1906 play. Significantly, however, the main female characters of Machado's novels are not, in the main, constructed as tyrants, seeking (as Azevedo's naturalistic ethos demanded) to dominate men as the strong dominate the weak, but as clear-minded advocates of the need to share power equally in an increasingly complex and evolving democratic Brazilian Republic, in which men and women of differing kinds of intelligence and skill sets must learn to work together for the common good.

In this new Brazil of the early twentieth century, no one can be permitted to be or remain subjugated, not for reasons of race, skin color, or gender. The 1906 comedy *Lição de Botânica* represents a major contribution to the author's continuing cultivation of this theme, specifically to the urgent question of female leadership in Brazil's rapid, if uncertain,

evolution as a progressive, modern republic. This late play further demonstrates Machado's belief that a new kind of woman—emancipated from
the old straitjacket of patriarchy, and yet, committed to working with a
new type of similarly emancipated man—was needed if this new Brazil was
going to achieve its true potential. As one of Machado's characters (the
liberal Paulo) makes explicit in the 1904 novel, *Esaú e Jacó* (Chap. 38),
it is not enough to free the slaves; their white masters (along with white
society, in general) have to be freed of their bigoted attitudes and beliefs
as well, and this latter emancipation will take longer and will be more difficult to achieve. Yet, it is crucial. And the same, Machado's texts suggest,
is also true of relations between women and men.

The parallel between this extraordinary declaration in the 1904 narrative and the argument more subtly (but also more effectively) advanced in
the 1906 play is too obvious to miss and too important to dismiss: women
can be liberated (or liberate themselves) from patriarchy, formally or informally, but, while laudable and just in itself, this move is ultimately insufficient; men, too, must be liberated, and from the same patriarchal thinking
that has ensnared women. Additionally (and a point surely not lost on
Machado), the same patriarchal thinking that has so damaged women and
held them back has also damaged and held back men, preventing them
from growing as egalitarian-minded human beings, domestic partners,
and citizens. No one is free until everyone is free, Machado seems to be
saying. As in the case of abolition, where it was one thing to free African
slaves, but quite another to free the white population from what it felt was
its natural right to enslave someone else, so, too, did the emancipation of
women in Machado's vision of a new Brazil depend on the emancipation
of the men (like the baron) around them. It is important to note that the
play does not end with the clear-cut happy ending that an audience or
reader of the time might well have expected. Rather, it ends (as is so typical
of the mature Machado) on a note of ambiguity: the now humbled baron
is asking Dona Helena to accept his hand in marriage, but, crucially, she
demurs, and it is not at all clear what her final decision will be. If he cannot
be "educated," or "liberated," and rise to *her* level of liberation and egalitarianism, then the baron will not become her mate—not romantically and
not politically. If he can, then he and Dona Helena, symbolizing a further
liberated and unified Brazil, can go forward together, as equals.

Like the white slave masters highlighted in the 1908 novel, who need
to be freed of their enthusiasm for enslaving and exploiting others, the
white male patriarchs of early twentieth-century Brazil must also be

freed of the crippling ideas about female inferiority that they harbor and perpetuate. Before Brazil can flower as a healthy plant (a key motif of the play), it will have to free not merely its slaves but its women as well. This is the message Dona Helena delivers at the very end of the play when she says to the baron and to her aunt (the older generation) that the decision he (representing patriarchy) and she (conventional thinking) must make is really a matter of "applied botany" (1187)—that is, how the new knowledge gleaned from the science of botany (how plants flourish and sustain life) can, if we will let it, teach us something about how a healthy, just society can be created and made to function. But it will be up to Brazil's citizens, its men *and* its women, to make it so. The singularity of the 1906 play is that the main male character, the baron, is presented (by Machado) as amenable to being taught by the exemplary young woman, Dona Helena, how to become the exemplary young man she would want to accompany her as, at the end of the play, she is about to move her own life (and, by extension, all of early twentieth-century Brazil) forward. The baron, in short, seems to be capable of doing what poor Félix, doomed by his doubt, his male status, and his power, could not do—allow himself to be reborn or resurrected by a superior ontology, based on a sense of equality and respect for others. The question that remains unanswered at the end of the play is this: will the Baron (and Brazilian patriarchy) be able to accept this new and deeply revolutionary change in status? As citizens of this nascent new Brazil, the audience will have to decide. The question is no longer academic or artistic; it is now civic in nature. As readers of Machado de Assis would have realized at this point, the trajectory between the male and female relationship that governs *Ressurreição* (1872), Machado's first novel, and the one that drives this late play, *Lição de Botânica*, is revealing of Machado's artistic and intellectual evolution with respect to the importance of his female characters and to his belief in the healthy progress and development of the Brazilian nation.

To appreciate how Machado moves his audience to consider this surpassingly important, if too long neglected, point, it is worth examining how he constructs and integrates the 14 scenes of this underappreciated— and quite surprising—one-act comedy.

Scene 1: To get the play moving, Dona Leonor, the tart-tongued but traditional matriarch, comes on stage reading a mysterious note she has just received from her neighbor, the Baron Segismundo de Kernoberg, a Swedish botanist whom she has never met, but who, she is now learning, wishes to speak with her about an issue of great importance. A paragon of the "old ways," Dona Leonor is dubious about granting what is, for her, the baron's rather odd request. To her love-smitten younger niece, Dona Cecília (who we can see is interested in the baron's nephew), Dona Leonor wryly declares of her as-yet-unseen neighbor that as a Swede and a botanist, he possesses two gravely boring qualities that make it less likely that his request will be granted. Her other niece, the older and feistier Dona Helena intervenes, however, and the power of her argument (that the baron is their neighbor, after all, and so they should meet him) wins out.

The plot thickens in scene 2, when Dona Helena mistakenly assumes that the baron wishes to ask Dona Leonor's permission for his nephew, Henrique, to court her niece, Cecília (who is Helena's sister). Clever dialogue between the two young women then ensues and Helena introduces the motif of the door (which, she makes clear, must, like the human heart, be either open or closed to new engagements, such as love) into the text by means of a perspicacious quote: "Il faut qu'une porte soit ouverte ou fermée" (A door must be open or closed; 1172). The fact that Helena delivers this line in French is important because it not only demonstrates her status as a well-educated young woman, but, given the context of the declaration itself, establishes her credentials as a sentient and imaginative young woman who is fully cognizant of all that is going on around her. This quality, moreover, is essential to her later transformation as a character. When Cecília retorts that she has lost the key to her door (heart), Helena comically discourses on how Henrique will respond to this allegation. In the back-and-forth of the dialogue, however, the reader also realizes that Helena is simultaneously talking about herself and her own situation as a young widow who, at this point, is adamant about not seeking a new mate. The scene ends with Helena declaring that the "pearls," that is, the high-quality suitors that are out there to select from must forever remain in the jewelry store.

Scene 3: The baron, stiff and formal and seeking a response to his earlier note, makes his initial appearance. Discovering that Dona Leonor is not available, he enters into an awkward chat with Cecília, whose funny asides to the audience enliven the scene. More importantly, the baron is bearing a scientific book about gramineous plants and whether such plants have perianths, the part that forms the external envelope of the flower. In another comic aside, Cecília observes that she will have to endure the boring baron because he might, one day, be her father-in-law. The scene ends with the baron observing, tellingly, that the word "perianth" is composed of two Greek words, *peri* (surrounding) and *anthos* (flower). The perianth, the reader understands, is thus like a couple—which is also composed of two parts, both of which must work together if the resulting flower is to bloom properly.

Scene 4: The witty banter continues as Dona Leonor joins her niece, Cecília, and the baron. Cecília exits the stage so that Dona Leonor and the baron can take up the question of the baron's still mysterious request for an audience with Dona Leonor.

Scene 5: At first, unsure of himself, the baron comically imitates Dona Leonor's every action as he sets about explaining himself and the reason for his note and visit. Stating rather tendentiously that books and science are his life, and that since his life has been devoted to science and scientific scholarship, he has had to remain celibate as far as love and matrimony are concerned, the baron then unexpectedly and rather bluntly declares that he has come to ask Dona Leonor to bar her door to his nephew, Henrique, who is enamored of one of Dona Leonor's nieces. If they were to allow Henrique to marry Cecília, it would, the baron insists, ruin him as a scientist, which he is being groomed to be. In a key aside, the baron mistakenly concludes that Dona Leonor does not understand his position (which she does not, but not for the reasons the baron supposes). His reaction (his misinterpretation of a woman) leads him into an absurdly extreme and unrealistic position—that science and marriage are incompatible. Machado here has the baron come off as overbearing and as the epitome of masculine arrogance, rigidity, extremism, and blindness. As Machado lays it out, the supposed tension between science and love amounts to a red herring that the alert reader understands must be obviated. From the perspective of the play's structuring, it is crucial that the baron, a man of learning, power, and position, present himself in this ridiculous fashion here in order that his later conversion to a more self-critical kind of being may seem more dramatic, and thus, effective. The presentation of the baron as offering the women nothing more than a fatuous ultimatum allows Helena to undo this kind of either/or thinking (one often associated with male psychology) and to show how brittle, threadbare, and unproductive it is.

Dona Leonor, a bit put off by the baron's asinine position and the brusqueness of its exposition, humorously declares that she does not have to be asked to shut her door; indeed, she would do it gladly, and to them both! After more clever word play involving images of doors, keys, flowers, and thorns, Dona Leonor effectively temporizes the baron and his risible request. But the fatuity of the baron's (male) outlook has been planted in the reader's mind. The scene ends with the baron graciously acknowledging that he is dealing with a woman of intelligence, strength, and spirit. And in the same vein—again, crucially, in terms of the scene's structuring—during the final exchange between Dona Leonor and the baron, the baron, who has just presented himself as a paragon of patriarchy, shows himself to be at least potentially capable of change, of adapting to a new environment, or, apropos of the scientific method, to alter his thinking in response to newly learned facts. A pivotal moment in the play, scene 5 is very artfully constructed.

In scene 6, Dona Helena and the Baron meet for the first time. They exchange pleasantries and the apparent central problem of the play up to this moment (that the baron does not want his nephew, Henrique, to be admitted into Dona Leonor's house since, in the baron's view, the young man must be kept celibate for science) is made manifest. Upon hearing this, Dona Helena begins to size up the situation in its totality and declares, tellingly, that she does not "understand." The reader, of course, realizes that while Dona Helena understands only too clearly the foolishness of the Baron's simplistic and unproductive position (which can be taken as being that of patriarchy), what she does not yet understand is how the Baron's unnecessarily rigid position might be altered and so parlayed to favor the life that her sister and young Henrique want to have together. The scene is very short because while the seed of Helena's intervention into what has been presented as the main conflict has been planted, it cannot as yet be shown to be blooming— either in terms of Dona Cecília, Helena's sister, and Henrique or with respect to herself and her own transformation as the play's main character. This must be more carefully set up, as it will be.

Scene 7: Dona Leonor, representing the past, and Dona Helena (a young widow), representing the future, show themselves to be smart, funny, and clear-minded as to the viability of the warming relationship between Cecília and Henrique. Interestingly, Dona Leonor, who finds the baron a tedious "bear," is adamant about nipping this relationship in the bud, whereas Helena argues in favor of "trying something" to see if the match between these two exemplary young people might be brought to fruition. Significantly (in terms of its symbolic value), this still inchoate plan involving a form of reconciliation with the baron (and the kind of male dominant thinking he represents) rests on the ability of a woman (Helena) to educate and enlighten a powerful man (the baron), to change his destructively narrow way of thinking and help him see that there are better ways to do things. The sociopolitical implications stemming from this scene are too strong to ignore. The irony in this new plot complication is that in making this effort for her sister, Helena is setting the stage for her own fate to change, which emerges as essential to the play's conclusion.

Scene 8: Dona Helena and her younger sister, Dona Cecília, are on stage together discussing, in a lively and engaging exchange that runs the gamut from the funny and clever to the serious and logical, how they might bring about a change of position by the baron. Throughout, it is Helena who, with every line, establishes her character as the wise woman who will find a solution to her sister's dilemma. In this scene, in fact, Helena, the experienced and more worldly woman, becomes the catalyst of change. Lest the reader or audience miss this important turn in her characterization, Machado has Cecília declare admiringly and unambiguously that Helena "is so intelligent" and that she is sure to "come up with, by dint of necessity, an idea" (1176).

With her intelligence clearly established, along with her social, economic, and sexual experience, Helena now moves over to a chair and "mechanically" (1177) picks up the book on gramineous plants and flowers that the baron had earlier left there. Tantalizingly, but also quite mysteriously and unexpectedly, Helena says, "Who knows if this book might save everything?" (1177). As she opens the book and leafs through it, an idea seems to come to her, and she begins to quiz her sister about the book's content and its relationship to the baron. While the love-struck younger woman does not yet grasp what Helena's plan will involve (this adding another comic element to the play), the scene ends very deftly, with Helena telling her sister to be patient a bit longer and she will then "see," that is, understand, everything. Like Cecília, the audience feels the suspense build and wants to know how this new plot twist, carried forth by Helena, will play out.

Scene 9: In what is, up to this point, the play's most complex scene, Dona Helena and the baron engage in a verbal duel—involving a subtle but slowly intensifying intellectual and emotional investment by both characters—that establishes their relationship, problematic though it is, as the heart of the play, the one the audience is most interested in. Very quickly, the image of the book (knowledge) is once again introduced into their dialogue, as are the facts about the book's content[7] and that since it is written in Swedish, it must be translated, or interpreted, into a language (one that will demonstrate the need for cooperation between Brazilian men and Brazilian women, who must, from now on, be equals, in marriage and under the law) that everyone (and not just one of the parties involved) can understand.

At first, in keeping with his character and all it symbolizes (patriarchy, even if it is of the benevolent sort), the baron comes across as vain, arrogant, and self-centered (the old problem, for Machado, of egoism). By the end of this key scene, however, he will be much less so. This transformation of his character is driven by what Helena slowly but steadily reveals about herself and about the kind of person she would like to be in the future. She says to the baron, for example, that while she is not trained in botany, she can read and she enjoys doing so—which of course, implies that she, a woman, already knows a great deal and that she is desirous of a better, more complete education. And, showing her strength of character, Helena does not hesitate to contradict the baron when he makes what he thinks (mistakenly) is a pithy comment, as when he rather tendentiously quotes Buffon to the effect that "Le génie, c'est la patience," to which she quickly and deliciously responds, "Not always." It is difficult to read this line and not feel that the time for women's rights to succeed in Brazil is now, in 1906, the time of the play, and that "patience," or further delay, is not what is needed. The "genius," one can feel, of the emancipation of women in the Brazil of the early twentieth century will not be attained by further "patience" with the old, unacceptable status quo; action now is what is needed. The baron is in a position to help bring about this long overdue and much-needed change, and so, with just a few carefully chosen words, Machado has been able to highlight the importance of Helena's plan to help him throw off the smothering, dead weight of patriarchy and enter into the more enlightened reality of a progressive and truly democratic Brazilian Republic.

The middle of this scene, which changes both the direction and the tenor of the entire play, hangs on Machado's symbolic use not of the flower per se (this will come later, in scene 12, when Helena speaks of how she desires her own bouquets to be), but of one particular part of the flower—the perianth. Known in botanical terms as the envelope of the flower, the perianth here takes on distinctly metaphoric properties that relate to the status of women (but also men, as we shall see) in Western society. As the envelope that encases the flower before it blooms, the perianth in Machado's play suggests that the concepts of protection and nurturing must eventually give way to liberation and flowering; protection and nurturing, in other words, must not become repression and imprisonment, which is what happens in a rigidly patriarchal environment. Machado makes symbolic use of the botanist's understanding of the word "perianth" to suggest that human society must nurture and protect its young—both its men and its women—but that, at a certain point, it must also allow these same young people (a nation's future) to "bloom," to become all they can be, separately but also together. A truly healthy society, like a healthy flower carefully tended in its fertile bed, where other flowers are also blooming, must be integrated and mutually supportive, not segregated and mutually opposed. It must not work against its own best interest, which is the distorted scenario maintained by patriarchy. In a way that effectively suggests the nature of a healthy, blooming society, Machado shows us that in a vigorous, blooming flower (the society in question), the perianth or calyx (that part of society charged with educating and caring for the young) naturally gives way to and supports the corolla, the most celebrated and attractive part of the flower, its colorful, sweet-smelling petals—that is, its young people. As part of this process, the stamens (the male part of the flower) work together with the pistils (their female counterparts) to produce something (a flower and a progressive, democratic republic) that is healthy and beautiful. We understand now why Machado had led the baron to reference the perianth so carefully in scene 4, but we also come to understand that the baron, as a man of science, can change his thinking about issues of both botany and life as new facts come to the fore (a point made clear via his commentary on the book, focusing on the perianth, that he and Helena discuss).

That the baron begins, in this scene, to consider his need to change his thinking about human relationships becomes clear in his wish to have Helena become his "disciple" (1178)—a word charged, in vintage Machado fashion, with multiple and sometimes clashing meanings. By comparing Helena to a violet—which he says is *formosa* (beautiful), but also *recatada* (modest, reserved, or subdued), qualities that will not describe Helena's "blooming" in this play (1178)—discovered by the great Swedish botanist, Carolus Linnaeus, the baron is well into his wooing of her. But we have already caught on to the dramatic irony being played out here, replete with its own sociopolitical significance for the newly emergent power of women in Brazil. While the baron, a symbol of not the old, obdurate patriarchy (the Brazil of the past) but one of a more malleable stripe, one that is somewhat more modern and flexible, and thus, capable of evolution and change,[8] thinks he is maneuvering Helena, it is really she who is maneuvering him (a fact made apparent by comparing what is happening here with what occurred in scene 8)!

A corollary to this reading of their fast evolving relationship, the reader also contemplates the word "disciple" and, in the process, wonders who is the true disciple here. Is Helena going to become the baron's disciple, as he thinks he wants and should have, or, in a delicious reversal, is he going to become her disciple—in order to learn to become the "new man" that she, as the new Brazilian woman, desires to have as her mate? Not accepting a position that is inferior to that of the baron, Helena continues to speak her mind and to challenge the baron's positions.

The idea of the traditional male-dominated marriage as a potential prison, for both men and women, is broached, as is the question of what kind of lesson is going to be given and received here and by whom. While the baron lays out his vision of why science and marriage are incompatible, Dona Helena, in what could be taken as the weakest point of her development as a character, effectively tells the baron that marriage is not necessarily the prison he makes it out to be, and that, in point of fact, a loyal wife can even strengthen her spouse (1179–80). What remains to be seen, however, is whether the reverse can also be true: can a loyal husband strengthen and support his wife?[9] This question, though implicit at this point in the play's development, will become all but explicit in its conclusion, where the couple's future, like that of modern Brazil itself, is yet to be determined. When Bosi writes of this play, for example, that its dialogue is lively, that its scenes are well-drawn, but that it still traffics in sentimentality, it is most likely this speech by Helena that drives his conclusion (1982, 273).

Yet, something else is going on here, something much more political and revolutionary in nature. While Helena's words here do present her in a most traditional way, without these very words, her transformation into the more independent woman we see at the end of the play would not be nearly as pronounced as it needs to be. In other words, I believe that Machado deliberately puts these words, with their very conventional ideas, into Helena's mouth because he needs to show how dramatically she changes, or "blooms," bursting out from the perianth that is, by now, (1906) a modestly progressive patriarchy (what the baron represents) later in the play. But Helena wants her freedom and she wants it now. With every utterance, she seems less and less inclined to wait for it any longer or to depend on her mate to give it to her. Read in this fashion, *Lição de Botânica* takes on distinctly feminist characteristics (see Lisboa 1996). Helena may or may not become a wife (the decision will be hers and hers alone), but if she chooses to do so, she will not be the dutiful and subservient wife of old Brazil. Either way, Helena is determined to become a modern woman, educated and emancipated and anxious to become a full-fledged citizen and domestic partner. How fast her emancipation will happen, and how he will respond to it, will become the source of the conflict between Helena and the baron, who must discover and embrace his own emancipation from the bonds of patriarchy.

The scene closes with Dona Helena exiting the stage and with the baron, seemingly perplexed, pausing to once again pick up the book, that powerful symbol of knowledge, power, growth, and intellectual liberation—but one that must, in the future, serve equally for both men and women! The scene's conclusion, with the baron contemplating the book (which, if he is able to embrace the lesson in it, could effect his own emancipation from the straitjacket that is blind, unthinking patriarchy), is pregnant with dramatic intensity. This is one of the play's best, most effective moments.

The baron's potential for change, his ability to become what Helena wants and expects him to become, thus constitutes the question that, unanswered even at the end, will live on into the final line of the play. Can old, traditional Brazil change with the times? Can it be educated and embrace the future? Can it learn to shrug off its old, patriarchal ways so that a modern and progressive Brazilian Republic can bloom? Can it attain the full, verdant flowering of its republican promise—one greatly strengthened by its newly emancipated women? These are the questions that are played out through to the play's unexpected conclusion.

Appropriately enough, scene 10 opens with the baron pensively mulling over the significance of what has just transpired with Dona Helena and how he feels about it. A critical part of his characterization here is that he does not simply get angry and reject Helena's position out of hand. Though the baron has not yet made up his mind about how he will respond, he is clearly considering a new ontology for himself, built on a new, and perhaps better, way of living and being. The question is, can he see his way clear to make this revolutionary decision, as his would-be wife has done? Heightening the plot tension, Machado presents the baron as leaning toward returning to his old isolation and his loveless life. He is on the verge of deciding to leave Dona Leonor's house forever when she suddenly joins him on stage. Clever banter ensues and the baron relates in all earnestness to a once again witty and perceptive Dona Leonor that her niece, Dona Helena, has asked him for some botany lessons. The scene thus ends with the audience able to enjoy a bit more the questions of who is giving lessons to whom and who will become whose disciple.

Scene 11: In another short, well-made scene, Dona Leonor asks (lest anyone miss it) the key question: what would her widowed niece, Helena, want with botany lessons?

Scene 12: With the audience wondering if it is really botany lessons that Helena wants, and if she wants to get them or give them, this scene has Helena declaring to her still-confused aunt that her chance to study botany (life itself?) will allow her, whether she gives or receives the lessons, to learn about the "flowers" in her bouquets (1182), a term that, used here in the plural form, suggests that Dona Helena is now thinking about the various forms, or flowerings, that her life will take—if only she can gain the freedom she needs to pursue them. This line of interpretation is given further credence when Helena next says that she needs to learn to not be confused by the diversity of life and to learn how to distinguish between things (e.g., truth and falsity or freedom and entrapment). When her aunt asks her what she expects to gain from learning all these things, Helena replies enigmatically, "Many things" (1182)—a response that can be taken as referring to the fullness of life itself, to all the possibilities for growth and development that the newly emancipated Brazilian woman (or man) might enjoy. Comically, however, neither Cecília, who stands to benefit if Helena's plan succeeds, nor Dona Leonor quite understands what Helena is up to here, and this allows Machado to conclude this scene in a way that augments the tension surrounding what—though still not evident here—will soon become the play's most important tension (the possibly blooming relationship between Helena and the baron).

Dubious about the value of the changes that the ideas coming from such botany lessons might bring, Dona Leonor, representing the ways of the past, urges her two younger female charges to reject these foreign influences and return to "being Brazilian women" (1182). This statement amounts to something of a crisis in the play in that we are now led to wonder whether Helena will be able to save the day and lead Brazil (and her own life) forward. Or will Brazil's oppressive past stifle its chance to create a better, more just future, being envisioned here by a strong young woman?

Scene 13: In this, the longest and penultimate scene in the comedy, Helena emerges as the dominant character, the one whose vision and strength will determine the outcome. She declares that she sees good qualities in the baron—who has not yet been able to liberate himself from his still restrictive patriarchal thinking, but who is now able to see in Helena the kind of person he wants to be with—but she realizes that this may not work out: their agreement about the giving and receiving of botany lessons (and in the minds of the imaginative audience, their potential future relationship and all it could symbolize for Brazil) now appears to be, if not undone, then, certainly placed in jeopardy. Significantly, it is the baron who, at this critical point, declares that she is the one who will decide (1183). The final decision will be hers, not his, and he, "free" (in some ways, yes, but not in others, we now realize), will accept it (1183). This is a moment of crucial import for the play, as it not only inverts the traditional power structure (the female is now agent), but also points clearly to the future and Brazil's need to change its old attitudes about male–female relations.

This same issue then gets reiterated as Machado (by means of Helena's character) uses the very charged term "master" (1183) to invoke the invidious and deeply entrenched master–slave relationship of exploitation and marginalization, which, for Brazilians of the period, would have certainly evoked painful memories of the pernicious institution of slavery. The term also invokes white patriarchy's control of knowledge and its role in the disenfranchisement of women and Afro-Brazilians through institutions and modes of thought.

The image of the book is suddenly re-entered into the complexity of this scene, where it serves to emphasize the kinds of liberation that come from asserting new, nonpatriarchal forms of knowledge. To learn (as from all manner of lessons) and to know (as from the gleaning of knowledge) is to free oneself from the violence of the past. It is, moreover, the baron himself who shows his own willingness to learn and to change his attitudes and behavior and declares that Helena can dispense with masters, and, if she wishes, educate (and liberate) herself with books (1183–84). It is Helena (and all Brazilian women) who will become free, and perhaps even more so than the baron himself, who has already been described, albeit ironically, as "free."

At this point, Machado enters into the text what is perhaps his most venerable human ill: *egoísmo* (1184), a term better understood in English as "selfishness" rather than its etymological kin, "egoism." For the modern reader, however, this charge leveled by Helena that the baron is an *egoísta* evokes the idea of the fragile if grandiose male ego, so frequently noted by feminist critics and social commentators. As Machado's play makes clear, the baron must learn to share power, to give up this crippling self-centeredness and rigidity of thought, and learn to live in a more egalitarian, just, and life-affirming fashion. This is the way forward—for the baron, for Helena, and for republican Brazil itself. Responding to this charge, the baron admits the deleterious effects of an existence based on selfishness, self-centeredness, and the pursuit of self-interest—the cornerstones of conservatism as a social and political philosophy and of capitalism as an economic system. He further dramatically confesses that his life has been little more than a "cloister" (1184) (a term that, in addition to its other meanings, also smacks of the quasi-religious qualities of self-centeredness) built on male appearances (1184) rather than on such democratic principles as justice, equality, and freedom.

This powerful and decidedly noncomedic scene comes to an end when, emphasizing once again the importance of knowledge as the "key" (1185) to unlocking one's mind from old prejudices and errors of thought and judgment, both Helena and the baron affirm that their relationship, if it is to continue at all, will not involve his being her master (1185). The real problem, we now realize, is the continuing existence of any kind of master–slave relationship. A modern Brazil cannot and should not abide by this. Making clear use of his play's main symbols, in the final lines of scene 13, Machado has the baron ask anxiously if he will never again pass through the door of Dona Helena's house (1185). She responds that he himself has closed that door with his own hands, suggesting his enervating ideas and attitudes. He then declares that the key to this door is in her hands, to which she responds, in one of the play's most fascinating lines, "I don't see it" (1185). Increasingly desperate, sensing that he is on the verge of losing something vital to his own development as a healthy human being (his own "flowering"), the baron pleads for the "hope" (1185) that Helena will grant him more time to change in the ways he must. Signaling its importance to the conclusion of this scene, this motif of hope appears no fewer than five times, but always in the context of the crucial question of whether the baron will insist on being, in one manner or another, the master of Helena, who says, finally and quite enigmatically, "I guessed that you want, at all costs, to be my master" (1186). The scene ends on a negative note with what is now the core question—Helena's relationship with the baron—very much in doubt.

In the play's relatively short final scene, there is no dénouement, no untying of the plot's core knot and no resolution of the basic conflict, which was clearly laid out in the previous scene. Our desire for a happy ending, or even a satisfactory or agreeable outcome, will be frustrated. The two main antagonists, Helena and the baron, are once again brought together, along with Dona Leonor and Dona Cecília, but the play's fundamental conflict, which swirls around Helena and what she will decide to do with respect to the baron, will remain unresolved—as will the true emancipation of women in Brazilian society. Is this where Machado's 1906 play takes us? There is good reason to think so.

In a delightful reversal of the action we saw in scene 1, where the baron asked that Dona Leonor bar her door to his nephew, who was beguiled by her niece, in scene 14, the baron asks Dona Leonor openly for Helena's hand. In making this (to Dona Leonor and Cecília) surprising declaration, the baron suggests that he is a changed man, though his statement of intent gets the ellipsis punctuation so distinctive of Machado's mature style when he wants the reader to think carefully about what has just been said: "I see all this now..." (1186). But the baron, sensing the uncertainty of his situation, also requests that Dona Leonor intervene on his behalf and pressure Helena to accept his request of her hand in marriage. When he appears to wish to dictate the terms of this exchange, Helena once again contradicts him, pointing out that it is not enough that he makes this request—she must accept it or not. Just as the baron (still suffering from a fatal arrogance or egoism, perhaps?) appears to be assuming that his request alone will be sufficient for him to gain what he now wants, Helena, the desired object, makes it clear that she controls the final outcome of this situation. Forceful and assertive in this final scene, Helena is still in command, though the future of her relationship with the baron is clearly clouded, even at this last minute, with what he intimates are his lingering problems with patriarchal thinking and the power it has long, if unjustly, afforded him.

When, seemingly surprised, he asks Helena if she will refuse him, she says she wants three months to think about it—something we feel she would not have said if she had been completely convinced that the baron was going to be able to break free from his own repressive ways and rise to her level of emancipation. Stressed, Helena responds tartly and firmly that 3 months is an "eternity" (1187) of 90 days, suggesting that she, the woman, lives in the world of reality while he, the man, lives in a world of self-delusion. Undeterred, the baron insists on knowing whether at the end of that time, he would have happiness or desperation. Dona Helena, approaching the play's final line, declares in a telling expression of power that *she* extends *her* hand to *him*, that the choice is up to him. But we understand that in saying this, Helena is not meekly giving the baron the old power he may think he has; to the contrary, she is telling him that this choice has to do with whether he will really change in all the ways he needs to change. If he does not, then he will lose what he now wants, or thinks he wants. His choice, then, is about him, not her. Helena has already made her decision. She has, in effect, liberated herself. What remains to be seen is whether her male counterpart can do the same.

The play ends with Helena's once again enigmatic comment to her aunt that "all this is applied botany"—a line that leaves us thinking that everything we have seen or read in this underappreciated one-act comedy concerning the complex relationship between the baron and Helena is also about how the laws of botany, that is, of science and life, can be applied to how they might wish to refashion, modernize, and democratize Brazilian society in ways that would make men and women equal as domestic partners and as citizens.

Although it is certainly true, as Bosi rightly suggests (1978, 273), that *Lição de Botânica* does not, within the confines of its own genre, exhibit the same level or degree of technical and formal innovation that we see so brilliantly exhibited in his post-1880 novels and stories, it is nevertheless an engaging, thought-provoking, and tightly constructed play—arguably his best. More importantly, it conveys, as only plays can, the urgency of one of his most important late themes—the status of women in the new Brazil that is struggling to emerge from its own colonial perianth. Only time would tell, of course, whether Brazilian men and women would achieve this new kind of emancipation, but in 1906, a writer and intellectual of no less stature than that of Machado de Assis showed them the way to proceed.

NOTES

1. It does, however, feature categories on his criticism, *crónicas*, stories, novels, and poetry.
2. All citations from the play are taken from the 1962 edition published by Editôra José Aguilar (*Obra completa*, vol 2).
3. Machado's relationship to science is complicated. While he seems to have had confidence in the ability of science to better understand the laws of biology and the physical universe and to solve problems of medicine, sanitation, and technology, he also seems to have disavowed the positivist view that science was some sort of panacea, that it would solve all of humanity's woes. In this play, the minutia of scientific study is given a ribbing, but the importance of science, and of scientific inquiry, is never in doubt. And, as Pontes points out, *Lição de Botânica* offers us the first instance in which Machado employs science to explain a human attitude (1960, 82).
4. Caldwell, in fact, believes that Machado's 1861 effort does not really constitute a true translation at all, arguing, with respect to Champcenetz, that,

in Machado's version, "there are only a few phrases taken from the original French, and the idea is somewhat different. Champcenetz concentrates on the (bad) nature of women; Assis, on the differences between the *tolos* and the *homens de espírito*" (Caldwell 1970, 232, ch 3 n2). She does not mention Hénaux. The point here relates less to the nature of Machado's translation and adaptation of Hénaux's work than it does to Machado's expansion, in the 1906 comedy, of the earlier concept of the man *de espírito* to include the woman *de espírito* as well. By the 1906 play and the characterization of Helena, Machado proffers a view of women that is far from that of Champcenetz.

5. The importance of these early feminist concerns in Brazil cannot be overestimated. When, in *Brazil: Five Centuries of Change* (1999), Thomas E. Skidmore writes that in the 1990s, "the largest, most radical, most diverse, and most effective of women's movements in Latin America" were coming from Brazil, he is arguing that far from being autogeneric of the late twentieth century, this organized feminist agenda has been a feature of Brazilian intellectual life since at least the early to mid-nineteenth century. It is all but inconceivable, therefore, that Machado de Assis would not have been fully informed about the importance of this great force for social progress.

6. Though it goes beyond the scope of the present study, Gledson offers the interesting theory that Fidélia and her second husband, Tristão, a naturalized Portuguese citizen, represent the abandonment of Brazil by its elite class (see Gledson 1986 215–55).

7. The book concerns itself with the nature of grasses, which recalls Whitman, for whom grass, like the concepts of democracy or human solidarity, was also a very durable and hardy plant, not delicate and susceptible to changes in weather, and, most important of all, capable of sustaining life—as the new Brazil must be.

8. In this sense, *Lição de Botánica* also connects to the advent of modernity and to the plethora of new ideas, technologies, and social transformations that characterized this revolutionary age.

9. A related question, surely not lost on Machado's audience, is whether a typical Brazilian husband, reared on the many betrayals characteristic of Brazilian patriarchy, could learn to be loyal to and supportive of a new kind of wife or partner.

References

Alencar, Mário de. 1962. O Teatrólogo. In *Obra Completa*, vol. 2, ed. Machado de Assis, 1135–1137. Rio de Janeiro: Editôra José Aguilar.

Assis, Machado de. 1962. *Lição de Botánica*. In *Obra Completa*, organized by Afrânio Coutinho, vol. 2, 1171–1187. Rio de Janeiro: Editôra José Aguilar.

Bosi, Alfredo. 1970. *História concisa da literatura brasileira*. São Paulo: Editôra Cultrix.

Bosi, Alfredo, José Carlos Garbuglio, Mario Curvello, and Valentim Aparecido Facioli (eds.). 1982. *Machado de Assis*. São Paulo: Editora Ática.

Burns, E. Bradford. 1980. *A history of Brazil*, 2nd ed. New York: Columbia University Press.

Caldwell, Helen. 1970. *Machado de Assis: The Brazilian master and his novels*. Berkeley: University of California Press.

Callahan, Monique-Adelle. 2011. *Literary transnationalism and African American poetics*. Oxford: Oxford University Press.

Fitz, Earl E. 2014. *Machado de Assis and female characterization: The novels*. Lewisburg: Bucknell University Press.

Gledson, John. 1986. *Machado de Assis: Ficção e história*. Trans. Sônia Coutinho. Rio de Janeiro: Paz e Terra.

Lisboa, Maria Manuel. 1996. *Machado de Assis and feminism: Re-reading the heart of the companion*. Lewiston/Queenston/Lampeter: Edwin Mellen Press.

Loyola, Cecília. 1997. *Machado de Assis: E o teatro das convenções*. Rio de Janeiro: UAPÊ.

Maia Neto, José Raimundo. 1994. *Machado de Assis, The Brazilian Pyrrhonian*. West Lafayette: Purdue University Press.

Menand, Louis. 2014. The Sex Amendment: How women got in on the Civil Rights Act. *New Yorker*, July 21, 74–81.

Pontes, Joel. 1960. *Machado de Assis e o teatro*. Rio de Janeiro: Serviço Nacional do Livro.

Sant'Anna, Affonso Romano de. 2000. Afterword to *The Slum*. Afterword translated by Adria Frizzi; book translated by David H. Rosenthal. Oxford: Oxford University Press.

Santiago, Silviano. 1978. *Uma literatura nos trópicos*. São Paulo: Perspectiva.

Skidmore, Thomas E. 1999. *Brazil: Five centuries of change*. New York: Oxford University Press.

CHAPTER 10

Capitu's Curiosity: Undecidability and Questions of Gender in *Dom Casmurro*

Marta Peixoto

Early in *Dom Casmurro*, the chapter "Capitu's Curiosity" takes the measure of a young girl's intellectual interests, eagerness to expand her horizons as well as her impatience with the constraints of her parents' quite modest situation and the limits on women's education in mid-nineteenth-century Brazil. The time is circa 1857; the place, the narrator Bento's wealthy childhood home.[1] Capitu, around 14 years old, has finished elementary school, where "she had learned reading, writing and arithmetic, French, religious doctrine and needlework" (1997, 59).[2] In the absence of public schools beyond the elementary level, as historian Emilia Viotti da Costa observes, "[u]ntil the end of the empire, secondary school education for women continued to be the privilege of the elite." (2000, 253) In Bento's household, Capitu can give free reign, or almost, to her intelligence and curiosity. She wants to learn Latin from Father Cabral, but is told it's not a language for girls, later admitting to Bento "that this very argument fired her desire to learn it" (1997, 59). "She read our novels, leafed through our books of engravings, wanting to know all about the ruins, the people, the military campaigns, the names, the place, the story behind everything" (1997, 60).

Capitu's open-ended curiosity and intelligence, however, configure only one side of the young woman this chapter and the first two-thirds

M. Peixoto (✉)
New York University, New York, NY, USA

© The Editor(s) (if applicable) and The Author(s) 2016   149
L. Aidoo, D.F. Silva (eds.), *Emerging Dialogues on Machado de Assis*, DOI 10.1057/978-1-137-54174-1_10

of the novel delineate. The other shows her applying her intelligence diligently to a specific issue: overcoming the obstacle to the marriage she and the narrator Bento ardently desire: his mother's promise to God that he would be a priest. She surveys the situation and their possible allies with a superior capacity for calculation and focus: "She gave it all her minute attention. She seemed to ruminate on everything...Or you could say that she was comparing, labeling and, as it were, pinning my account up in her memory" (1997, 59). Capitu's two guises—not, at this point contradictory—as a charmingly assertive and curious young girl and someone intent on circumventing authority figures so as to accomplish her own ends are supported by the same evidence. Her interest in the piano, the books, the paintings in Bento's house, as well as in his mother's jewelry and stories about when she wore them, could also be taken as a grasping survey of the material advantages her marriage to Bento would bring her. From her two youthful guises, Capitu's development involves contradiction: she becomes either a properly submissive married woman and loving mother, content with having reached the object of her adolescent dreams, or a woman whose subversion of authority continued to operate on the sly, leading her to bear the child of her lover Escobar, as Bento finally accuses her of doing.

Most contemporary readers now hold that because of the radically subjectivized mode of narration—a story of betrayal told by the man who thinks he was betrayed and admits to an obsessive jealousy—the central question of whether an adulterous liaison actually took place is ultimately left open, for readers or re-readers to realize that this issue cannot be solved on the basis of the evidence in the novel. This is also a mark of the novel's more complicated realism, as it looks toward modern fictional strategies. Roberto Schwarz observes that like Henry James, Machado invents "narrative situations or narrators placed inside a given fictional circumstance, creating fables whose drama is only complete when we take into account the interested nature, the active partiality of the storyteller himself" (2012, 61).

Yet, some readers persist in opting for a "yes" or "no" answer to the adultery question and all that it entails. The novel instigates (while, for some, it frustrates) the interpretative powers of readers, so much so that this can be considered a central effect of this provocative text. As Hélio Seixas Guimarães acutely observes: "It's as if the texture of the novel opened up and its fissures—contradictions, omissions, amendments, gaps—constructed an internal space capable of gathering into itself discordant readings that will vary in accordance with the projections that empirical readers create, affirming their own values and beliefs about the radically ambiguous text of the novel" (2004, 216).

While keeping in mind this radical ambiguity or undecidability, this chapter focuses on how the novel's dilemma is configured, attempting to understand the mythic and historical dimensions of Capitu's multiple characterizations, reading the impossibility of closure—and the pressures to assent to or reject the closure the narrator offers—as a crucial part of the artistic construct of the novel.

In two well-known 1878 reviews of Eça de Queiroz's novel *Cousin Basílio,* Machado takes issue with the Portuguese writer's naturalist-inflected depiction of the protagonist Luísa, who is driven by forces that make of her a puppet rather than a moral being. "For Luísa to attract and captivate me, she herself must be the source of her misfortunes: she might be rebellious or repentant, remorseful or raging, but by God!, give me her moral person" (1972, 906–07). By the time Machado wrote *Dom Casmurro,* he was at the height of his power to delineate characters of dazzling moral complexity. In drawing Capitu and leaving the question of her possible adultery undecidable, Machado creates a woman character with irreconcilable moral tempers, where even her actions are left open to speculation. In this sense, Capitu is unique among Machado's female characters. In the celebrated short story "Midnight Mass," published in the same year as *Dom Casmurro,* and like the novel, a retrospective narrative by a mature man remembering an incident of his youth, the protagonist Conceição has often been compared to Capitu, in terms of her enigmatic and seductive power. Machado, however, leaves no doubt as to Conceição's actions, although the motivations for them remain shrouded in mystery (2008, 231–40).

Critics that view Bento with suspicion,[3] and, taking a further step, acknowledge the novel's indeterminacy, have sometimes pronounced the question of Capitu's guilt or innocence irrelevant. Silviano Santiago, for instance, discusses in a seminal article the implications of the narrator's dubious rhetoric of verisimilitude, where what matters is a surface persuasiveness, and urges us to see Bento's moral substance as the only relevant subject of inquiry (1978, 29–48). Other critics who see Bento as an unreliable interpreter of the central events in his life, such as John Gledson (1984) and Roberto Schwarz, find that his jealousy manifests complex social motivations. Schwarz summarizes Gledson's thesis, with which he agrees: "Behind the emotional ups and downs that dominate the foreground of the novel, Gledson identifies the presence of strictly social factors linked to the structure of a paternalist order and its crisis. Instead of a new Othello, who out of jealousy destroys and defames the love of his life, there appears a rich young man, from a declining family, a mummy's boy, for whom the energy and free opinions of a more modern girl prove in the end intolerable. In this sense, the jealousy signifies a broad, historically specific social predicament and represents the convulsions of a patriarchal society in crisis" (Schwarz 2012, 60). For both Gledson and Schwarz, once the full implications of Bento's objectionable traits come into view, a kind of undertow leads them to move in the direction of considering Capitu blameless. John Gledson puts this plainly: "For anyone who has some sympathy with Capitu—and I think many, if not all, readers will feel that at some time in the novel—there is one moment when she has such dignity that, whatever the arguments of the head—which I've argued can lead nowhere—the heart will likely declare her not guilty" (Gledson 2008, 106). The moment in question comes in chapter 138, when Bento reveals to Capitu that he believes Ezequiel is not his son; she admits to a chance resemblance between the boy and Escobar, but not to an affair, and takes as a foregone conclusion that after such an insulting accusation, their marriage is over. Also in reference to that final confrontation, Schwartz, too, slips into a seeming acceptance of Capitu's innocence, when he speaks of "Capitu's final, lucid and moving resignation" (Schwarz 2012, 80). But if we view the novel as an undecidable construct, this crucial scene can also be read as Bento reads it, to the assent of generations of critics, as another instance of Capitu's skilled and bold deceptiveness.[4]

To read the novel in full awareness of the undecidability of the adultery question and therefore of Capitu's moral conduct, we need to see that although the two central characters have multiple guises, they are not multiple in the same way. In Bento's case, they make up a coherent fictional personality, developing and changing over time. Bentinho, the timid and enamored youth, already prone to fits of jealousy, gives way to Bento the adult, Capitu's impulsive and authoritarian husband (though perhaps not more so than most mid-nineteenth-century Brazilian upper-class husbands); by the time he accuses Capitu of having borne Escobar's child, his actions display a confident self-righteousness, closed off to the perspectives of others. When Bento takes on his third guise as Dom Casmurro and our narrator (who, as such, serves as filter for the presentation of his younger selves and for everything else in the novel), he regains some of the mildness of his youth and even a kind of repressed suspicion he may have judged Capitu harshly on the basis of insufficient evidence. He is certain, yes, but doubts (expressed as contradictions, blindnesses or gaps in his reasoning) seem to pursue him on the threshold of awareness; such is Machado's masterful creation of this complex character. As narrator, Casmurro is genial, engaging, addressing readers of various kinds, taking us nonchalantly on seemingly unrelated digressions that only after further readings of the novel, reveal their pertinence to the more urgent matters of the narrative. It's crucial to the novel's effect that Casmurro, while possibly wrong-headed, and certainly in many ways objectionable, be sympathetic to the reader, who would otherwise not be drawn into the push and pull of contrary emotions the novel depicts and elicits.

As a character, Capitu's multiplicity implies two "natural," though contradictory, developments of her moral substance and personality. Although all our views of her are mediated by Bento's intense emotions, two of her guises are displayed, with an abundance of detail, as actualities in the novel: Capitu as a clever teenager, capable of mind, possessing superior social skills, and later, as a devoted and properly submissive wife and mother. Her third guise, as the woman who bore a son to Escobar, is merely a hypothesis potently imagined by Bento. As the novel offers no conclusive proof to the contrary, as a literary character, Capitu is incomplete without the possibility that yes, she did bear Escobar's child.

In the first part of the novel, up until Bento and Capitu's marriage, women occupy positions of authority. Bento's mother, Dona Glória, a wealthy widow, lives off the property (real estate and slaves) left by her late husband and governs a household of dependents. In Capitu's far more modest house next door—the father is a civil servant—the women, mother and daughter, are practical and reliable, whereas the father lacks those qualities completely. The prevalence of dependents in Bento's household, who must please those that provide them with their means of subsistence, has, as a consequence, the complete absence of sources for a trustworthy second opinion on Capitu's character or the resemblance of the five-year-old Ezequiel to his best friend and next-door neighbor, Escobar. José Dias, chief among the dependents, lives at the house and looks after the young Bentinho "with a mother's affection and a servant's attentiveness" (1997, 47). At first, dead-set against the socially unequal marriage, he focuses all of his limited influence over Dona Glória and Bento in trying to prevent it. He calls Bento's attention to Capitu's eyes, "those eyes the devil gave her" (1997, 48), and hints, to Bento's despair, that while he is away at the seminary, she flirts with the neighborhood boys, eager to find a husband among them. But when José Dias sees that the marriage is inevitable, he declares her an "angel," and backtracks decisively: "I confused her childish ways with expressions of character, and didn't see that the mischievous girl, already with her thoughtful eyes, was the capricious bloom which would produce such a sweet, wholesome fruit" (1997, 176).

Not even Dona Glória can be relied on for perceptive opinions. While she occupies a position of authority, as do other widows in Machado's fiction—the Baroness in *The Hand and the Glove* and Valéria, in *Iaiá Garcia*, for instance—she does not, like them, display force of intellect or personality. Her mind, in fact, seems less than acute, as when she fails to see the connection between Bento's sudden opposition to the priesthood and his attachment to Capitu: "My mother was innocent as the world's first dawn, before the first sin, and certainly she was not capable even intuitively of seeing the connection between one thing and another..." (1997, 80). Dona Glória's lack of intelligence and perceptiveness are framed as a kind innocence, granting her an imagined immunity from sin. In a fine comic moment, Bento insists in having "A saint" inscribed on his mother's gravestone, despite some resistance from the cemetery administrator and the parish priest. The hovering suggestion is that Capitu's quite opposite mental attributes—clear thinking, sensitivity to the interests of others, and the ability to marshal them to her own ends—constitute in themselves a tendency toward sin.

The female dominance in the early part of the novel is not, however, complete. Escobar, the boy Bento meets in the seminary who soon becomes his friend and confidant, introduces a forceful though dubious male presence in Bento's world. Hints of Bento's homoerotic attraction to Escobar (Valente 2001, 16–17) take their part in constituting a total configuration that leave him in the sway of his friend and girlfriend, who end up determining the early course of his life. It is Escobar who comes up with the ruse that extricates Bento from the duty to become a priest, freeing him for the marriage that even Dona Glória had come to desire.

A reversal in the balance of power favoring Capitu follows fast on the heels of their marriage. In a fanciful representation of their honeymoon as an entry into heaven, among the quotations from the Bible that convey Bento's rapture, a distinct change of direction emerges. Bento imagines Saint Peter reciting to them from the First Epistle verses that exhort a wife to be in subjection to her husband, to turn away from material ornaments and to adorn herself only with the man she carries hidden in her heart. The husband, in turn, should honor his wife as "the weaker vessel." Capitu learns by heart words from the Song of Solomon: "With great delight I sat down under the shadow of him I had so much desired" (1997, 178).

The idea of Capitu as a weaker vessel, or someone content to live in Bento's shadow, signals a new dispensation, and the appearance of Capitu's second guise as a proper and submissive wife. As she settles into married life, Capitu learns to accommodate Bento's habitual jealousy, incited by the most commonplace events (Capitu's waiting at the window for him in the evening or showing her bare arms when wearing an evening dress) by simply refraining from all that distresses him. If social climbing and access to wealth were key motives for her marriage, she does not now show undue interest in finery or elegant society. The couple leads a quiet life and Capitu seems to adjust her behavior completely to her husband's whims and will. Indeed, after the marriage, Bento takes hold of patriarchal power with fierce determination and to Capitu's apparent satisfaction.

Capitu, in her married life, conforms closely, in terms of outward appearances, to the prevailing wisdom around the time the novel was written as to the proper behavior of wives. Julia Lopes de Almeida's *Livro das Noivas* (A Book for Brides, 1896) counsels a young bride: "if your husband doesn't like you to dance or to attend balls,...resign yourself and keep away from that kind of entertainment. Your blond tresses will have more poetry by the light of the sweet household lamp...than brushing against the black cloth of dress coats that would take you twirling around rooms too full of flowers, of light, heat and gossip; but if by any chance, you don't have the strength to resist, and will dance, and if afterward, your husband should be jealous and compare you to the wives of his friends, all very resigned, kind and virtuous, etc., don't get furious...." (Almeida 1896, 87). Over this bride too hover the phantoms of temptation and jealousy; the task of keeping them in check by vigilant self-sacrifice falls squarely on the woman.

After the marriage, Capitu's third guise as an adulterous woman, while invisible in her actual behavior, possibly operates behind the scenes. The couple, having strengthened more than ever their ties to Escobar and his family, after two years of marriage, persists in their hope for a child. While focusing mostly on his own jealousy and Capitu's skillful adaptations, Bento as narrator provides insidious hints of her possible covert behavior. For instance, before she became pregnant, during a lesson on astronomy Bento is delivering to her, Capitu's attention drifts (1997, 184–86). She confesses she was thinking of an exchange of her leftover household allowance into pounds sterling, a transaction accomplished that very day with Escobar's help while Bento was away, and meant, she says at this point, as a gift to Bento. Bento claims he calls attention to this incident as evidence of his wife's thrifty ways, leaving to the reader the malicious interpretation that during this meeting, or others, transactions of a different nature could also have taken place.

The extreme incompatibility between Capitu's demeanor as a good wife who wanted more than anything (in Bento's view) to bear his child ("Capitu begged for it in he prayers, and more than once I caught myself praying and begging too") (1997, 182) and her possible other guise as a woman who would be, at that very moment, engaged in an affair with Escobar are impossible to reconcile and leave the attentive reader and re-reader unable to decide on who she "truly" is. There is much in the novel that supports a view of Capitu as a Desdemona figure, grievously wronged, as Helen Caldwell first proposed. Could the resemblance of Ezequiel to Escobar be a chance resemblance? Who looks like whom in a family is, after all, a matter fraught with wishful thinking and subjective opinions. It's impossible to determine the degree of similarity, as Machado has made sure that none of the other characters are capable of an independent opinion. The other closely interested party, Escobar's wife Sancha, who could perhaps have weighed in on the matter, leaves Rio after Escobar's death, when Bento's jealousy begins to take truly frightening proportions, growing along with his supposed son Ezequiel.

The novel certainly delineates Capitu's negative guise more robustly than her positive one, supporting it with the narrator's conscious opinion and narrative designs, harking back to age-old strictures placed on women and to misogynist myths of women's inherent treachery. In Judeo-Christianity, her prototype Eve disobeys God's injunction and listens to the serpent and to her own transgressive desires. One of the legion of critics who have emphasized this subtext, Augusto Meyer, while affirming that "*Dom Casmurro* is Capitu's book," points to her "unfathomable treachery" and holds that she "slips and slithers" through the novel (1958, 141, 146–47). The mermaid or siren, another ancient image of women's treachery in her double nature, half-fish and half-human, is another central subtext, also dear to Victorian literature and visual culture (Auerbach 1982, 90–96). It appears, first and foremost, in the celebrated metaphor that compares Capitu's eyes to the treacherous undercurrents of the ocean. We might note that their power to pull Bento in, more than any property of the eyes themselves, reveals Bento's subjection, his sense that his will is no match for the force that draws him to her. Indeed, at the beginning of the courtship, he feels that "they held some kind of mysterious, active fluid, a force that dragged one like the undertow of a wave retreating from the shore on stormy days...[T]he wave emerging from them grew toward me, deep and dark, threatening to envelop me, draw me in, and swallow me up" (1997, 63). Following the logic of the siren who destroys those she manages to seduce, Escobar, a strong, habitual swimmer, falls prey metaphorically, in Bento's imagination, to Capitu's demonic power, and dies while swimming in an a stormy sea. In a second chapter, with the title "Undertow eyes" (lest the reader fail to make the connection), at Escobar's funeral, Bento minutely observes Capitu's face, trying to decipher the lineaments of her emotion: "There was a moment when Capitu's eyes fixed on the body of Escobar...large and wide open like the waves of the sea out there, as if she too wanted to swallow up the morning's swimmer" (1997, 212). As additional evidence of Capitu's siren power to seduce and destroy, Bento says that when he came to believe that Ezequiel is Escobar's son, their relationship is ravaged by storms that were "continuous and terrible"; Bento underlines with an apology the metaphor once again: "Excuse these metaphors; they smell of the sea and the tide which brought death to my friend, my wife's lover, Escobar. They smell, too, of Capitu's undertow eyes. So, though I have always been a landsman, I recount that part of my life as a sailor would recount his shipwreck" (1997, 223).

Regarding the strong bipolarity of Capitu's images—submissive, tactful wife and mother, as well as smoothly deceptive adulteress—we might consider first that it would have been very easy for Machado to foreclose one of these images, as he did with the other seductive women of his major novels. There's no doubt that Virginia (*Posthumous Memoirs of Brás Cubas*) eagerly participates in a long-lived adultery, successfully hidden from public view. In *Quincas Borba*, the narrator specifies precisely the moral implications of Sofia's actions, as she flirts with Rubião, encouraged by her husband who wants access to his wealth: "Let us not make her more of a saint than she is, nor less so" (Assis 1998, 47). Capitu's actions and their moral implications, left open to the artistic advantage of the novel, might, however, also be considered from a more nuanced perspective than the two extremes often favored by critics. As Bento observes when Capitu's attention wanders during that astronomy lesson, "there's an infinite gradation where blame is concerned." "It's well known that people's distraction may be to blame, or half to blame, or a third, a fifth, or a tenth to blame" (1997, 186). Did Capitu succumb to Escobar's decisive seduction? Did she fall prey to strong sexual urges, such as the one described in the short story "A Pair of Arms," when Dona Severina surprises herself by kissing the lips of her husband's apprentice while the boy sleeps, then, horrified by her action, has him immediately fired? (Assis 2008, 181–93) Did Capitu fall passionately in love with Escobar and unluckily conceive in few encounters a boy, who unluckily came to bear a strong resemblance to his father? These questions are left open, suggesting not a double, but a multiple Capitu, whose share of blame, if any, is impossible to determine. In any case, unlike the vain and frivolous Sofia and Virginia, Capitu is established as intelligent and mature; her slips, if she did slip, have to be considered in this context.

Why would Machado have worked out the undecidability of Capitu's motives and actions in such meticulous detail? Capitu's impossible to determine nature could also be placed in the context of another version of women's multiple possibilities impinging on morality that agitated public opinion in late nineteenth-century Brazil. Women's education and suffrage evoked the hope (or the specter) of capable female citizens who would possibly be less reliably family-oriented and subservient to their husbands. This possibility was a concern for women writers as well as men, for those who opposed women's education and suffrage and those who favored it.

Viotti da Costa observes that, after the fall of the monarchy (1889), women's suffrage was discussed in the Constitutional Assembly. "The idea of extending the right to vote to women seemed to many delegates to be immoral or anarchic. Some predicted that to grant the right to vote to women would be to decree the dissolution of the family. Woman should not have the right to vote because their mission was to educate children. For them, participation in the public sphere seemed incompatible with women's domestic role. As a result, women would have to wait for forty years (until 1932) to gain the right to vote" (Costa 2000, 264).

Machado, although not speaking up frequently on this question and often couching what he did say in playfulness or irony, unmistakably favored both women's education and suffrage (Stein 1984, 126–27). Like the majority of other contemporary writers on the issue, including women, including feminists or proto-feminists, as Viotti da Costa terms them, Machado viewed with disquiet the possibility of any shake-up in women's established roles. In "A Book for Brides" mentioned above, Julia Lopes de Almeida, herself a highly regarded and prolific writer (prose fiction, theater, newspaper articles) and a defender of women's education, puts it at the service of her child-rearing functions: "To learn in order to teach! Such is woman's sacred mission!" (Almeida, 1896, 39).

In a 1881 sonnet, Machado proposes that women's education should carefully maintain in delicate balance two opposing natures or pursuits, embodied in the biblical figures of Martha, "distracted by much serving," and her sister Mary, who raptly listens to the teachings of Jesus. When Martha complains that she is getting no help, Jesus determines that Mary "has chosen the good portion, which shall not be taken away from her." (Luke, 10:42) In this sonnet, "Give to Martha's work a portion of Mary's," Machado redirects these biblical figures to the issue of woman's education and also rebalances the weight of a traditional "service" role versus intellectual (or spiritual) pursuits, proposing that Mary's portion—a small portion—should enrich Martha's primary task:

Give to Martha's work a portion of Mary's,
Give a kiss of sunshine to the untended shrub,
As you see a flowering of the dried up trunk,
So you will find in Martha greater interest and more worth.

The sweet mother loses none of her imposing role,
Nor the conjugal home its perfect harmony.
Two will live there instead of only one,
And labor will exact less difficult a cost.

You must face life without apathy or weakness,
O woman! Within your gracious bosom,
Within your warm breast, a valiant heart must beat!

Neither solitary darkness nor ill-lit day.
Just a ray of sunshine to the untended shrub.
To Martha's work a part of Mary's will suffice.[5]

While addressing mainly those with the power to grant or withhold the ray of sunshine that would allow women to flower, the poem posits as the ultimate goal the enhancement of her function as mother, companion, and wage earner, so as to ease and improve men's lives. In a chronicle of the same year, directed to the female readers of the periodical *A Estação*, Machado reaffirms the "great social necessity" for women's education, while at the same time, demarcating strict limits: "we don't want you as social reformers, preachers of abstruse ideas which you hardly understand, and that in any case detract from your role; but between this and ignorance and frivolity, there's an abyss: let us fill the abyss" (Assis 1957, 125–26).

Machado ends by saying he will avoid an obvious exposition of the value of woman as "daughter, wife, mother, sister, nurse," to make only one sufficient statement: "to educate woman is to educate man himself; the mother will render her son more complete" (1957, 127). Affirming cautiously the value of women's education, Machado takes for granted (though he does not refrain from underlining) that it must not in any way detract from her traditional role. In the essay, as in the poem, the envisioned beneficiaries are not so much women themselves as men.

On the brink of the twentieth century, when, in 1932, women would finally gain the right to vote and become full-fledged citizens, Machado imagines a woman character of great energy and seduction, but with a finally undeterminable nature—one who, simultaneously and in a contradictory fashion, harks back to traditional and misogynist myths of women's devious power, but who is also mature, intelligent, and possibly behaves in utter conformity with the role considered appropriate for upper-class wives in late nineteenth-century Brazil. Capitu's multiple guises might place some readers in a difficult position.[6] To continue to see in the adult Capitu the defiant spirit that enabled her to reach her adolescent goal of marrying Bento against the constraints of a religious vow and a considerable class divide, one would have to agree with Bento's patriarchal reading of her moral nature: her rebelliousness was only apparently extinguished by marriage; she continued to scheme and seduce, reaching her own ends hypocritically, deviously, "not with a single bound, but with lots of little jumps" (1997, 38). But to disagree with Bento's oppressive interpretation, the reader needs to come to a sad realization: Capitu's intelligence and lucidity were not up to the task of countering Bento's fantasies and she became his victim, no more and no less than the compliant wife and devoted mother we see on the surface, incapable even of negotiating for herself and her son a better outcome than exile in Switzerland. So we have, then, either a clever and rebellious adulteress or a meek and resigned wife. Or, if we take the novel's indeterminacy seriously, we have both, and perhaps still other more nuanced possibilities for her behavior and moral nature.

Fiction, even realist fiction, doesn't only reflect, or reflect on, social conditions—either of the time the novel is set or at the time of its writing—but, going beyond that, captures affective dispositions of its author, both conscious and unconscious, as well as ideas, hopes, and fears visiting society at large. Machado suggests this when he has Casmurro exclaim, quoting Goethe's *Faust*, as he begins his writing project: "Ah, come ye back once more, ye restless shades?" (1997, 6) Casmurro's project (and we might recall that the novel was published the year before Freud's *The Interpretation of Dreams*) is haunted by forces he doesn't entirely fathom or control. Perhaps there could be no better vehicle for those other restless shades, the hopes and fears regarding women as the nineteenth century drew to a close, than the multiple Capitu, whose images hark back to the most ancient misogynist myths of woman as destructive seducer, but who also appears as a kind, irreproachable matron and mother, as well as someone who intelligently, willfully, transgresses society's norms in her sexual conduct—all stemming from her first guise, the decided young lady who "thinks clearly and fast" (1997, 93).

NOTES

1. This chapter develops and modifies an interpretation of the novel I proposed in an earlier essay (Peixoto 2005).
2. Page numbers and the abbreviation DC refer to Gledson's translation (Assis 1997). All other translations are mine, unless otherwise noted.
3. Abel Barros Baptista discerns and interrogates key assumptions of that criticism in an incisive metacritical analysis (Baptista 1998, 367–400).
4. See also Alfredo Bosi's insightful and nuanced reading of that crucial scene (2000, 33–37).
5. This sonnet was first published in a volume of short tributes celebrating the inclusion of women as students in the Liceu de Artes e Ofícios in Rio in 1881 (Machado 1957, 60–61).
6. Paul Dixon has analyzed this dilemma precisely; it interests him with regard to the ideology of the novel (Dixon 1989, 128–29).

REFERENCES

Almeida, Júlia Lopes de. 1896. *Livro das noivas*. Rio de Janeiro: Companhia Nacional Editora.

Assis, Joaquim Maria Machado de. 1957. In *Poesia e prosa*, ed. J. Galante de Souza. Rio de Janeiro: Civilização Brasileira.

Assis, Joaquim Maria Machado de. 1972. Eça de Queiroz: O Primo Basílio. In *Obra Completa*, Vol Three. Organized by Afrânio Coutinho, 903–13. Rio de Janeiro: Aguilar.

Assis, Joaquim Maria Machado de. 1997. *Dom Casmurro*. Trans. John Gledson. Oxford: Oxford University Press.

Assis, Joaquim Maria Machado de. 1998. *Quincas Borba*. Trans. Gregory Rabassa. Oxford: Oxford University Press.

Assis, Joaquim Maria Machado de. 2008. *A Chapter of Hats and Other Stories*. Trans. John Gledson. London: Bloomsbury.

Auerbach, Nina. 1982. *Woman and the demon: The life of a Victorian myth*. Cambridge: Harvard University Press.

Baptista, Abel Barros. 1998. *Autobibliografia: solicitação do livro na ficção de Machado de Assis*, 367–400. Lisboa: Relógio D'Água.

Bosi, Alfredo. 2000. *Machado de Assis: o enigma do olhar*. São Paulo: Ática.

Costa, Emília Viotti da. 2000. Patriarchalism and the myth of the helpless woman in the nineteenth century. In *The Brazilian Empire: Myths and histories*, revised ed. Chapel Hill: The University of North Carolina Press.

Dixon, Paul B. 1989. *Retired dreams: Dom Casmurro, myth and modernity*. West Lafayette: Purdue University Press.

Gledson, John. 1984. *The deceptive realism of Machado de Assis*. Liverpool: Francis Cairns.

Gledson, John. 2008. Capitu: A personagem. In *Quem é Capitu?* ed. Alberto Schprejer. Rio de Janeiro: Nova Fronteira.

Guimarães, Hélio de Seixas. 2004. *Os leitores de Machado de Assis: O romance machadiano e o público de literatura no século 19*. São Paulo: Nankim Editorial/ Edusp.

Meyer, Augusto. 1958. *Machado de Assis: 1935–1958*. Rio de Janeiro: São José.

Peixoto, Marta. 2005. Dom Casmurro by Machado de Assis. In *The Cambridge companion to the Latin American novel*, ed. Efraín Kristal, 219–231. Cambridge: Cambridge University Press.

Santiago, Silviano. 1978. Retórica da Verossimilhança. In *Uma literatura nos trópicos*, 29–48. São Paulo: Perspectiva.

Schwarz, Roberto. 2012. Capitu, the Bride of Dom Casmurro. Trans. John Gledson. In *Two girls and other essays*, 57–91. London: Verso.

Stein, Ingrid. 1984. *Figuras Femininas em Machado de Assis*. Rio de Janeiro: Paz e Terra.

Valente, Luiz Fernando. 2001. Machado's wounded males. *Hispania* 84(1): 11–19.

PART IV

Machado on Masculinity and Queer Relations

CHAPTER 11

Machado's Wounded Males

Luiz Fernando Valente

For quite some time, critics such as Dirce Cortes Riedel (1959), Antonio Candido (1970), Maria Luísa Nunes (1983), Earl Fitz (1989), Roberto Reis (1992), and others have called attention, with good reason, to the modernity of Machado de Assis's fiction, in matters of both literary technique and theme. According to this view, Machado was not only a precursor of the modern novel, but was also far ahead of his contemporaries in his treatment of such modern questions as, for example, the concept of human (as opposed to clock) time, the instability of the self, and the absurdity of human existence. Over the past 20 years, however, scholars such as Roberto Schwarz and John Gledson have demonstrated conclusively that notwithstanding the modern elements in his work, Machado was attuned to all the crucial issues facing Brazilian society of his time. Despite appearances to the contrary, these two critical positions regarding Machado's works are far from incompatible. Indeed, Machado's modernity is inseparable from the author's profound understanding of the dilemmas and contradictions faced by Brazilian society during the Second Empire and the early years of the First Republic. As Machado himself reminds us in a

Reproduced with permission from *Hispania*, the official journal of the American Association of Teachers of Spanish and Portuguese, Inc.

L.F. Valente (✉)
Department of Portuguese and Brazilian Studies,
Brown University, Providence, RI, USA

© The Editor(s) (if applicable) and The Author(s) 2016
L. Aidoo, D.F. Silva (eds.), *Emerging Dialogues on Machado de Assis*, DOI 10.1057/978-1-137-54174-1_11

well-known essay (2013), the universal and the local dimensions of literary works are intertwined, and writers are most universal when they are most faithful to the contexts in which they practice their craft.[1]

There is no question that Brazil achieved political stability and material progress during the Second Empire—the setting for most of Machado's works—but an old mentality remained influential in social, economic, and political matters. Although Brazil was officially a constitutional monarchy, Brazilian liberalism was, to use Schwarz's classic formulation, a misplaced idea (1992), as the failures of a progressive entrepreneur like Mauá[2] and the continued dependence on slavery left no doubt. The majority of Brazilians were citizens in theory only, since the requirements of property ownership and literacy limited the number of those who were enfranchised. Moreover, Brazil was unable to effectively integrate most of its population into a peripheral economy geared primarily toward supplying the export sector rather than developing the domestic market. Finally, though the urban population had been growing for more than 100 years and Rio de Janeiro had become the largest city in Latin America by the second half of the nineteenth century, Brazilian society continued to be affected by a conservative mentality that Sérgio Buarque de Holanda has attributed to Brazil's inability to discard its "rural heritage": "Slaveholding-planters and their sons, who were educated in liberal professions, monopolized politics during the monarchy. They elected their own candidates or had them elected, and they dominated parliaments, government departments, and generally all positions of authority. The stability of their institutions was based in their uncontested realm of influence and power" (Holanda 2012, 44).

Schwarz's and Gledson's analyses give a perceptive account of Machado's incisive portrayal of the Brazilian patriarchal family as the microcosm of this rigidly hierarchical social, economic, and political structure, based on a paternalistic conception of reality and resting on the two pillars of slavery, on the one hand, and the emperor's moderating power, on the other. As Gledson has suggested, Machado's fiction "explores the limits of the paternalism which was the official justification, not only for oligarchic control, but for the very existence of slavery itself" (Gledson 1984, 7). What has not been properly emphasized, however, is that Machado's depiction of the Brazilian patriarchal family also reveals a keen sensitivity to the harmful psychological consequences that such a traditional, conservative, and strictly regulated society imposes on males, particularly—though by no means exclusively—on white males from the dominant classes. Machado detects a subtle connection between male sensibility and the system that both engenders and is engendered by the destructive and self-destructive behavior in which males often engage. Thus, Machado forsakes a simplistic, manicheistic view of the patriarchy in which white men are always regarded as victimizers and never as victims, for a sophisticated social and psychological portrayal of Brazilian patriarchal society in which men appear as vulnerable to the ills of the patriarchal order as women. Just as Machado's fiction moves beyond nineteenth-century technical and thematic parameters, Machado's trenchant representation of the patriarchal family during the Second Empire and the early years of the First Republic displays a surprisingly modern awareness of questions of masculinity.

In this chapter I will address these issues by first examining two short stories, "Wedding Song" ([1883] 2014) and "Midnight Mass" ([1863] 1966), as a preamble for a more detailed discussion of the novel *Dom Casmurro* ([1899] 1953). Published over a period of a little more than a decade and a half, these three texts depict males struggling to come to terms with society's high expectations and inflexible norms, and haunted by a fear of failure and a sense of inadequacy. While reflecting on the complex and often painful process of constructing a male sense of selfhood, these texts offer a powerful indictment of the patriarchal system, which insidiously wounds even those who supposedly uphold it, control it, and benefit most from it.

Although, on the surface, the subject of "Wedding Song" is the trials and tribulations of the artist in the throes of the creative process, the tale symbolically addresses issues of masculinity, to which Machado will return in the other two texts to be considered. It tells the story of Romão Pires, the renowned conductor of the orchestra at the Carmo church, who, despite being revered by Rio society, feels unfulfilled due to his inability to author a musical piece of his own: "Ah! If Maestro Romão were able, he would be a great composer. It seems that there are two kinds of vocations: those that have a voice and those that do not. The former are fulfilled; the latter represent a constant and sterile struggle between the inner impulse and the absence of a mode of communication with mankind. Romão was of this kind. He had an intimate vocation for music; he had within him many operas and masses, a world of new and original harmonies that he could not manage to express and put onto paper" (Assis 2014, 168). The reader soon learns that the piece that Romão has struggled to complete throughout his life is an epithalamium on which he started to work only three days after his own wedding. In keeping with Romão's inability to finish that nuptial song, the story is laden with images of sterility and impotence. The sexual overtones are too obvious to miss:

> Three days after they married, Maestro Romão felt inside him something akin to inspiration. Thus, he came up with the idea of the wedding song and wanted to compose it, but the inspiration could not find a way out. Like a bird that has just been confined and strives to escape the walls of the cage, flitting up and down, impatient and terrified, thus beat the inspiration of our musician, locked up inside him with no way out, unable to find a door, nothing. A few notes ended up coming together, he wrote them down, resulting in a single sheet of paper, nothing more. He kept on the following day, ten days later, twenty times during his marriage. (169).

Although Romão loves his wife, the relationship remains emotionally, if not sexually, unfulfilled, as she dies young and the couple is unable to conceive a child. Since the death of his wife, Romão has shared living quarters with a black man, Papa José. Their household is characterized by a sterile atmosphere: "Naturally, the house was neither rich nor cheerful. It did not have even the slightest trace of a woman, old or young, nor birds that sing, nor flowers, nor lively or pleasant colors. A somber and bare house" (168).

Returning home after a successful concert, but feeling old, dejected, and ill, Romão tries once again to garner enough energy to finish the nuptial song. Sitting at the clavichord, unable to compose, he notices through the window a newlywed couple embracing. Romão is immediately moved by a desire to complete the musical piece as his gift to the couple: "I will compose at least this song that they can play" (171). The vicarious experience of tenderness, however, is not enough to free Romão from his artistic impotence: "Maestro Romão, breathless from the illness and impatience, turned to the harpsichord, but the sight of the couple did not provide him with inspiration, and the subsequent notes did not sound" (171). As Romão walks away in distress from the harpsichord and tears up the sheet on which, as is always the case, he has been able to write only a few notes, the young woman begins to sing. Ironically, her song includes the exact musical phrase that Romão had unsuccessfully attempted to write: "At this very moment, the young woman, absorbed in her husband's gaze, began to hum at random, unconsciously, something never before sung or known, in which a certain *la* was followed by a lovely musical phrase, the exact one that Maestro Romão had sought for years without ever finding"

(171). Overcome with sadness, Romão dies without having produced the artistic offspring that he intended as the confirmation and perpetuation of his genius, just as he was unable to father a child.

Though Romão is an accomplished conductor, he regards himself as a failure due to his inability to be a composer in his own right. Incapable of converting the passive (and therefore feminine, according to the rules of patriarchal society) sensibility of the conductor into the active (hence, masculine) stance of the composer, Romão views himself as less than a full artist, and, by extension, less than a full man.

An economical writer par excellence, Machado is known for eschewing superfluous details, especially in his more mature texts. Indeed, he is one of those writers who, to use Lukács's classic terminology, "narrates" rather than "describes"[3]; that is, he never wastes words that do not advance the plot. With this in mind, it is fair to assume that the reference to the fact that Romão was born near the Valongo, the site of the heinous slave market in Rio de Janeiro, abolished only in the 1860s, is a significant detail, allowing Machado to anchor the symbolism of Romão's creative impotence and sterility in concrete historical and social reality. Machado appears to be reminding us that slavery has bound Brazil to an old, decaying order inherited from its colonial past, which is incompatible with Brazil's status as a newly independent nation.[4] The mainstay of the Brazilian patriarchal system, slavery is a disease that infects every aspect of society. Just as Romão has been unable to fully realize his promise as an artist and to assert himself as a complete man, slavery has stunted Brazil's growth, weakened its moral fiber, and prevented it from fulfilling its destiny. Romão's death suggests that only with the demise of the old order will the promise of renewal, represented by the young couple (who, unlike Romão, can literally and figuratively make beautiful music), be realized.

Whereas Maestro Romão is pathetically disconsolate and frustrated, Nogueira, the narrator of "Midnight Mass," is defensively bitter and sardonic. Nogueira wants to convince the reader of his version of a conversation he allegedly had with Conceição Meneses, a woman 13 years his senior, on Christmas Eve many years before, while, as a 17-year-old guest of the Meneses family, he awaited the arrival of a friend who was to accompany him to midnight mass. Because Nogueira is an unreliable narrator, it is impossible to ascertain whether the narrated events happened precisely as he presents them. Nevertheless, the narrator's unreliability is exactly what makes this story so compelling, for it allows Nogueira to reveal much more about himself than he intended. What should interest us, then, is not so much the accuracy of Nogueira's narration of the events as Nogueira's perception of what took place. Obviously, the reader cannot be sure whether Conceição really attempted to seduce an unsophisticated, sexually inexperienced teenager, as the narrator wishes us to believe. Nevertheless, the reader can easily infer that the events of that night have left an indelible psychological scar on Nogueira, and have permanently colored his view of the world and his attitude toward women, as his caustic, and at times, derisive characterization of Conceição indicates.

Nogueira, who is staying with the Meneses family while studying for his college entrance examination, comes from Mangaratiba, a small rural town some 50 miles west of the capital city of Rio de Janeiro. As such, Nogueira was most certainly raised according to the traditional rules of the patriarchal family, so aptly described by Sérgio Buarque de Holanda in *Roots of Brazil* and Gilberto Freyre in *The Masters and the Slaves* (1946). It can be safely assumed, then, that Nogueira learned at an early age both to defer to the absolute authority of his father and to emulate his behavior. Likewise, Nogueira was surely taught to venerate the white women of the big house as unassailable saintly mothers and sisters, whose honor must be preserved at all costs, in contrast with the black women from the slave quarters, who were supposed to be readily available for sex. In both cases, women were regarded as men's possessions, with few rights of their own. Transplanted to the urban environment of the Meneses household, however, Nogueira is confronted with a new set of circumstances that destabilize the safety of his patriarchal and rural heritage. For, despite the continued influence of a traditional, rural-based mentality, a distinct urban culture had developed and established itself in nineteenth-century Brazil, as Raymundo Faoro (1976) has argued.[5] It is ironically significant that Nogueira is in Rio to complete his preparatory studies, for his experiences in the Meneses household are also a rite of passage into a new world. Thus, the transposition of Nogueira from a rural to an urban setting, which calls into question the values that informed his upbringing, creates a sharply focused new lens through which Machado can examine male behavior in a patriarchal society in the process of undergoing important transformations.[6]

It is public knowledge that Meneses keeps a mistress, a separated white woman with whom he shamelessly spends one night a week under the pretense of attending a theatrical performance. At the same time, Meneses neglects his wife, Conceição, who, lacking economic and social options, not only has been forced to close her eyes to her husband's infidelity, but also, according to the narrator, "came almost to accept the affair as proper" (Assis 1966, 94). On that Christmas Eve, Nogueira is shocked to learn that despite being named after the Virgin Mary and called a "saint," Conceição is a sexual being who is capable of showing an interest in men other than her husband and of awakening a young man's libido. The conversation between Nogueira and Conceição is a masterfully orchestrated sexual dance during which Conceição gazes at Nogueira, licks her lips, closes her eyes, moves about the room, and finally, leans toward the young man, revealing her arms and sexually arousing him, as the following passage clearly suggests: "One thing I remember vividly is that at a certain moment she, who till then had been such engaging company (but nothing more), suddenly became beautiful, so very beautiful" (98).

Elisabeth Badinter has pointed out that patriarchal society has engendered a "mutilated man" by constructing masculinity in opposition to femininity: "The patriarchal system gave birth to a mutilated man incapable of reconciling x and y, his paternal and maternal heritage. The construction of masculinity merged with the process of differentiation. One was recognized as a man worthy of the name once one had cut all one's ties with maternal femininity, in other words, with one's original soil. No one dreamed, then, of gluing back together the 'pieces' of one's primary and secondary identities" (1995, 121). This story challenges, however, such construction of masculinity by making the demarcation between stereotypical male and female sexual behavior increasingly fuzzier. As Nogueira perceives his encounter with Conceição, it is she who assumes the masculine role of the pursuer, whereas he plays a passive feminine role. It is not necessary to determine what, if anything, really happened between Conceição and Nogueira. Whether we take that silent moment toward the end of the story—"We stopped talking and for some time (I cannot say how long) sat there in silence. The only sound was the gnawing of a rat in the study" (100)—literally or read it as a clue that the seduction was consummated is irrelevant. What is important is that a slave to the rigid rules of his upbringing, Nogueira is twice a loser. Looking back on the events of that night, he seems sensitive enough to be contemptuous of Meneses's behavior and to appreciate that having been neglected by her husband, Conceição justifiably craves attention. Nevertheless, having internalized the lessons of the patriarchy about the relationship between men and women, Nogueira is not only incapable of tenderness, but he also behaves as though his identity as a male is compromised because he finds himself in the unusual position of being the object of Conceição's sexual interest.[7] Realizing later that he did not behave the way a manly man was expected to, he experiences a mixture of shame and contempt for Conceição, and, by extension, for women in general.

Thus, the story subtly demonstrates how the roots of misogyny may paradoxically lie in the reverential attitude toward women, propounded by the patriarchal code. By placing women on a pedestal, such reverence obscures women's concrete social, historical, and psychological situation, and therefore, denies women their status as complete, independent, and equal human beings. Temporarily subverting gender roles, Machado disputes that males and females are as diametrically opposed as patriarchal society has constructed them to be. With enormous prescience, the author suggests, furthermore, that the supposedly universal patriarchal rules are, rather, artificial creations, that is, constructions crafted to justify male domination and to protect men's fragile sense of identity. In the end, these rules harm males and females alike by misunderstanding women's sexuality, mutilating men's sensibility, and denying both men and women the freedom to make their own choices.

In *Dom Casmurro*, Machado returns to a bitter, insecure male narrator. Not surprisingly, like Nogueira, Bento Santiago is unreliable, for such narrators serve Machado's intention perfectly. Unreliability exposes the mechanisms of deception and self-deception that control the narrators' warped view of themselves and of the world around them. Just as it was unnecessary to decide to what extent Nogueira's narration was accurate, it is unnecessary to ascertain whether Bento's wife Capitu committed adultery with Bento's friend Escobar, for—as was the case with "Midnight Mass"—what is really at stake are the movements of the narrator's mind.

As in Machado's other mature novels, *Dom Casmurro* offers a subtle yet trenchant critique of the decay of the patriarchal family through a combination of literal and symbolic elements. By the time the narrative opens, Bento's father is dead, a symbolic situation that Roberto Schwarz (1988, 151) has observed as being frequent in Machado's fiction, and before the narrative closes, Bento's son Ezekiel will also have passed away. The place of the father has been usurped by José Dias, who arrogates the role of Bento's mentor, but, as an *agregado* ("dependent," in Caldwell's translation), is not a full member of the Santiago family. Finally, in addition to the feminized José Dias, the other members of the family—Bento's mother, Dona Glória, Uncle Cosme, and Cousin Justina—live in a chronic state of widowhood.

In many respects Bento is the logical offspring of this asexual, fatherless household. With the exception of his adored mother—"The truth is that my mother was candid as the first dawn, before the first sin" (Assis 1953, 101)—he views women as sources of evil and corruption. Throughout the narrative, Bento portrays Capitu as devious and manipulative. He also hints that Cousin Justina has a prurient interest in him: "Only then did I realize that Cousin Justina's eyes had seemed to feel me as I spoke, listen to me, smell me, taste me—do the offices of all the senses" (61). Besieged with wet dreams, Bento decides that "these female visions would henceforth be looked upon as simple incarnations of the vices" (132). Finally, he claims that Escobar's wife, Sancha, has made sexual advances toward him: "And yet Sancha's eyes did not ask for fraternal expansiveness—they seemed sultry and imperious, they said something quite different, and soon she moved away from the window, where I remained looking pensively toward the sea" (236).

From as early as his adolescent games with Capitu, women appear, for the misogynist Bento, to be little more than vehicles designed for men to assert their manhood. This becomes clear in the episode where, after kissing Capitu for the first time, 15-year-old Bento darts back to his bedroom, where he proudly proclaims to himself: "I am a man!" (85). Significantly, no sooner has Bento made that declaration than, assuming the traditional male role, he begins to view Capitu as his possession. He suddenly becomes uncharacteristically aggressive—indeed, borderline violent—and tries to coerce Capitu into giving him a second kiss. At the same time, he uses terms such as "oblige her," "made a move to pull her to me," "hold on to her hands with force," "struggle," and so forth, to describe his actions. Capitu, however, stands up to Bento, allowing herself to be kissed only when Bento ceases forcing himself on her: "But Capitu, before her father could come into the room, made an unhoped for gesture, she placed her mouth on mine, and gave willingly what she had refused to yield to force" (93).

In *The Reproduction of Mothering* Nancy Chodorow has observed that "boys in father-absent and normally father-remote families develop a sense of what it is to be masculine through identification with cultural images of masculinity" (1978, 176). Besides, as American psychologist Ruth Hartley has noted, from a very early age boys learn to define their male identity in a primarily negative manner, that is, young males are taught to conceive of masculinity in opposition to the feminine (1989, 458). Thus, in order to become real men, males are supposed to discard any characteristics that society deems as feminine, or, as Robert Stoller has ironically suggested, "A man's first duty is not to be a woman" (1989, 311). This attitude generates a view of everything that is believed to be feminine as being opposed, rather than complementary, to what is believed to be masculine, creating a warped value hierarchy in which the feminine is associated with weakness, inferiority, and dependence, and cutting men off from what Elizabeth Badinter has called the ties with one's original soil (1995, 121).

Not surprisingly, Bento appears to be more at ease with his friend Escobar than with Capitu. In fact, the friendship between Bento and Escobar contains a strong homoerotic component: "The padres liked me, the boys too, Escobar more than the other boys or the padres" (144–145), Bento comments to Capitu about life in the seminary. A few pages later, Bento refers to a day when Escobar came to visit as "the day of pleasant sensations,"[8] describing Escobar in stereotypically feminine terms, and clearly in far more detail than he ever described Capitu:

> Escobar's eyes, which were clear, as I have said, were also very sweet. That is the way José Dias defined them after he left, and I maintained the word in spite of the forty years that have passed over it. In this case there was none of the dependent's exaggeration. Escobar's shaven faced showed a fair, smooth skin. His forehead perhaps was a trifle low (the part in his hair came just above his left eyebrow) but it was still high enough not to swallow up the rest of his features and lessen their grace. Actually it was an interesting face: a fine mouth with a salty lift to it, a curved, slender nose. (157)

According to Bento, Escobar returns the compliment. Commenting on Dona Glória's appearance, he tells Bento, "Forty! She doesn't look thirty, so youthful and pretty. And no wonder! You had to take after someone with those eyes God gave you; they are exactly like hers" (190). Bento is more affectionate toward Escobar than toward Capitu: "We separated with great affection: inside the omnibus, he still waved goodbye. I stayed at the door to see if he would look back from the distance, but he did not" (158). Capitu does not fail to notice this: "She had seen our unabashed and affectionate goodbyes and wanted to know who it was that meant so much to me" (158). The close association between Escobar and Bento is evident during their time in the seminary: "Escobar, you are my friend: I am your friend too. Here, in the seminary, you are the person who has made his way into my heart; and outside, except for the members of my family, I do not, properly speaking, have a friend" (166). Even as an adult, Bento acknowledges that his heart beats faster when he is in Escobar's presence: "Friendship does exist: it was in my hands as I shook those of Escobar on hearing him say this, and in the total lack of words with which I thus signed the pact. The words came afterward, in a rush and refined by the heart, which was beating hard" (218–19). There is, moreover, a great deal of physical touching between Bento and Escobar: "I was so enthusiastic over the mental ability of my friend that I could not help giving him a hug. It was in the patio; other seminarists noticed our effusiveness; a padre who was with them did not like it" (194). Right after describing Sancha's alleged advances toward him, Bento caresses Escobar's arms, which are obvious phallic symbols: "I felt his arms, as if I were feeling those of Sancha. This confession is painful for me to make, but I cannot suppress it; it would mean distorting the truth. I not only had this idea— but also, feeling his arms, I found them thicker and stronger than mine, and I envied them" (237).

Regardless of whether the adulterous relationship between Capitu and Escobar was real or merely a product of Bento's paranoia, adultery represented the welcome possibility of a vicarious fulfillment of Bento's attraction to Escobar. The prospect of Bento's own adulterous relationship with Sancha can be viewed as a similar fantasy of vicarious fulfillment. It is not necessary, however, to try to ascertain Bento's sexual orientation because Machado is less interested in sexual identity per se than in psychological and behavioral processes. Thus, it is significant that Bento claims not to have suspected Capitu's alleged infidelity until after Escobar has died, and that it is only after Escobar's death that Bento rejects his son Ezekiel, to whom previously Bento was admittedly very close, for Escobar's death is both a real and symbolic moment of crisis. Until he drowns, Escobar has stood for an abstract model of masculinity, which functions as a reference point for Bento in his struggle to define himself as an individual. Therefore, pushing Escobar out of his inner circle was out of the question for the insecure Bento even if Bento believed Escobar to be Capitu's lover. Nevertheless Bento's precarious sense of self cannot be brought into balance through Escobar's specular mediation. Suddenly and violently deprived of the mirror image represented by Escobar, Bento is forced, in spite of himself, to confront alone his problematic relationship with others, particularly with women. Bento is obviously threatened by difference, for he takes "different" to be synonymous with "contrary" or "opposite." Unable to come to terms with difference, he remains psychologically and morally mutilated, permanently nostalgic for his lost connection with his mother and unable to establish a mature relationship with other women. As psychiatrist Gerald I. Fogel suggests in the introduction to *The Psychology of Men*, Bento may be afflicted by a condition that goes beyond the confines of nineteenth-century Brazilian society:

> Masculinity is often defined in relation to and in contrast to women; as boys and men we are dependent upon, threatened by, vulnerable to, and envious of women--in far more conscious and unconscious ways than we can ordinarily bear. Not only must men struggle with the real and fantasy-distorted powers of women as objects, but also with those qualities and impulses within themselves that are perceived as womanly or womanish. Thus men's view of women becomes further twisted and confused. If women are not enough of a problem in their own right, they become so in their assigned role as the bearers or symbolic representatives of various disavowed, warded off, projected, degraded, unacceptable aspects of men. (1986, 9)

Ultimately, Bento's undoing is his inability to relate to others who are different from himself—something that he tries to postpone indefinitely until Escobar's death forces him to attend to it, with disastrous results.

Machado's fiction offers a compelling assessment of the effects imposed on male sensibility by a patriarchal order that conceives the world in terms of oppositions and makes it difficult to incorporate difference. Unable to fulfill the rigid expectations of what a man should be and how a man should behave, many of Machado's male characters are haunted by the specter of inadequacy and impotence—a situation that inflicts painful psychological and moral wounds. These wounds perversely control their sense of self and permanently distort their relationships with others, particularly with women. Although Machado's fiction is set in a society spatially and temporally removed from us, his treatment of the relationship between the sexes remains convincing, in part, because despite all the social and historical changes that have occurred since the nineteenth century, we have not managed to free ourselves from conventional views of both the feminine and the masculine. In other words, though Machado grounds his analysis in the actual historical, social, and economic circumstances of Brazilian society during the Second Empire and offers an astute and sophisticated critique of that society, the situations portrayed in his fiction are by no means restricted to nineteenth-century Brazil. Indeed, Machado's fiction invites his readers, including those of us in the new millennium, to consider the destructiveness of a patriarchal legacy based on a strict system of oppositions that stubbornly refuses to go away. Faced with the dire consequences of the old ways of doing things, embodied in the fate of Machado's male characters, we are encouraged to realize, even while acknowledging the differences between men and women, that difference does not mean antagonism, and are challenged, likewise, to contemplate a more productive reconciliation of the masculine and the feminine.

NOTES

1. "And I would like to ask further if *Hamlet, Othello, Julius Caesar* and *Romeo and Juliet* have anything to do with English history or take place on British soil, and if, Shakespeare is not, in addition to being a universal genius, also an essentially English poet.... What we should expect of the writer above all is a certain intimate feeling that renders him a man of his time and country, even when he addresses topics that are remote in time or space" (Assis 2013, 89).
2. In *Roots of Brazil,* Sérgio Buarque de Holanda comments that Mauá was "out of place" in nineteenth-century Brazilian society: "In a certain sense, the commercial failure of Viscount Mauá is also an eloquent indicator of the radical incompatibility between lifestyles copied from more socially advanced nations, on the one hand, and Brazil's centuries-old patriarchalism and personalism on the other" (2012, 60).
3. In his classic essay "Narrate or Describe," Georg Lukács suggests that the great realist writers, such as Balzac and Tolstoy, forsake description for narration; that is, details are introduced into their texts "only as they play a part in the destinies, actions and passions of men" (1970, 137). On the contrary, naturalists such as Zola rely heavily on description, a mode of composition in which the writer "loses himself in a whirlwind of details of apparently equal significance" (128). Machado's mature texts are excellent examples of what Lukács calls narration, since details are always significant. It is probably not a coincidence that like Lukács, Machado had a strong distaste for naturalism.
4. Significantly, the story is set in 1813, when Brazil's legal status as a Portuguese colony is about to end. Although it can be argued that Brazil ceased being de facto a colony in 1808—when the Portuguese royal family abandoned Lisbon due to the invasion of Portugal by Napoleon's army and the capital of the Portuguese Empire was transferred from Lisbon to Rio de Janeiro—it is only in 1815 that Brazil is officially raised to the status of a kingdom, united with Portugal and Algarves.

5. "From Brazil's early days, a class of merchants and capital investors developed alongside the 'rural nobility.' That class, which grew in tandem with the landowners, thrived on greed and speculation; heir to the Portuguese capitalists, it was…responsible for the supply of slaves, equipment and capital for the rural establishments, and purchased their products…. More than the rural landowners, who were often absent from their properties, it was these merchants and capitalists that spurred the founding and growth of cities." (Faoro 1976, 23; my translation)

6. During the Second Empire (1840–89), Brazilian society underwent significant social and economic transformations. These changes were first noticeable in the urban centers, particularly in Rio de Janeiro, the capital of the empire and the largest city in Brazil. Despite the continued influence of a conservative mentality, as historian June Hahner has argued, some changes in the traditional role of women also began to be felt, due, in part, to an increased literacy rate among women: "During the second half of the nineteenth century, as urban society in Brazil became more complex and diversified, a small band of pioneer advocates of women's rights voiced their dissatisfaction with the traditional male-determined roles assigned to women. Largely through their newspapers, they endeavored to awaken other women to their potential for self-advancement and to rate their level of aspirations. They sought to spur changes in women's economic, social, and legal status" (1990, 40–41).

7. "We must learn to dissociate sexuality from a sense of manliness, in order to break up the identification between sexual performance and masculinity. The latter can be confirmed by something other than an erect penis" (Badinter 1995, 125).

8. Helen Caldwell translates this passage as "the day of pleasant surprises" (Assis 1953, 156), which does not convey the double meaning intended by Machado.

References

Assis, Joaquim Maria Machado de. (1863) 1966. Midnight mass. In *The psychiatrist and other stories*. Trans. William L. Grossman and Helen Caldwell, 94–100. Berkeley: University of California Press.

Assis, Joaquim Maria Machado de. (1883) 2014. Wedding song. In *Stories*, edited and translated Rhett McNeil, 167–171. Champaign: Dalkey Archive Press.

Assis, Joaquim Maria Machado de. (1899) 1953. *Dom Casmurro*. Trans. Helen Caldwell. New York: Noonday.

Assis, Joaquim Maria Machado de. 2013. Reflections on Brazilian literature at the present moment: The national instinct. Trans. Robert Patrick Newcomb. In *Brasil/Brazil: A journal of Brazilian literature* 47: 85–100.

Badinter, Elizabeth. 1995. *XY: On Masculine Identity*. Trans. Lydia Davis. New York: Columbia University Press.

Candido, Antonio. 1970. Esquema de Machado de Assis. In *Vários escritos*, 13–32. São Paulo: Duas Cidades.

Chodorow, Nancy. 1978. *The reproduction of motherhood*. Berkeley: University of California Press.

Faoro, Raymundo. 1976. *Machado de Assis: A pirâmide e o trapézio*. São Paulo: Companhia Editora Nacional.

Fitz, Earl. 1989. *Machado de Assis*. Boston: Twayne.

Fogel, Gerald I. 1986. In *Introduction to The psychology of men*, ed. Gerald I. Fogel, Frederick M. Lane, and Robert S. Liebert. New Haven: Yale University Press.

Freyre, Gilberto. 1946. *The masters and the slaves: A study of the development of Brazilian civilization*. Trans. Samuel Putnam. New York: Knopf.

Gledson, John. 1984. *The deceptive realism of Machado de Assis*. Liverpool: Francis Cairns.

Hahner, June E. 1990. *Emancipating the female sex: The struggle for women's rights in Brazil, 1850–1940*. Durham: Duke University Press.

Hartley, Ruth. 1989. Sex role pressures in the socialization of the male child. *Psychological Reports* 5: 458–468.

Holanda, Sérgio Buarque de. 2012. *Roots of Brazil*. Trans. G. Harvey Summ. Notre Dame: University of Notre Dame Press.

Lukács, Georg. 1970. Narrate or describe. In *Writer and critic and other essays*, edited and translated by Arthur D. Kahn, 110–148. New York: Grosset & Dunlap.

Nunes, Maria Luisa. 1983. *The craft of an absolute winner: Characterization and narratology in the novels of Machado de Assis*. Westport: Greenwood.

Reis, Roberto. 1992. *The Pearl Necklace: Toward an Archaeology of Brazilian Transition Discourse*. Trans. Aparecida de Godoy Johnson. Gainesville: University of Florida Press.

Riedel, Dirce Cortes. 1959. *O tempo no romance machadiano*. Rio de Janeiro: São José.

Schwarz, Roberto. 1988. *Ao vencedor as batatas: Forma literária e processo social nos inícios do romance brasileiro*. São Paulo: Duas Cidades.

Schwarz, Roberto. 1992. *Misplaced Ideas: Essays on Brazilian Culture*. Trans. John Gledson. London: Verso.

Stoller, Robert. 1989. *Masculin ou féminin?* Paris: Presses Universitaires de France.

CHAPTER 12

Homoaffectivity Exemplified in *Dom Casmurro*

Camilo Gomides

Many readers do not contemplate the psychology of the characters in the works of Machado de Assis (1839–1908). The stories are enjoyable simply for their humor and pathos (González Echevarría and Pupo-Walker 1996). Nevertheless, the characters are meticulously constructed and invite psychological analysis. The most inviting such work is the novel *Dom Casmurro* (1991), in which a lonely middle-aged man narrates how he married his childhood sweetheart and how she came to cheat on him, with none other than his best friend. Bento Santiago is the narrator; Capitu, the wife; and Ezequiel de Souza Escobar, the friend. Bento is an attorney whose professional skills are brought into play as he makes his case—not wholly convincing—against Capitu.

Commentary on that thumbnail description is basically how the work was read from its launch in 1899 until 1960, when Helen Caldwell published her *Brazilian Othello of Machado de Assis: A Study of Dom Casmurro*. Beneath the poignant narrative and credible portrayals, Caldwell explored the psychology of what is said and left unsaid in *Dom Casmurro*. The story morphs into the plight of a woman hounded by her husband's jealousy. Two readings are equally plausible—from the perspective of the aggrieved husband or with sympathy for the wife of an insanely jealous man. In the duality, a philosophical message emerges: a

C. Gomides (✉)
University of Puerto Rico-Río Piedras, San Juan, Puerto Rico

© The Editor(s) (if applicable) and The Author(s) 2016
L. Aidoo, D.F. Silva (eds.), *Emerging Dialogues on Machado de Assis*, DOI 10.1057/978-1-137-54174-1_12

181

life is too complex to be accurately understood by the individual, much less by others.

The ambiguity of the story engages the reader to reflect on what may or may not have happened. Psychological analysis thereby becomes a Rorschach inkblot test where attempts to decipher intentions may end up revealing more about the analyst than about the characters. With that caveat, I explore the homoeroticism and homosocial bonds that go beyond the jealousy of a husband who believes himself cuckolded. My uneasiness in exploring the psychology of the characters also has antecedents in Caldwell's analysis. Roberto Schwarz says of Caldwell, "An American professor (for being a woman? for being a foreigner? perhaps for being Protestant?) tackles the persona of Bento Santiago—Casmurro—warily with mixed feelings" (1991, 85).

My analysis begins with a classification of psychological roles. Capitu is a conduit for Bento's love-desire-hate toward Escobar. The classification conforms to a pattern observed by Gayle Rubin about such female conduits: "The total relationship of exchange which constitutes marriage is not established between a man and a woman, but between two groups of men, and the woman figures only as one of the objects in the exchange, not as one of the partners" (1975, 174). In other words, the woman enables bonding between men, where the true partner is another man. By mediating the homosocial relationship, the woman enhances the men's virility. Rubin's insight casts the intentions of the characters of *Dom Casmurro* in a very different light. With Capitu as conduit, Bento wishes to secure his homosocial bond to Escobar, whom he describes as "a slender fellow of blue eyes, a bit fugitive, like his hands, like his feet, like his speech, like everything about him" (72).[1] Capitu becomes the apex of a love triangle, with Bento and Escobar at the base.

Bento's meticulous descriptions of Escobar, often homoerotic, support the inference of homosocial bonds. Bento seems to be searching for the father figure whom he never had, in Freudian terms, a "homoerotic identification: a position of feminized subordination… as a condition for finding a model for his own heterosexual role" (Sedgwick 1995, 23). Although such Freudian analysis is often dismissed because it does not easily generate testable hypotheses, psychology does serve well to explain Bento's behavior toward Escobar. In that vein, Julio Ramos clarifies Bento's fixation on the image of Escobar: "The history of Bento's adult life develops a duality in the figure of the mediator. Escobar as confidant is also a father figure of authority for Bento. In the beach house, Bento hangs

Escobar's portrait next to his mother's…. The transformation is noteworthy: Bento places Escobar's portrait over the blank space of the father's portrait" (1996, 110; my translation). Bento would have Escobar become the paternal figure who was absent in his upbringing: "When my father died, [José Dias's] grief was enormous, that is what I was told, I do not remember" (11). Too young to remember his father's death—much less his daily presence—the young Bento would be looking for a father figure in Escobar "as a condition of finding a model for his own [indefinite] heterosexual role" (Sedgwick 1995, 23). The absence of a strong masculine *pater familias* continues over Bento's formative years.

An idea from Michel Foucault complements the Freudian explanation: a man "under the power of his own appetites and of others" (1990, 85) will let himself become overwhelmed by the appetites that either attract or distract him, becoming sick through jealousies and suspicions. Seen thus, Bento's masculinity is destabilized because of a feeling of inadequacy and lack of control over his own pleasure. Applying Foucault, Bento would be classified as "a man who is not sufficiently in control of his pleasures" (1990, 85). To regain control over ungovernable pleasure, Bento attempts to persuade the reader, via the first-person narrative, of Capitu's guilt. In making this case, Bento does not reflect on the etiology of his own effeminate state and lack of control over his own predilections.

Caldwell comes to a simpler explanation: Bento is not only sick from jealousy, but also frustrated by a desire to take control. Unable to define himself sexually, he assumes the masculine role in his relation with Capitu, which he had never achieved in a family home dominated by his mother, a female cousin, and the somewhat effeminate, dependent, and easy-going uncle. A homosocial and homoerotic reading departs subtly from such an analysis. Escobar becomes the vehicle for Bento to discover his own masculinity. From there, much fascination with his friend develops through "confessional speech" (Ramos 1996, 104), in which Bento defines himself sexually before Capitu and society. To achieve the heterosexual prototype for marriage, a paternal figure becomes necessary, which Bento establishes in his homosocial bond with Escobar.

The homoerotic dimensions and homosocial bonds between Bento and Escobar emerged in their adolescence at the seminary and are reinforced over many vignettes. A connection quickly takes hold that supports the alternative analysis. Chapter 65, "The Deceit," relates, "The padres liked me, the boys too, Escobar more than the other boys or padres" (130–31). From that point forward, Bento informs the reader that Escobar makes greater efforts than any of the other seminarians or padres to win his affection. The admiration becomes mutual in chapter 94, "Arithmetic Ideas." Bento is in awe of Escobar's mathematical abilities and embraces him with warmth. However, Escobar worries about the resultant jealousy among the seminarians. The padre reproaches both of them:

> I was so enthusiastic over the mental ability of my friend that I could not help giving him a hug. It was in the patio; other seminarists noticed our effusiveness; a padre who was with them did not like it.
> —"Modesty," he said to us, "does not countenance these excessive gestures. You may show regard for each other, but with moderation." (180)

It is noteworthy that the two friends do not desist from their homosocial bond. Of the two, Bento is the more persistent, suggesting to Escobar that they strengthen their friendship despite the reprimand. Escobar also perceives that the padre and other seminarians are jealous. He fears their opinion and wants to act with greater caution in order to sustain his tender feelings:

> Escobar remarked to me that the others and the padre spoke out of envy and suggested that we keep apart. I interrupted him and said 'no,' if it was envy, so much the worse for them.
> "We'll fix them!"
> "But..."
> "Let us be greater friends than ever."
> Escobar furtively gripped my hand so hard that my fingers still tingle. (180)

Read as homoeroticism, Bento seals the pact with a quasi-sadomasochistic act.

Many other vignettes cohere with a reading of homoerotic and homosocial dimensions. In chapter 93, "A Friend for a Dead Boy," Bento receives a visit from Escobar after a friend succumbs to leprosy: "A friend thus made up for a dead boy, and *so much a friend that he stood for almost five minutes with my hand in his*, as if he had not seen me for months" (175; italics added). The overt demonstration of affection is called a *chamego* in Brazilian Portuguese. The gesture confirms the preexisting longings between the two and long predates the triangulation of desire among Bento, Escobar, and Capitu.

Rather than elaborate the psychology associated with homoeroticism and homosocial bonds, Caldwell sees mostly a disturbed psyche in

Bento's attraction, albeit "detect[ing] also an element of vanity, or of homosexual jealousy, in the Escobar-dandy sequence" (Caldwell 1960, 66). For example, she analyzes Escobar's departure from the Santiago family home in chapter 71, "Visit from Escobar," when Bento is left staring toward the bus that Escobar has just gotten on, wanting to see if Escobar is sufficiently attached to him to turn around and wave good-bye again. Escobar does not turn around, even though they have departed "with great affection" (144). The incident is soon put into high relief in chapter 73, "The Stage Manager." A dandy on horseback rides through the neighborhood and admires Capitu leaning out of the window of her house. Smitten with her beauty, the dandy turns around and takes another look. Bento narrates: "The rider was not content to pass on, but turned his head in our direction, the direction of Capitu, and looked at Capitu, and Capitu looked at him. The horse went on but the man's head continued to stare back. This was the second fang of jealousy that sank into me" (147). One can surmise that what Escobar did not do for Bento from the bus—turn around to wave good-bye again—the dandy did profusely on horseback toward Capitu. Ambiguity emerges. Although Bento claims that he suffered jealousy, which Caldwell accepts, the context implies more envy than jealousy. Bento seems to envy Capitu in that Escobar did not think about him in the same way that the dandy thought about her.

A similar interpretation of homosocial bonding, rather than a manifestation of jealousy, can be inferred in chapter 18, "The Mother of Sancha." Bento supposedly lusts for Escobar's wife, Sancha, as a means of retribution, "imagining the possibility of revenge: the possibility of a love affair with Sancha the wife of the other," as Ramos writes (110). The alternative interpretation is that Bento's desire for Sancha is his desire for Escobar, expressed through another love triangle—this time, with Sancha as the conduit. The following excerpt supports such an inference:

> "Tomorrow, the sea will be a challenge," it was the voice of Escobar, who was standing at my side.
>
> "You intend to swim in that sea tomorrow?"
>
> "I've gone in worse, much worse. You can't imagine what a good wild sea is like. One must swim well, as I do, and have these lungs," he said beating his chest, "and these arms. Feel."
>
> I felt his arms as if I were feeling those of Sancha. The confession is painful for me to make, but I cannot suppress it without distorting the truth. I not

only felt them with this thought in mind, I received another sensation: I found them thicker and stronger than mine and I envied them—besides, they could swim. (223)

Bento, upon feeling Escobar's arms, says he thinks about Sancha. Given his erotic thoughts associated with the possible swap of couples, one may suspect that Bento imagines Sancha enveloped in Escobar's arms, reminiscent of Capitu's dandy admirer. Through triangulation, Bento would desire Escobar in his professed desire of Sancha, where she becomes the new mediator for the homoerotic desire between the two men, imagined through an embrace.

To tackle the personae of *Dom Casmurro*, a theoretical construct is needed that accommodates both the consistencies and inconsistencies in the narrative with Freudian analysis, homosociality, and homoeroticism. Inasmuch as the charm of the work lies in achieving ambiguity with stylistic clarity, the construct must facilitate multiple interpretations. "Homoaffectivity" affords such breadth and audience reception. It is a neologism whose meaning is sufficiently self-evident that its creator, Denilson Lopes (2002), did not define it with any precision, which also coheres with the theme of intended ambiguity. We can, thus, invite similar readings of the other works of Machado de Assis. The relationship between Bento and Escobar in *Dom Casmurro* is its exemplification.

NOTE

1. All citations from the novel are taken from the 1991 Farrar, Straus and Giroux edition translated by Helen Caldwell.

REFERENCES

Assis, Machado de. 1991. *Dom Casmurro*. Trans. H. Caldwell. New York: Farrar, Straus and Giroux.

Caldwell, Helen. 1960. *The Brazilian Othello of Machado de Assis: A study of Dom Casmurro*. Berkeley: University of California Press.

Foucault, Michel. 1990. *The use of pleasure. Vol. 2 of the history of sexuality*. New York: Penguin.

González Echevarría, Roberto, and Enrique Pupo-Walker (eds.). 1996. *Brazilian literature. Vol. 3 of the Cambridge history of Latin American literature*. New York: Cambridge University Press.

Lopes, Denilson. 2002. *O homem que amava rapazes e outros ensaios*. Rio de Janeiro: Aeroplano.

Ramos, Julio. 1996. Anticonfesiones: deseo y autoridad en Memórias Póstumas de *Brás Cubas* y *Dom Casmurro* de Machado de Assis. In *Paradojas de la letra*, ed. Julio Ramos, 97–115. Quito: Ediciones Excultura.

Rubin, Gayle. 1975. The traffic in women: Notes on the 'political economy' of sex. In *Toward an anthropology of women*, ed. Rayna R. Reiter, 157–201. New York: Monthly Review Press.

Schwarz, Roberto. 1991. A poesia envenenada de Dom Casmurro. *Novos Estudos* 29: 85–97.

Sedgwick, Eve Kosofsky. 1995. *Between men: English literature and male homosocial desire*. New York: Columbia University Press.

CHAPTER 13

Masculinity and Matrimonial Secrets in *Dom Casmurro*

Richard Miskolci

At first glance, Machado's novel *Dom Casmurro* (Lord Taciturn 1900) appears to be an intimate portrait of a retired university graduate,[1] Bento Santiago, who narrates his life story, which is deeply impacted by a romantic relationship in his youth. It is a relationship that alters a boy's path to the priesthood, molding him, instead, into a *pater familias*. It also leads to a double betrayal by his wife, Capitu, with his best friend, Escobar. By analyzing this love triangle, we can better grasp the tensions and paradoxes tied to matrimony as the founding bond of a new ideal family structure for Brazilian society at the end of the nineteenth century.

According to Eni de Mesquita Samara (2004), concubinage was rampant in nuclear families of the urban popular classes of the time, while legal marriage was more common among wealthier families. As is evident in Machado's novel, released at the dawn of the twentieth century, it was among the elite that one could find larger domestic groups, thanks in large part to the presence of slaves and domestic workers known as *agregados*. The increasing prevalence of social hygiene discourse tended to encourage legal unions among the poor, underscoring the mother's responsibility for child rearing and domestic unity.

Translated by Daniel F. Silva and Lamonte Aidoo

R. Miskolci (✉)
Federal University of São Carlo, São Paulo, Brazil

189

The novel's plot can be regarded as a noteworthy source for research on the tensions that affected the institution of marriage among Brazilian elites at the dawn of the twentieth century. Despite their respectability and role as family ideal, legal unions continued to be unpopular in Brazilian society. Hegemonic discourses, however, posited heterosexual marriage as the foundation of civilized social life, ignoring and blurring the inequalities and restrictions that were internal to the institution—particularly those that disenfranchised women.

The growing concern with sexuality pointed to a larger endeavor to reestablish the terms by which sex intersected systems of societal utilitarianism and regulation. Such systems, emanating from the national status quo, articulated marriage (and its idealization) as a family model, based on a more solid relationship between partners. According to Margareth Rago, in such a family model, the woman is "elevated to the central figure of her space,"[2] but in a strictly limited role in which, "vigilant, attentive, sovereign in her space, she becomes responsible for the health of both her children and her husband, for the family's happiness and the home's hygiene, at a time of growing obsession with germs, dust, waste and all else that aids the spread of disease. The house is considered a privileged place where the character of the children is formed; where they acquire the defining behavioral traits of the nation's new workforce. Hence the significant moral responsibility attributed to the woman for the betterment of the nation" (1997, 80).

In *Lord Taciturn*, the reader follows a deconstruction of these ideals pertaining to marriage and family during the empire's decay, especially in the midst of issues stemming from the power structure of a formerly slave-based society that created a particular grammar of social, romantic, and sexual relations. Despite this, the novel was largely read as a story of betrayal, a sad narrative coming from a respectable representative of the Brazilian elite that relates to us the infidelity of his wife—a woman of lower social class—with his best friend.

This sort of reading reveals not only the credulity of the readers of the twentieth-century's first decades, but also the Brazilian cultural consensus in condemning the wife, whose humble origins posit her as the a priori guilty party. This hegemonic interpretation of the novel lasted more than half a century until an American scholar, Helen Caldwell, published *The Brazilian Othello of Machado de Assis* (1960/2002), finally pointing out Machado's critical stance toward the narrator and society.

According to Caldwell, Bento Santiago is a character eroded by jealousy who labors to prove to both himself and to us readers that he was, in fact, betrayed by those he most trusted. The biased narration does not allow us access to the perspectives of the other characters involved, leaving us only the narrator's version of the story, along with his conjectures and judgments. Caldwell's shrewd reading paved the way for other reinterpretations of Machado's work, finally recognizing the author as a (subtle) critic of Brazil's elite.

Since then, we have understood that Machado's novels continue to present unresolved enigmas. Unfortunately, the reception of Caldwell's book in Brazil was limited to Capitu's transformation from adulteress to woman under suspicion, thus maintaining a masculine-oriented interpretation of *Lord Taciturn*. Readers no longer interpreted the narrator's confidently created account as a clear-cut condemnation of an adulterous wife. Instead, the novel began to be read as a narrative based on a husband's suspicions regarding his wife's fidelity. Confidence in the protagonist was displaced, but the focus on the possibility of betrayal was not, transferring the point of observation from the narrator to the reader.

The majority of previous analyses maintained this masculinist perspective by way of a focus on the Bento–Capitu marriage, and, at the very most, considering the possible love triangle through a heterosexual optic that nonetheless paid little attention to the relationship between Bento and Escobar. I propose, below, a reading of the novel through a feminist and queer perspective—more aware, in other words, of both the social condition of women in turn-of-the-century Brazil and the novel's homosocial components left unexamined by previous analyses.

Portrait of a Brazilian Marriage

Lord Taciturn is a memorialist account, the life story of a retired and solitary *bacharel* who, in his old age, decides to face the ghosts of his past by writing his memoirs. John Gledson astutely observes that despite the plot taking place in the 1850s and the beginning of the 1870s, it is impossible to affirm that Machado de Assis somehow abandoned his own period in a manifestation of nostalgia. According to the English scholar, the protagonist "Bento is the escapist, but who nonetheless writes in 1899, when the city of Rio was growing to the outskirts where he resides, when there was already a republican constitution that separated church and state, and so on, and so forth" (Gledson 2006, 340–41).

The protagonist's account, therefore, is constructed through the historical lens of the turn of the century, even if the beginning of the account dates back to the mid-nineteenth century, when his father died and his family resided in urban Rio de Janeiro. Bento's widowed mother, Dona Glória, promises her son to the priesthood despite his lack of religious vocation. Unable to undo this maternal promise on his own, he offers an amorous justification to avoid the path of priesthood: his love for his neighbor, Capitu. The brilliant idea for such an excuse came, of course, from his seminary classmate, Escobar. Young, blessed with business savvy, and also, without religious vocation, Escobar proposes that Dona Glória sponsor a poor boy's entrance to the priesthood in her son's place. The arrangement, which reveals the influence of economic power in religious matters, frees Bento from the maternal promise and enables him to marry the young girl of humble means.

In deconstructing the enigma that is the transformation of a naïve Bento into the bitter Lord Taciturn, Roberto Schwarz (1997) affirms that the turning point can be found in his marriage to Capitu. The climax of the couple's marriage is ultimately Bento's ascent to the role of heir and proprietor—in other words, his rise to the top of the nation's socioeconomic hierarchy. Schwarz, thus, dares to transfer the suspicion of marriage for financial gain from Capitu to Bento. This is an important and plausible reading, but one that can nonetheless fail to fully comprehend the novel if we are limited to a logic of economic desire. Even though Bento aspires to and manages to attain socioeconomic stature through marriage, we must consider another event as that which truly alters his life: the death of his friend. Escobar's drowning deeply unsettles Bento and raises, for him, suspicions regarding Capitu, ultimately transforming him into the old Taciturn (Assis 1992, 205).

The very title of the short chapter containing the news of Escobar's death could not be clearer in this regard: "The Catastrophe." The chapter also alludes to the year 1871, which saw a new governmental cabinet take power, one that would declare the Law of Free Birth, ultimately signaling the beginning of the end for the empire. In the following chapter, relating Escobar's wake, the narrator reiterates, in more explicit terms, the impact of the date: "One person or another discussed the new Rio Branco Cabinet; it was March of 1871. I never forgot neither the month nor the year" (207). The first significant sign of the imperial regime's demise intersects with the main shift in the novel's plot: the transformation of Bento into Lord Taciturn. Thus, social and psychic change clash and inform one another, revealing deep-seated fears about the future.

Bento's panic regarding his wife's possible infidelity is not reduced to a fit of jealousy against his wife. After all, there is a fine line between desiring what someone else has (Capitu) and desiring that very someone (Escobar). Therein lies the key to Bento's inner conflict: the suspected betrayal by his wife cannot be divorced from his uncertainties regarding his own relationship with Escobar. Perhaps because his jealousy may not be necessarily due to Capitu betraying him, but due to the fact that the betrayal involved his secretly desired friend.

It is worth reflecting on this sort of relationship between men in which women appear as intermediaries for male homosociability and the reconsolidation of masculinity. Even in betrayal, implying a shift in the relationship between the two men, the betrayed man retains his masculine social privilege and power. The façade of heterosexual marriage, in other words, sanctions the homosocial bond while allowing the two men to perform heteronormativity. The flip side of such an arrangement, which offered men a particular type of power, implied a new layer of female subordination. Masculinity was acquired and reconsolidated vis-à-vis femininity—itself projected solely on women.

Eve Kosofsky Sedgwick famously coined this tie that binds masculine relationships "male homosociability" in her classic *Between Men* (1985, 25). In this foundational text of queer theory, Sedgwick argues that in societies influenced by masculine power, one can find an intimate bond between male homosociability and the phallocentric power structures that maintain their control over women. Such homosocial bonding or desire tends to be an ambiguous and, at times, conflicting combination, which helps us understand why at the end of the nineteenth century, relationships between men changed considerably (Foucault 2004; Ortega 1999; Carrara 1996). These became objects of greater social control, leading to a decrease in intimacy between men and the restructuring of male friendship as secondary to a man's relationship with a woman within the nuclear family.

The emergence of sports and sporting activities, already evident in the late nineteenth century, has a direct correlation with the control over male relationships. These became increasingly based on disciplined collective activities that were, unsurprisingly, encouraged as a form of "social hygiene."[3] At home, men were pacified by the civilizing presence of their wives. Meanwhile, in the public space and in the presence of other men, their relations were closely monitored by the public gaze. Their desires were thus channeled toward the household, to be realized with the opposite sex and with the goal of reproduction.

Such a reality underscores the growing collective fear around intimacy between men. In this context in which relationships between men are seen as socially problematic, two interrelated phenomena emerge: on an individual level, the refusal to be amorously or sexually involved with someone of the same sex and, on a societal level, the institutional positing of heterosexuality as the natural order in which desire manifests itself. Together, these phenomena fomented a dynamic mode of social control over relationships between men so that such bonds could continue functioning for masculine domination over women, rather than falling into the "dangerous" desire for a partner of the same sex.

Such a dynamic directed desire toward its socially expected forms, constituting not only a mode of simple control, but more importantly, of the formation of subjectivity—or subjectivation. The social construction of the subject and the implied manipulation of desire became central to the creation and maintenance of a particular power structure, one based on control over women and insistence on the fragile monogamous union that constituted the nucleus of the idealized reproductive family. In other words, the domestication of desire ultimately depended on the institution of marriage.

Brazilian society of the early twentieth century, the inspiration behind Machado's final decade of work, witnessed the emergence of this new order of sexuality[4] evident in the archives and their hygienic emphasis on marriage, the family, and the health of the nation. This new order could also be seen in the literary production of the period, which allows us to better grasp subjectivation and the division of desires as accepted versus prohibited. In the case of *Lord Taciturn*, this process of subjectivation based on accepted versus prohibited desires is evident in the relationship between Bento and Escobar, from their adolescence in the seminary to their adult lives as married men.

Close to the turning point in the novel's plot, Escobar plans a group trip to Europe, causing Bento to have erotic thoughts about a possible spouse swap. Following this conversation, Escobar tells Bento that he will go for a swim in the ocean the next morning, bragging about the strength and stamina of his arms. Escobar eventually asks Bento to feel his arms. Bento relates what follows: "I squeezed his arms as if they were Sancha's [Escobar's wife]. This confession is particularly difficult, but I cannot suppress it; that would be crippling the truth. Not only did I squeeze them with that fantasy, but I also felt something else: I found his arms to be thicker and stronger than mine, and I was jealous of them; on top of that, they knew how to swim" (Assis 1992, 201).

Bento learns of Escobar's drowning the following day. The blow to Bento is dramatic. Upon seeing Capitu in front of Escobar's coffin at the wake, he notices her shed a tear. For Bento, this tear begins to raise suspicions regarding his wife's fidelity. He starts to imagine the betrayal. This, coupled with the death of his friend, brings him to sobbing tears that make him incapable of delivering the eulogy. He walks aimlessly through the streets, and it is then that his marital paranoia emerges, ultimately transforming Bento into the taciturn narrator.

From then on, Bento expresses his doubts about his wife's fidelity and the paternity of his son, named after his best friend. These are doubts that begin to destabilize his position in the marriage, within the family that he and Capitu constructed, and within society at large. This undoubtedly contributes to Bento's growing paranoia, which is not only a psychic response to his delicate situation, but also the internalized expression of social forces and regulations, such as the refusal to accept his desire for Escobar. The imposition of heterosexual relationships demanded the rejection of any possible ties between people of the same sex, increasingly considered abject.

Bento's paranoia leads him to voice the violence that constructs the asymmetries of class and gender. Such violence is directed not only toward Capitu, but also, toward himself, obliging him to fear his desire for Escobar. At the time of Machado's writing (1896–1899), the issue of homosexual desire grew in visibility and societal importance. Even though homoerotic desire was potentially present in anyone, sexual theories of the time attributed it mainly to celibates, masturbators, blacks, and other "degenerates."

Among elites—given their societal role as models of whiteness—the need for self-control was even greater. We can thus recognize the cultural conventions regarding gender and sexuality of Brazilian elites in Bento's fear and refusal vis-à-vis his homoerotic desire. His personal dilemma—between suspecting his wife and fearing his attraction toward his friend—lays bare the quotidian exigencies of white elite masculinity.

Following Escobar's death, Capitu is seen as the unscrupulous and opportunistic adulteress who even robbed Bento of his virility due to the doubts surrounding their son's paternity. She embodies his failure and threatens his power and privilege. Escobar, meanwhile, becomes the specter that compromises Bento's masculinity, haunting him from the facial features of his own son and leading him to contemplate suicide by poisoning.

It is worth noting that at the end of the nineteenth century, self-poisoning was a form of suicide attributed mainly to women, while men preferred suicide by hanging or gunshot. In this regard, even his greatest act of desperation, although not concretized, demonstrates how his paranoia emasculated or even feminized him.

In terms of power relations (inseparable from those of gender), Bento's life was affected by the experience of being the son of a widow, having his identity and place in society mediated and controlled by a woman—to the point of being promised to the priesthood. The ecclesiastic future was like a form of castration. He was able to sidestep such a future, thanks to two masculine figures: the *agregado* José Dias and, most importantly, Escobar. Dias helped convince Bento's mother that she should accept his love for the neighboring Capitu, while Escobar proposed, of course, allowing a poor boy to take Bento's place in the seminary. Further ahead in the novel, Capitu's possible betrayal strips him of his patriarchal power and places a question mark over his paternity. In this regard, throughout his life, only other men were able to legitimize and validate his masculinity, while women posed a threat to it.

Bento's paranoia—and uncertainty concerning his power and masculinity—is the signifying chain that propels a narrative in which Capitu becomes the center of attention for being the social object that allows him to avoid the priesthood and become a husband, heir, father, and patriarch. Nonetheless, Capitu is merely one of the corners that compose the novel's love triangle, in which Escobar has a no less important role. After all, it was he who helped free Bento from the priesthood to a secular life, and it is his death that engenders Bento's suspicions toward Capitu.

Ironically, without Escobar, Bento would arguably have been unable to lead a confident life as husband and father. Machado carefully articulates the importance of the bond between the two friends, be it through the sarcastic statement, "The priests liked me, the boys did as well, and Escobar liked me even more than the boys and the priests did" (Assis 1992, 122), or through the declaration in the seminary:

"Escobar, you are my friend, I am yours friend as well; here in the seminary, you are the person who has most entered my heart. Out there, aside from my family, I do not have a friend."

"If I say the same thing," he responded with a smile, "it may seem less special; as if I am simply repeating. But the truth is that I do not have any acquaintances here; you are the first and I believe they have already noticed, but I am not concerned with that." (Assis 1992, 139)

Bento adds, "Emotionally moved, I felt as though my voice jumped out of my throat" (Assis 1992, 139). Following the reciprocal admission, they continue to reveal secret after secret until they both confess they do not wish to follow the priesthood. It is worth noting the title of this chapter, "Secret by Secret," which evokes the increasingly private space to which affectivity among men was relegated. Their mutual revelations resemble a confession, which is particularly relevant, considering the space of the seminary: a religious locale in which any sort of affect toward someone of the same sex was not only a secret, but more importantly, a sin.

In one particular visit, Bento describes how Escobar held his hand between his for five minutes, "as if he had gone long months without seeing me" (158). There are numerous passages that illustrate the centrality of this relationship in Bento's life. The relationship between the two exemplifies the tenuous nature of homosociability, in which bonds between men constituted the privileged mode of masculine socialization and shared power over women.

The betrayal would eventually threaten to remove Bento from the social position of control that characterized white fatherhood at the turn of the twentieth century. The specter of betrayal guides the narrative, and, as outlined at the beginning of this chapter, profoundly influenced the dominant interpretations of the novel.[5] We can, nonetheless, separate the ghost of Taciturn from such heteronormative and heterosexist perspectives, thus revealing the nuances behind his paranoid account of the past. In other words, the alleged opacity of the relationship between Bento and Escobar is not always easy to pin down, but a thorough theoretical unpacking can extract some of power's inner workings. It is worth questioning: does maintaining the obscurity of the relationship in the vast majority of analyses not justify and maintain what the novel asks us to question—the "secret" through which such politically and socially relevant relationships were constructed?

A system of power's degree of effectiveness is directly proportional to its degree of misrecognition. In terms of sexuality in the late nineteenth century, power relations were molded by a moral and normalizing discourse that created a division between acceptable and condemnable desires. To effectively unpack the logic and values behind such a division, we must trace the spectral images of betrayal as shifting expressions of the societal fears that emerged with the end of the Empire.

FEARS WITHIN THE BRAZILIAN FAMILY
AT THE TURN OF THE CENTURY

The same set of civil laws that ruled the country during the historical period that concerns the novel's plot—the beginning of the empire's decay—remained in force at the time of the book's publication.[6] According to King Phillip's Ordinances and the Penal Code of 1830, the law against adultery was rigid and aimed, above all, at control over women, their fidelity, bodies, and desires. Punishment of the adulteress depended on proof of the act and the husband's will to prosecute his wife. After all, the social status of the betrayed husband was as much a dishonor as it was an affront to his masculinity. Considering such damage to a man's public image, it is no wonder that public trials over adultery were quite rare, the majority brought by women of the elite against their husbands.[7]

As a lawyer, Bento Santiago was aware that according to existing legislation, adultery was only lawfully recognized when both parties were alive. Therefore, the possible betrayal by Capitu and Escobar is relegated to the realm of suspicion, especially because it emerges by way of a simple tear running down his wife's face. The suspicion of betrayal is born in a purely spectral form, destined to haunt the narrator until his old age, when he decides to put it in writing.

The conditions that materialize his suspicions constitute their own secret—also a burden from which he seeks refuge by way of his memoirs—an account of his interpretations of the world, his interpersonal and romantic relationships. The aged and distrustful Bento becomes the embodiment of the existing social order, in which power relations, namely those between classes and genders are defended as in a tribunal against Capitu and Escobar. His paranoid account also serves to reprimand the naïveté of his youth, his feelings for Capitu, and his erotically ambiguous friendship with Escobar.

To this very day, Capitu continues to be discussed as a mysterious character, which makes her exotic, strange, and the Other vis-à-vis Bento and the Brazilian society of the time. At the turn of the twentieth century, dominant representations of women posited them as figures of disorder. Their social marginality placed them at the interstice of masculine order and what was considered chaos—a space outside of patriarchal culture. This helps explain the centrality of the femme fatale figure in the arts of the period. The overly intelligent woman, guided by a desire for autonomy, was seen as a threat to matrimony, and according to the discourse of the time, she was destined to have her brain enslaved by the flesh and dominated by the uterus.

The mystery that surrounds Capitu mythologizes her experience as a woman in the late nineteenth century, ultimately masking the nuances of her social mobility and submission to Bento, the patriarch. Many scholars have demonstrated how the narrator attempts to prove Capitu's betrayal by underscoring the disparity between her class origins and the social status she reached through marriage. Amidst all the analyses the novel has undergone, one issue appears to have gone unmentioned: Capitu is not necessarily accused of having married for financial gain, but of betraying her commitment to the idealized family, within which the married white woman was to be desexualized and her honesty equated with purity.

The adulterous woman was a trope that sparked significant social anxiety, since she was neither wife nor prostitute. In a historical period that cultivated rigid social roles and identities, the adulteress ambiguously floated across moral fixities, losing her bourgeois respectability while remaining in a sort of limbo that was uncomfortable for her class congeners. This was especially the case for her husband as Capitu challenged the meaning of marriage and destabilized its most fundamental hierarchy: what is constructed through masculine power, depending on the woman as a figure "infantilized as an image of helplessness, of an incapacity for free thought, and of a naturally servile spirit" (Rago 1997, 68).

The description of Capitu's eyes at Escobar's wake ties eroticism to the mystical danger of the ocean, which, in actuality, takes Escobar's life. In this regard, seduction becomes a discourse of class in which masculine weakness is justified by supposedly irrational forces or by economic interests masquerading as a woman's amorous intents. Capitu is presented as the intersection of both. Her intelligence intermingles with her sensuality behind the implied accusation that she seeks her own autonomy socially foreclosed as a transgression against masculine power and privilege. Part of the reproduction of masculine hegemony traced the man "as a victim at the hands of women: ignoble, accessible, lying, scandal-mongering, and seductive creatures that stop at nothing to satisfy the passions by which they are controlled. Women are deemed culpable for the failure of marriages" (Nunes 2000, 118–19).

In the European context, Elaine Showalter (1993) characterizes the end of the nineteenth century as a period marked by the fear of sexual anarchy, and outlines the main figures to which feared gender chaos was attributed: the new woman and the homosexual. The overarching fear was that sexuality would no longer be conveniently contained and tied to fixed gender identities and hierarchies. Emerging identities were seen as threats to the institution of marriage, to the bourgeois family, and especially to the rigid and hierarchized gender binary that articulated an entire social, economic, and symbolic order.

In European literature, this is manifested in the shift in readership at which novels are directed. Starting in the 1880s, the individual reader displaces the family as the potential consumer of novels. If, as Nancy Armstrong (1987) affirms, the history of the novel cannot be divorced from the history of sexuality, one can connect the rise of the individual reader to the centrality of gender and sexuality in the novelistic plots of the end of the nineteenth century. In Brazil, the fact that the country's first census revealed an illiterate majority at the time undoubtedly influenced how writers approached their implied readers. Machado was certainly no exception; and following the census results, his narrators become increasing more provocative (Guimarães 2004, 177).

Within the literary trends of the time, we can identify a psychological turn toward split subjectivities that were central to many plots at the turn of the century. The demise of a linear and stable ego can be even be found in *Lord Taciturn*, in the shift from young Bento to Taciturn, the narrator. Even though the transformation is clear and comprehensible, we can still question its veracity, considering the perspective of a partial and biased narrator. After all, why does the death of his best friend coincide with the emergence of his suspicions toward his wife? Perhaps because the loss of Escobar threatened to reveal a secret Capitu discovered many years earlier, when she observed him watching Escobar's departure in entranced admiration following a warm visit:

> We separated with much affection: he, inside the bus, waved good-bye. I remained at the door, to see if, from far away, he would look back, but he did not.
> "What friend can be so great?" asked someone from a nearby window. Needless to say, it was Capitu. (Assis, 1992, 106)

The relationship between Bento and Escobar in their youth can be regarded as a passionate friendship. These were common among elites and tolerated because they were seen as a phase that would pass on the way to adulthood. In Machado's novel, however, there is no indication that such a transition has occurred or that the friendship has lost importance. On the contrary, the trauma of Escobar's death underscores how their ambiguous friendship developed on the border between the societal expectation and societal fear. Bento was thus aware of the socially perilous consequences that his secret could bring if Capitu were to divulge it.

His wife thus knew too much. Her tear over Escobar's coffin brought him to contemplate the specter of betrayal, but not just any betrayal—a double betrayal of his wife and best friend. Moreover, the friendship shared by Bento and Escobar invites us to rethink the common understanding of a love triangle. This is not simply a case of the partial model, one woman for two men, but a more complete and complex "the same man for him and her."

Bento desires Escobar and is desired by him, but to that reciprocity, one must add the rivalries that constitute hierarchies of masculinity. In this vein, we can recall the scene in which Bento feels Escobar's arms and expresses his desire. Bento must affirm his masculinity, so he mimes Escobar's desire by affirming that he squeezed his arms as if they were Sancha's. His desire for his friend is presented as if it were directed toward his friend's wife, thus heterosexualizing his desire by way of feminizing Escobar in order to accept him as object of desire. Also, he immediately notices that Escobar's arms were stronger than his, sparking envy—which can be read as emasculating, thus feminizing and transforming himself into a viable object of his friend's desire.

In this peculiar erotic grammar, the desire of one man for another is only comprehensible within a gender binary in which masculinity and femininity are not attributed to the biological sex of those involved, but rather, convey positions of domination and submission. The desire between the friends is mutual, constituting a sort of homosocial equality that is nonetheless supplemented by the expectation of inequity at the heart of erotic relations at the time. To be more or less of a man was a dispute to be decided by the conquest of the other's wife or, more drastically, in the paternity of the other's child. The combination of desire and rivalry deeply affects Taciturn's narrative and exposes his logic based on a model of intelligibility from the slaveholding experience.

The taciturn narrator's attempt to dissimulate the role of his relationship with Escobar as the driving force behind his narrative offers an incipient reflection on the emerging social and sexual relations in Brazil at the turn of the century. First, it is clear that patriarchy had not lost any ground in the social order of the nascent republic. The old order of slave society can be found in Taciturn's deliriums regarding his wife, friend, and child.

Haunted by the ghost of betrayal, he brutally exercises his power as if he could, in that way, recover what he lost with Escobar's death: his confidence in the position of power afforded to him by a seigniorial order. This in turn helps us understand how slavery influenced the inception of Brazil's model family, which sought to mirror that of Europe.

If there is a biographical mark in the novel, one can find it in the way Machado foregrounds relations of dependence in turn-of-the-century Brazil. Although he did not include any reference to his particular experience of social dependence as a mulatto, it can be argued that he transposed racial dependency to that of gender. The logic of hegemony went beyond forces of production, having obvious racial and gender components. The relationship between masters and slaves was founded on, and maintained through, the belief in white supremacy, just like the dependence of women was based on notions of their natural subordination to men.

The novels that comprise Machado's so-called first phase are largely centered on the social destiny of the free woman within slave-based society, while the works of his second phase arguably focus on the masters. Nonetheless, one important element remains: his strategy of substituting the racial component—far more controversial at the time—for that of gender as the signifier of difference. Such notions of alterity often relegated his female protagonists to the social limbo also experienced by free blacks and mulattoes in the slaveholding nation.[8] This uncertain social integration (even when realized, it is constantly suspected, if not under threat of revocation without justification) marks the experiences of dependent women in Machado's novels. Hence the theory that race is substituted for gender as the artistic strategy used to lay bare the modes of social domination at the turn of the century.[9]

This also provides a rebuttal to the oft-levied accusation that Machado avoided writing about Afro-Brazilian experiences, instead, choosing to novelize stories of white men (Costa 2000). Within the realm of artistic choices afforded by the empire in its final throes, the decision to center stories on white (dependent) women in the slave-based hierarchy can be seen as conforming to the trends of the artistic field while still highlighting the privileged place of patriarchy. This place of power was, of course, informed by both masculine domination and racism. In this regard, Machado's investment in his white female characters is tied to his constant criticism of the emergent Brazilian family—inextricably structured by slavery's social order.

Lord Taciturn is Machado's first novel written during Brazil's republican period, and it is no coincidence that it also marks the return to his plots centered on the struggles of women for social mobility. The transition from one political regime to the other structures the novel. Bento, thus, embodies the crises of the old order, especially as a bourgeois lawyer. Taciturn's brutality meshes with the view that Machado held regarding the nascent republic—that it represented merely the transferring of power and inequality to the republican regime by way of rooted oligarchies. Without any hint of imperial nostalgia, *Lord Taciturn* is a social and psychological analysis of an intimate component of Brazilian elite life, the same life that witnessed political change without losing its authoritarian character.

The novel addresses a period of societal transformations in terms of gender and sexuality that are tied to the political shifts enacted during the end of the empire (1870–1889) and consolidated during the republic. Existing hierarchies and subalternities were rehistoricized under new headings. For instance, the emerging narrative of "our peculiar 'racism' "—and later, the myth of racial democracy—continued to tie skin color to the moral demands of whiteness as social ideal. At this moment of historical reinscription, Machado sought real political change. He supported, for instance, in a 1895 op-ed, the women's suffrage movement in Brazil as well as women's right to run for office.[10]

The so-called *Nova Mulher* (New Woman) was a figure of contestation vis-à-vis the old order, as well as a counterpoint to the republic, which aspired to bourgeois notions of progress while maintaining the authoritarian stance of the past and continuing to deny citizenship to the majority of the population. In *Lord Taciturn*, Machado takes up the trope of the free yet dependent woman, approaching her place in both imperial society and the new republican present now through the framework of an erotic triangle, underscoring new fissures and discrepancies that undergird society.

In such a paradoxical period of political shifts and social continuities, Lord Taciturn's paranoid narrative serves as an example of how betrayal implied a deeper set of hegemonic fears, starting with his own identitarian fractures that haunt him, all the way to his union with a woman armed with her own ideas and desires. This is to say nothing of the potentially disastrous consequences brought on by the death of his best friend should the secret of that bond have been publically revealed. What these specters indicate regarding late-nineteenth-century Brazilian society is the deep-seated fear among white male elites of losing their societal power and privilege.

Significant psychoanalytic thought intimately ties paranoia to particular phobias, especially pertaining to homosexual desire. Freud notably defined paranoia as a neurotic manifestation of the repressed homosexual component of infantile sexuality, which can reemerge in adulthood via fears of being dominated by another man. From a more sociological perspective, such paranoia can become tied to other sources of personal or collective anxiety.[11] In this sense, we can posit the paranoid subject as one who foresees the risks in an existing conception or social narrative, neurotically pointing out possible threats to their place in society—its political, economic, and symbolic order.

Taciturn's narrative can, therefore, be considered not simply as a narrative on homosexuality, but on how modern moral values are reinforced at the level of the subject via the sustained refusal of homosexual desire. Due to this interdependent dynamic, fears regarding the desire for someone of the same sex were tied to the threatening possibility of losing power, over both women and other men, due to the construction of white masculinity stemming from slavery.

Machado's ability to create a work so critical yet so acclaimed by the elite public he criticized is grounded in the fact that this account of a failed marriage could have been read in opposition to the idealized model of married life. The narrative of a white man and family father was immediately received with sympathy and interpreted as the story of a man unjustly betrayed. What the reading public took time to understand was that the plot lends itself to potentially disruptive readings vis-à-vis the cultural conventions of power.

Machado's novel offers a nuanced look into how the problematics of relationships between men can emerge. From here, the plot's main source of tension shifts from Bento–Capitu (the focus of the majority of analyses) to the Bento–Escobar friendship. Machado's deeper social critique emerges from the positing of Escobar as the wife's lover, becoming the specter that haunts Taciturn and destabilizes his comfortable integration into the nation's power dynamics and its hegemonic models of love and friendship.

Haunted by this specter, and by the subsequent loss of power over Capitu, Bento relegates his wife and son to forced exile. His paranoid account embodies bourgeois civilization, acting to impose his masculine power in the midst of a changing erotic order that posited heterosexual relations and marriage as the first step toward a new social era. Marriage would create a new family, distinct from that of the colonial and imperial epochs, but always tied to the legacies of the past. This account of suspicion and condemnation of the past makes Taciturn's narrative the materialization of the fears and anxieties that shaped end-of-the-century discourses, spawned by the ideals of Brazil's political, economic, and intellectual elites.

NOTES

1. Translator's note: "University graduate" is translated from the Portuguese *bacharel*, referring to someone with a bachelor's degree (usually in law or medicine). At the turn of the twentieth century, to be a "bacharel" implied being a white male member of Brazil's socioeconomic elite.
2. Translator's note: All translations of quotes are ours.
3. The growing corporal and masculine discipline became another argument in favor of sporting practices, which connected activity among men under the gaze of society with the gaze of medical discourse. The section "Um pouco de sciencia" ("A Little Bit of Science") in the January 22, 1897 edition of the newspaper *O Estado de S. Paulo* included a translation of rules from a manual of athletic hygiene, originally written by Fresson and published by the Commission on Hygiene of the Union of French Societies of Athletic Sports (cited Schwarcz and Costa 2007, 86).
4. This evokes what Steven Seidman refers to as the contribution of queer theory to sociology to invite others to the "study of those knowledges and social practices that organize 'society' as a whole by sexualizing—heterosexualizing or homosexualizing—bodies, desires, acts, identities, social relations, knowledges, culture, and social institutions" (1996, 12–13). For historical and sociological references on transformations in the realm of sexuality in Brazil during this period, see Balieiro (2009); Beluche (2008); Green (2000); Gledson (2006); and Lara (2009).
5. Among these interpretations, it is worth underscoring the meticulous way in which Raymundo Faoro (2001) presents social mobility as the central motivation of female protagonists in Machado's novels. According to Faoro, such characters viewed marriage as the trapeze for climbing the social pyramid.
6. The republic soon created the Criminal Code, but the Civil Code took a bit longer, being approved only in 1916. The laws inherited from the empire were used in the interim.
7. During my research in the National Archives, I came across a very negligible number of trials for adultery during the second half of the nineteenth century.

8. As Raymundo Faoro observes, "Sadder is the luck of women—for them, options and opportunities are far more limited, with little hope. If they are not blessed with an opulent godmother or the generosity of a wealthy husband, only marriage awaits, often with a futureless *bacharel*, an employee with limited finances, or the employee vexed by the threat of unemployment" (2001, 346).

9. Pierre Bourdieu notably argues that in literature, the biographical becomes an object of study, of self-analysis, or even, socioanalysis (Bourdieu 2005).

10. "If a woman can vote, why could she not run for President? Birth gave Catherine of Russia and Elizabeth of England the right to rule. Why can't the suffrage of a nation elect a capable woman to the Presidency?" (Assis cited in Piza 2005, 283).

11. For more regarding such psychoanalytic thought, consult Sedgwick 2003.

References

Armstrong, Nancy. 1987. *Desire and domestic fiction: A political history of the novel.* Oxford: Oxford University Press.

Assis, Machado de. 1992. *Dom Casmurro.* Rio de Janeiro: Livraria Garnier.

Balieiro, Fernando de F. 2009. A pedegogia do sexo em o ateneu: O dispositivo de sexualidade no internato da "Fina flor da mocidade brasileira." Master's thesis, Universidade Federal de Santa Catarina.

Beluche, Renato. 2008. *O corte da sexualidade: O ponto de viragem da psiquitria brasileira do século XIX.* São Paulo: Annablume.

Bourdieu, Pierre. 2005. *As regras da arte: Gênese e estrutura do campo literário.* São Paulo: Companhia das Letras.

Caldwell, Helen. 2002. *O otelo brasileiro de Machado de Assis.* São Paulo: Ateliê Editorial.

Carrara, Ségio. 1996. *Tributo a Vênus.* Rio de Janeiro: Editora Fiocruz.

Costa, Emília Viotti da. 2000. *Da monarquia à república: Momentos decisivos.* São Paulo: Brasiliense.

Faoro, Raymundo. 2001. *Machado de Assis: A pirâmide e o trapézio.* Rio de Janeiro: Globo.

Foucault, Michel. 2004. Michel Foucault, uma entrevista: Sexo, poder e a política da identidade. *Verve* 5: 260–277.

Gledson, John. 2006. *Por um novo Machado de Assis.* São Paulo: Companhia das Letras.

Green, James N. 2000. *Além do carnaval: Homossexualidade masculina no Brasil do século XX.* São Paulo: Editora UNESP.

Guimarães, Hélio Seixas de. 2004. *Os leitores de Machado de Asis: O romance machadiano e o público de leitura no século 19.* São Paulo: Nankin Editorial.

Lara, Oswaldo. 2009. Entre o instinto e a falta de hábito: A psiquiatrização da sexaulidade em Bom Crioulo. Master's thesis, Universidade Federal de São Carlos.

Nunes, Silvia Alexim. 2000. Psicopatologia da feminilidade: Histeria. *O corpo do diabo entre a cruz e a caldeirinha: Un estudo sobre a mulher, o masoquismo e a feminilidade*. Rio de Janeiro: Civilização Brasileira.

Ortega, Francisco. 1999. *Amizade e estética da existência em Michel Foucault*. Rio de Janeiro: Graal.

Piza, Daniel. 2005. *Machado de Assis: Um gênio brasileiro*. São Paulo: Imprensa Oficial.

Rago, Margareth. 1997. *Do cabaré ao lar: A utopia da sociedade disciplinar*. São Paulo: Paz e Terra.

Samara, Eni de Mesquita. 2004. *A família brasileira*. São Paulo: Brasiliense.

Schwarcz, Lilia Moritz, and Angela Marques da Costa. 2007. *1890–1914: No tempo das certezas*. São Paulo: Companhia das Letras.

Schwarz, Roberto. 1997. *Duas Meninas*. São Paulo: Companhia das Letras.

Sedgwick, Eve Kosofsky. 1985. *Between men: English literature and male homosocial desire*. New York: Columbia University Press.

Sedgwick, Eve Kosofsky. 2003. *Touching Feeling: Affect, Pedagogy, Performativity*. Durham: Duke University Press.

Seidman, Steven. 1996. *Queer theory/sociology*. Oxford: Blackwell.

Showalter, Elaine. 1993. *Anarquia sexual*. Rio de Janeiro: Graal Rocco.

PART V

Machado, Allegory, and the Narration of Violence

CHAPTER 14

Machado's Tales of the Fantastic: Allegory and the Macabre

M. Elizabeth Ginway

First gathered in a volume edited by Magalhães Júnior in 1973 and relaunched by Bloch Publishing in 1998, Machado's fantastic stories have been the object of renewed interest by critics and students alike. However, not all of the assessments have been entirely positive. Marcelo Fernandes, for example, characterizes the stories as "quasi-macabre" (2003, 1), since they neither follow the parameters of the gothic horror tale nor incorporate the Todorovian hesitation between the natural and the supernatural explanation of events (Todorov 1973, 44–46). In this chapter, I suggest that three of Machado's macabre stories—"O capitão Mendonça" (Captain Mendonça, 1870), "A vida eterna" (Eternal Life, 1870), and "Os óculos de Pedro Antão" (Pedro Antão's Glasses, 1874)—far from being merely diluted or flawed tales of the macabre, were originally designed to disguise political criticism of Dom Pedro II and his regime. Machado's tales employ the uncanny not to endorse the presence of the supernatural and ghostly, but rather, to unsettle and unnerve, offering depictions of violence, especially in images of the body, and, I argue, the body politic—precisely the kind of abjection that is central to Benjamin's concept of allegory.

In *Ficção e história* (Fiction and History), John Gledson examines the presence of historical allegory in Machado's mature work (1986, 72, 94),

M.E. Ginway (✉)
University of Florida, Gainseville, Florida, USA

© The Editor(s) (if applicable) and The Author(s) 2016
L. Aidoo, D.F. Silva (eds.), *Emerging Dialogues on Machado de Assis*, DOI 10.1057/978-1-137-54174-1_14

so it should come as no surprise that Machado experimented with allegory in his early work as well. For Walter Benjamin, the presence of allegory is set forth in the image of the ruin, which conveys the passage of time and failed moments in history, of which Brazil, with its history of colonialism and slavery, has had no dearth (Stead 2003, 56). Each of Machado's three tales evokes a ruin or other setting associated with the past—an old house in Rio, an aristocratic hall, an abandoned mansion. The stories are also populated with corpses and skulls, mirroring Benjamin's observation that allegory often involves an image of the "death's head," as a result of which "the observer is confronted with the *facies hippocratica* of history as a petrified primordial landscape. Everything about history that, from the very beginning, has been untimely, sorrowful, unsuccessful, is expressed in a face—or rather in a death's head" (1977, 166).

Machado's macabre tales use allegory to contest the official version of history, according to which Dom Pedro was an intellectual, scientifically progressive monarch who unified Brazil and reigned over a peaceful nation from 1840 to 1889. As Bradford Burns summarizes, "Historians praise the honesty, integrity and moderation of Dom Pedro II" (Burns 1980, 215). Following a serious of rebellions during the Regency period (1831–40), Dom Pedro II's rule brought about political unity in the 1840s, reinforced by foreign military victories in the 1850s, establishing the political stability of the Second Empire, which was sustained by the coffee boom. The success of the 1851–52 Guerra do Prata against the dictatorial Argentine leader Juan Manuel de Rosas (1793–1877) served, in part, to consolidate the power of Dom Pedro II, who became an icon of the peaceful, moderate parliamentary monarch and used his moderating power to maintain peace and balance between the liberals and conservatives (Burns 1980, 217–18). However, two events—the Paraguayan War of 1865–70 and the cabinet incident of 1868—tarnished the emperor's reputation when the former, which ended up being far bloodier, longer, and more costly than originally projected, caused the latter when Dom Pedro II upset the balance of power in congress by naming the conservative Itaboraí to head his new cabinet in order to appease Caxias, his faithful commander-in-chief in the Paraguayan War. As Burns notes, by replacing a liberal who was designated to the position in accordance with tradition, Dom Pedro cost the liberals an electoral victory, exposing the weakness of the parliamentary system and provoking outrage among members of the party who viewed the act as a coup (1980, 221). In retaliation, they subsequently demanded direct elections, the expansion of suffrage, an independent judiciary, and steps toward abolition (Carvalho 2007a, 126–7). This period, portrayed in depth in Machado's novel *Quincas Borba* (1891), was characterized by a regime that professed liberty, equality, and progress while refusing to acknowledge its dependence on slavery and privilege (Gledson 1986, 91). Machado's wariness of the misuse of power, science, and secret societies emerges in these stories of the macabre, where they are used to suggest political exclusion and manipulation.

Machado's keen interest in politics has not been overlooked by historians. In an essay discussing the importance of history in Machado's work, Jefferson Cano (1998) revisits several stories and novels that Machado published during the 1870s and 1880s while working at the Agricultural Ministry. Cano shows that Machado used his fiction to portray a broad social array of characters and to demonstrate his engagement with the issues surrounding slavery, especially the Law of the Free Womb of 1871, which granted freedom to children born to slaves as a gradual solution to the central issue facing Brazilian society (1998, 60–61). I suggest that Machado carried out similar, albeit simpler, projects in these earlier fantastic tales of the 1870s, many of which appeared in the women's magazine *Jornal das Famílias* (Family Journal),[1] where he published some 70 stories (Gledson 2006, 37). Many of the apparently arbitrary names, literary figures, dates, and other symbols in these macabre tales actually provide clues to historical and political events.

"O CAPITÃO MENDONÇA" (1870): ROBOTS AND POLITICAL MACHINATIONS

Students of Brazilian science fiction will be interested to know that Machado penned Brazil's first proto-robot story in "O capitão Mendonça," although it eventually turns out, as in many of Machado's stories of the fantastic, that the events are part of a dream. Loosely based on E.T.A. Hoffmann's 1816 "The Sandman," "Captain Mendonça" is the story of a young man named Amaral who is obsessed with an inventor and his invention, a female automaton. The story begins when Amaral accepts an invitation to dine with Captain Mendonça, a friend of his father's who had fought alongside him in the 1851–52 campaign against Rosas. Captain Mendonça's house, with its dark rooms, taxidermied animals, and labs for alchemy experiments and other sinister operations, is reminiscent of gothic horror. Amaral describes the house as having a "purgatorial character" (187),[2] thus casting Mendonça as a Faustian figure whose faraway look, bushy eyebrows, and eccentric manner recall that of a mad scientist. Soon, Amaral meets Augusta, a beautiful, green-eyed female automaton whom Mendonça introduces as his daughter. Eventually, Amaral falls in love with Augusta and proposes marriage. Captain Mendonça consents, but only under the proviso that Amaral undergoes a brain operation to match his intelligence with that of his future wife. When he is immobilized for the operation with Mendonça preparing to perforate his scalp, Amaral suddenly awakens to find that he had fallen asleep while at the São Pedro Theater, where he dreamed the entire episode.

Augusta is an unsettling figure for Amaral, who feels that she is beautiful but strange, at times "smiling maliciously" (187). Her green eyes are the same color as those of a stuffed owl. Captain Mendonça asks if Amaral would like to examine them, and when Amaral assents, Mendonça removes the eyes of his "daughter" for Amaral to inspect. Her face looks like a skull to Amaral: "a living skull, talking, smiling, fixing her two empty sockets on me" (188), yet he is drawn to her despite the deathly image. As mentioned above, this is typical of the allegorical frame. It shows Machado's "de-idealizing, melancholic drive . . . which goes below the surface of the face, in a fascination with what is material and deathly" (Tambling 2010, 112). James Krause claims that Hoffmann's and Machado's "monstrous" females, both of whom feature removable or "enucleated" eyes, evoke Freudian anxieties (2009, 55), but such a reading does not preclude an allegorical one.

The story's allegorical portrait of corruption tied to the monarchy is based on its settings: the São Pedro Theater (recalling the name of the emperor), the Rua da Guarda Velha (Old Guard Street), and the building of the Câmara dos Deputados (Chamber of Deputies). While Sandra Maria Steilein feels that the contrast between the recognizable geographic landmarks of Rio mentioned above and Captain Mendonça's eerie house serves the purpose of creating an uncanny or fantastic atmosphere in the story (1992, 33), their primary purpose may be rather to call attention to the fact that Dom Pedro was supported by the "old guard" and literally meddled in the politics of the Chamber of Deputies, resulting in the electoral loss by liberals in the 1868 scandal.

It is significant that the story makes a number of references to the colors green and yellow—colors associated with Brazil's royal house—which contrast starkly with the otherwise dark setting: the female automaton's eyes are green and her hair is gold; the tablecloth and the eyes of the stuffed owl in the living room are green (186); Amaral sees strange green and yellow lights as he is anaesthetized (202). If Captain Mendonça is an allegory of Dom Pedro II, then the State could be Augusta, his beautiful daughter—an artificial entity that must entice and seduce her suitor, Amaral, who represents the public. Augusta claims, "I am not a bastard daughter. . . . I alone can brag about being a legitimate daughter, because I am the daughter of science and of man's will" (192). Thus, when Mendonça removes Augusta's eyes for Amaral to examine, he momentarily reveals his machinations, as Dom Pedro did in the cabinet affair.

Finally, the idea of the old guard in both theater and politics is also a target of Machado's criticism. Amaral awakens in the theater, cursing ultraromantic dramas, and when he subsequently receives a written invitation from Captain Mendonça to dine at his home, he refuses, suggesting a wariness of the old guard of his father's generation. Perhaps readers should regard Mendonça with suspicion as well, as the shadow side of the emperor, who used the enlightened rhetoric of science and progress to hide coercion. Brazil's first robot story evokes the idea of marionettes whose strings are pulled by the old guard, using the power of science to justify machine politics.

"A VIDA ETERNA" (1870): IMPERIAL MADNESS IN THE DECADENT TEMPLE

Machado's "A vida eterna" is a dress rehearsal of sorts for his best-known tale of the fantastic, "A chinela turca" (The Turkish Slipper), whose first version (1875) was rewritten and published in its definitive form in the collection *Papéis avulsos* (Collected Papers, 1882/1966). Both "A vida eterna" and "A chinela turca" involve a kidnapping and forced marriage under threat of death, and, in both cases, the situation turns out to be a dream. "A vida eterna" begins when a tall man named Tobias appears at the home of a respectable bachelor, 70-year-old Dr. Camilo. Dressed in a green and gold suit—again, the imperial colors—Tobias is described as looking as if he had escaped from the Praia Vermelha (Red Beach) hospital—the popular name of the Hospício de Pedro II mental asylum that was inaugurated in 1852. Tobias forces Dr. Camilo at gunpoint to accompany him to a palace where he will marry a much younger woman, his own daughter Eusébia. Soon after the brief marriage ceremony, his young bride informs Dr. Camilo that she has been forced to serve as bait for a secret cannibalistic society of elders that plans to dine on him that very evening. Bound and transported to a lavishly decorated dining room,

Dr. Camilo listens in horror as the society's members plan his assassination and dismemberment so that he can be fit into an oven to be cooked and eaten, thereby giving them eternal life. When this uncanny experience turns out to be a dream, Dr. Camilo recounts his adventures to his old friend Dr. Vaz, who, in a metafictional touch, recommends that Camilo write it down for the *Jornal das Famílias* so that he can send it personally to the publisher.

Luiz Roncari has speculated about the political meaning of the story in noting that Tobias, who appears dressed in the colors of the Brazilian flag, is logically an allegory of the emperor and recognizing that Machado used allegory in order to avoid being a victim of the imperial censors (2005, 243). Perhaps it is no coincidence that Tobias looks as though he has escaped from the Praia Vermelha asylum, because orthodox conservatives of the political old guard were known as "vermelhos" (reds) (Carvalho 2007a, 126), a color also associated with blood and the feeding motif of Machado's cannibals in the story.

Historian José Murilo de Carvalho quotes an anonymous conservative of the old guard in a pamphlet called "Os partidos" (The Parties) from 1866: "According to this, the liberal and conservative elements were eternal [and] 'represent the two great human forces of political life, reason, which holds it back, and passion, which moves it forward. 'Without the liberal party, the government is an automaton, and without the conservative, it is a precipice" (2007b, 6). In "A vida eterna," Machado critiques this sanguine political perspective. Here the secret society of "reds" cannibalizes the past—hence its preference for septuagenarians such as Dr. Camilo—in an allegory of a decadent and ghoulish body politic.[3] The worshippers even chant, "In the name of the black eagle and the seven children of Septentrion" (111)—an esoteric reference that includes the eagle as an allegory of regal power. While it is known that the emperor was active in Freemason circles—his father served as Grand Master of the order (Gollo 2013, 158)—the story's secret society is of a far darker ilk. The Tobias/Dom Pedro figure and his conservative supporters use the 22-year-old Eusébia—whose age is likely an allegory for the year of Brazil's political independence in 1822—as a means for the regime to justify and sustain itself.

Finally, the architectural features of the setting of the secret ritual reinforce the theme of political decadence (Roncari 2005, 243). The palace has symbols of democracy such as Greek-style Doric columns and statues of the Roman gods Mercury and Minerva. As Tobias cynically explains, "They are emblems, my dear son-in-law: Minerva means Eusébia, standing for knowledge; I am Mercury, representing commerce" (103). Thus, for Tobias, Eusébia represents wisdom that can be used to make money for him and his followers. The main salon features an eagle as part of the frame of a great mirror adorning the central part of the room, but, as Roncari noticed, the eagle—an allegory of imperial authority—is actually made of wood and painted to look like bronze, suggesting a false or ersatz power (2005, 244). As an allegory of the hollow nature of Brazil's imperial power, it portrays a regime that feeds off of the living— perhaps an allusion to slavery—in order to continue to survive. The mirror is also used to great effect in the allegorical story appropriately named "O espelho" (The Mirror, 1882/1986). As Gledson notes, the mirror in Machado's later story dates from 1808, the date of the arrival of the royal family in Brazil, and its frame, now rotten and hollow, is only ornamental, reflecting the dependent, imitative colonial structures of power (2006, 74). While "A vida eterna" does not possess the same semantic richness or literary quality of "O espelho" or "A chinela turca," it nevertheless offers a clear indictment of imperial power. Given its hidden message, Machado recognized that this earlier story was suited for an ephemeral venue like *Jornal das Famílias*, as Dr. Vaz quips in the final line, where it would be safely read as a macabre tale to be enjoyed by a mostly female audience.

"OS ÓCULOS DE PEDRO ANTÃO" (1874): SLAVERY AND A HAUNTED HOUSE

Machado's "Os óculos de Pedro Antão" (Pedro Antão's Glasses) has been characterized as the only one of the author's macabre tales that could be categorized as detective fiction (Fernandes 2003, 9); yet, in my view, it uses detection more for literary and political critique than for solving crimes. Similar to Poe's 1844 "The Purloined Letter," Machado's text centers on a lost letter that is purported to explain the mysterious death of reclusive Pedro Antão and his servant. While Poe's detective, Auguste Dupin, is successful in protecting the royal family from scandal by outwitting his challenger in "The Purloined Letter," Machado's amateur detective, somewhat confusingly also named Pedro, fails to solve any crime, instead inventing a theory that is eventually proven wrong. The key clues on which he bases his theory turn out to have been intentionally planted in order to create a mystery, rather than solve one. However, the details of the intercalated tale based on the false clues—like the dreams of the previous stories—serve to refer to political struggles related to slavery and imperial power as well as to outdated romantic esthetics.

The title of "Os óculos de Pedro Antão" draws attention to a pair of glasses whose green lenses can also be associated with the main color of the flag of Brazil's royal house. Like Poe's dark glasses in "The Purloined Letter," they can be used to hide or reveal the truth about a drama taking place within the royal court. In Poe's story, detective Dupin uses dark glasses to prevent his nemesis from detecting his eye movements as he scans the room to recover the missing letter, which turns out to be hidden in plain sight on the mantle. In Machado's story, Pedro Antão's glasses are left behind as a clue to be deciphered by the amateur detective Pedro, who is a close friend of Antão's nephew and heir, Mendonça. By examining the clues left behind in the house, the narrator, Pedro, plays the role of literary detective in order to explain the mysterious demise of the eccentric Pedro Antão and his servant, who perish in the creepy setting of his home, which has remained unoccupied ever since.

Pedro bases his theory about Antão's death on selected objects left behind in the house: the glasses, a set of books on the occult, a lock of hair, and a rope ladder. In his fictional reconstruction of events, the amateur detective speculates that 40-year-old Antão, ashamed of having fallen in love with 18-year-old Cecília, must have shut himself up in his home in order to dedicate himself to esoteric studies. Further, Cecília continued to pursue him, and he eventually succumbed to her seduction plot, using a rope ladder to reach her room, where she begged him to elope in order to save her from an arranged marriage. However, when Antão discovered that his servant had overheard their plans, he suffocated him and had his body buried by a neighbor the following day. The narrator calls the murdered man Antão's "servant," but the fact that the murder is not considered a crime indicates that, in fact, the man was a slave—a key element in the allegorical interpretation of the story. When Antão went to Cecília's window to elope with her, a mysterious dark figure appeared and saved Antão from being shot by her father. Later, at home, Antão was surprised to discover that his savior was none other than the ghost of his murdered servant. Terrified, he tried to flee, but, held fast by the ghost, he stumbled and took a fatal tumble down the stairs, leaving the glasses behind.

If we consider Machado's text as a variation on Poe's "The Purloined Letter," with its reference to a royal family and the use of doubles, then we have something quite different from a mere critique of romantic drama, which is what Mendonça thinks of Pedro's explanation, accusing his friend of parodying Portuguese poet and playwright Almeida Garrett (1799–1854). In fact, Pedro's invented tale does indeed resemble the life of the Portuguese poet, who, at age 40, ran off with a girl of 17, Adelaide Deville, with whom he had an illegitimate daughter. Her tragic life inspired his 1843 romantic play, *Frei Luís de Sousa* (Friar Luis de Sousa) (Nabais 1995, 25). With its ghosts, murder, and acts of revenge, the play recalls the incidents of the intercalated story in "Os óculos de Pedro Antão." While this literary homage is one form of doubling, Edgar Allan Poe is known for another: he doubles his detective Dupin with his nemesis, the minister D., who share the first letter of their last name (Irwin 1994, 342). Perhaps Machado is engaging in a similar game by repeating the name Pedro in both the narrator and main character of his tale—a stratagem that also calls attention to the given names of both Brazilian emperors, Dom Pedro I and II, which may give us another clue to the story's allegorical ties to Pedro I's legacy and Pedro II's rise to power.

Significantly, the only explicit date mentioned in "Os óculos de Pedro Antão," March 23—the day on which Mendonça is allowed access to his uncle's house—has resonance for the young Dom Pedro II's political ascent. This is the month and day on which the conservatives took power in 1841, beginning the consolidation of Dom Pedro II's regime along conservative lines, supported by the ultra-conservative group called *regresssistas,* who were opposed by the liberals (Silva, 2013, 5). The idea of gaining access to "the old house" and its conservative patriarchal values is similar to themes that Machado would later develop in "Casa velha" (The Old House, 1885/1986), in which a priest gains access to the library of a deceased counselor of Dom Pedro I in order to write about the First Empire. As a historical allegory of Brazil's royal house and the conservative nature of the Brazilian elite, the priest, who expected a more liberal heir, is stunned by the entrenched conservatism of the family (Gledson 1986, 50).

"Os óculos de Pedro Antão" appeared in 1874, three years after the passing of the Law of the Free Womb. This measure, designed as a step toward abolition, gave Dom Pedro II the appearance of being an enlightened liberal monarch while representing only a small concession toward the long-term problem of slavery. In Machado's story, when Antão murders his own servant, he is "saved" by a ghost that ends up indirectly causing his death, perhaps representing how Dom Pedro II, hoping to be saved politically by the Law of the Free Womb, was eventually its victim. As Gledson points out, the law at first appeared to save the regime, but actually brought about the beginning of its demise (1986, 103). In October 1876, in one of Machado's chronicles—newspaper columns that he wrote throughout his life—the author reflects on the five years since the passing of the Law of the Free Womb: "If it had come to pass some thirty years ago, we would be in a different situation. But thirty years ago, the law did not pass, but the slaves certainly continued to come, by contraband, and were sold openly in Valongo" (2009, 24). Here, Machado calls attention to the fact that although the slave trade had been forbidden since 1850, the practice had continued at Rio's Valongo docks. The reference to a 30-year interval since 1871 again calls attention to the year 1841, the year of the consolidation of power by the March 23 government, the date referenced in "Os óculos de Pedro Antão," when Dom Pedro II secured his power.

The final message of "Os óculos de Pedro Antão," however, has nothing to do with the narrator Pedro's theory. As it turns out, the letter written by Antão, once opened, reveals that he had left the clues in his home for amusement only. The uncle had hoped that someone would make up a more exciting story about him in order to cloak the banality of his life, which Pedro certainly did, indirectly using the story to reveal a deeper truth about Brazil's slave-based society. Just as Pedro Antão's letter ultimately offers no simple explanation of the mystery of his death or his servant's, the issue of slavery had no simple solution for Brazil's emperor and the landed elite.

Disguised as titillating tales of the quasi-macabre, Machado's stories incorporate his typical arsenal of metafiction, intertextuality, and references to literature and history, elements that he would continue to refine in his later work. Here, infused with the idea of unresolved political impasses in settings of ruin, the stories emit a sense of failure typical of Benjamin's sense of allegory, of disrupted history, death and loss. "Captain Mendonça" is an allegory that reveals the emperor's political machinations and his desire to manipulate public opinion. "A vida eterna" tells the tale of the leader of a cannibalistic society as an allegory of a political system that has resorted to feeding on the past, rather than attempting to forge new parties, policies, and alliances. "Os óculos de Pedro Antão," with its warning against false appearances and the two deaths at the center of its plot, serves as a reminder that Brazil will be haunted by the ghost of slavery for years to come. In this sense, Machado's work is enriched by Benjamin's concepts of allegory, in tales that "stand outside the chronological narrative of progress that makes up official history" (Tambling 2010, 117), thereby portraying untimely disruptions or discontinuities through uncanny evocations of near-death experiences in "Captain Mendonça" and "A vida eterna" and failed explanations in "Os óculos de Pedro Antão."

Perhaps the reason that Machado's tales do not entirely follow the conventions of the horror genre of the fantastic is precisely their goal of allegorically depicting a political state of affairs. Indeed, they may be read as fictional versions of literary critiques found in Machado's essays "Ideias sobre o teatro" (Ideas on the Theater, 1859/1986) and "Instinto de nacionalidade" (The Instinct of Nationality, 1873/1986). As political allegories related to the imperial regime, what better place to hide them, like Poe's "purloined letter," than in plain sight in the *Jornal das Famílias?*

NOTES

1. Raymundo Magalhães Júnior's 1966 compilations of Machado's early stories, *Contos avulsos* and *Contos Recolhidos*, cite the *Jornal das Famílias* as the source of the three stories examined here.
2. Page numbers for Assis's stories refer to the 1973 edition of *Contos fantásticos de Machado de Assis*, edited by Raymundo Magalhães Júnior. All translations from the Portuguese are mine.
3. It is notable, perhaps, that at the age of 70 in 1870, Dr. Camilo is of the generation of Dom Pedro II's father, Pedro I, who was born in 1798.

REFERENCES

Assis, Joaquim Maria Machado de. 1882/1966. *Contos Avulsos*, ed. Raymundo Magalhães Júnior. Rio de Janeiro: Edições de Ouro.

Assis, Joaquim Maria Machado de. 1973. *Contos fantásticos de Machado de Assis*, ed. Raymundo Magalhães Júnior. Rio de Janeiro: Bloch.

Assis, Joaquim Maria Machado de. 2009. *Crônicas selecionadas: Machado de Assis.* São Paulo: Martin Claret.

Benjamin, Walter. 1977. *The Origin of German Tragic Drama*. Trans. John Osborne. London: New Left Books.

Burns, Bradford. 1980. *The history of Brazil.* New York: Columbia University Press.

Cano, Jefferson. 1998. Machado de Assis, historiador. In *A história contada: Capítulos de história social da literatura no Brasil*, ed. Sidney Chaloub and Leonardo Affonso de Miranda Pereira, 35–66. Rio de Janeiro: Nova Fronteira.

Carvalho, José Murilo de. 2007a. *Dom Pedro II*. São Paulo: Companhia das Letras.

Carvalho, José Murilo de. 2007b. Liberalismo, radicalismo e republicanismo nos anos sessenta do século dezenove, University of Oxford working paper CBS-

87-07. Oxford: Centre for Brazilian Studies. http://www.lac.ox.ac.uk/sites/sias/files/documents/WP87-murilo.pdf

Fernandes, Marcelo. 2003. Machado de Assis: Quase Macabro. *Poesis-Literatura, Pensamento e Arte* 85 (April). http://www.netterra.com.br/poiesis/85/machado_de_assis.htm

Gledson, John. 1986. *Ficção e história*. Trans. Sônia Coutinho. Rio de Janeiro: Paz e Terra.

Gledson, John. 2006. *Por um novo Machado de Assis: Ensaios*. São Paulo: Companhia das Letras.

Gollo, Rodney Rhodes. 2013. The birth of a new political philosophy: Religion and positivism in nineteenth-century Brazil. In *Latin American positivism: New historical and philosophical essays*, ed. Greg Gilson, Irving Levinson, and Eduardo Mendieta, 153–167. Lanham: Lexington Books.

Irwin, John T. 1994. *Mystery to a solution: Poe, Borges and the analytic detective story*. Baltimore: Johns Hopkins University Press.

Krause, James R. 2009. Enucleated eyes in 'Sem olhos' and 'O capitão Mendonça' by Machado de Assis. In *Border crossings: Boundaries of cultural interpretation*, ed. Pablo Martínez Diente and David Wiseman, 51–63. Nashville: Vanderbilt University Press.

Nabais, Palmira. 1995. *Introduction to Frei Luís de Sousa*. Lisbon: Biblioteca Ulisseia.

Roncari, Luiz. 2005. Machado de Assis: O aprendizado do escritor e o esclarecimento de Mariana. *Revista Brasileira de História* 25(50): 241–258.

Silva, Regina Felix da. 2013. Revoltas liberais no início do Segundo Reinado: Francisco de Salles Torres: Homem, imprensa e política. Paper presented at the *XXVII Simpósio Nacional de História*, Natal, Rio Grande do Norte, July 22–26. http://www.snh2013.anpuh.org/resources/anais/27/1364528647_ARQUIVO_TextoAnpuh2013.pdf

Stead, Naomi. 2003. The value of ruins: Allegories of destruction in Benjamin and Speer. *Form/Work: An Interdisciplinary Journal of the Built Environment* 6: 51–64.

Steilein, Sandra Maria. 1992. 'O capitão Mendonça': Um conto fantástico de Machado de Assis. *Travessia* 25(1): 32–39.

Tambling, Jeremy. 2010. *Allegory*. London: Routledge.

Todorov, Tzvetan. 1973. *The Fantastic: A Structural Approach to a Literary Genre*. Trans. Richard Howard. Cleveland: Case Western University.

CHAPTER 15

Machado de Assis and the Secret Heart of Literature

Paulo Moreira

Machado de Assis's short story "A causa secreta" was first published on the front and second pages of the Saturday edition of the *Gazeta de Notícias* on August 1, 1885. This was the last of four years of remarkable output in Machado de Assis's short fiction production—no less than 67 new stories were published in various venues between 1882 and 1885. "A causa secreta" passed Machado de Assis's own rigorous selection[1] and was featured with a few minor revisions in the first edition of *Várias histórias* in 1896.

In the English-speaking world, "A causa secreta" has enjoyed notable prominence, having been translated twice by reputable English-language scholars, one on each side of the Atlantic. In 1963, Helen Caldwell's translation "The Secret Heart" appeared in the anthology *The Psychiatrist and Other Stories*[2] (1963, 66–75), and her translation features nowadays in the *Oxford Anthology of the Brazilian Short Story* (2006, 68–74), edited by K. David Jackson. In 2008, John Gledson retranslated the story, now entitled "The Hidden Cause," and included it in his anthology *Chapter of Hats: Selected Stories*, published by Bloomsbury in the United Kingdom.

I have used both versions in the classroom and carefully compared them to the original in Portuguese. Caldwell and Gledson differ mainly in the diction with which they approach Machado's prose. Caldwell leans toward a slightly more formal and wordier rendering of Machado, possibly to

P. Moreira (✉)
Yale University, New Haven, Connecticut, USA

© The Editor(s) (if applicable) and The Author(s) 2016
L. Aidoo, D.F. Silva (eds.), *Emerging Dialogues on Machado de Assis*, DOI 10.1057/978-1-137-54174-1_15

suggest the sense of a nineteenth-century text, removed (but not too far) from mid-twentieth-century readers—hence, for instance, her decision to render the title of the story as "The Secret Heart."[3] Gledson prefers a less formal, more direct translation, avoiding, as much as possible, significant changes in the syntax and wording, as seen in his translation of the title. In the passages I quote here, neither translator outperformed the other consistently and I decided to use bits of both translations, choosing the one that seemed closest to Machado's meaning and style.

In several aspects, "A causa secreta" is typical of Machado de Assis. There is the familiar, understated motif of an ambitious young man from the lower classes having to negotiate favors and compromises in order to ascend socially. Then, there is his (and our) gradual realization that the peculiar chain of events triggered by his ascension leads to an ironic fate, a set of impossible conundrums that pit interests and their justifications against stated principles and desires. In the presentation of this under-stated tragic drama, there is, in "A causa secreta" (as in many other stories by Machado), a subtle but insidious choreography of carefully calibrated, shifting times, points of view, and narrative voices that gently but firmly lead the unsuspecting reader to become more and more closely involved with the story and its complex characters, affecting our reading experience as well as our understanding of the story.

All these typical traces point to "A causa secreta" as the story of Garcia, the young medical graduate from whose perspective the story is told for the most part. Garcia is an ambitious man with a particular obsession: a penchant for what could be called analytic voyeurism (explained below). His ambitions and inclinations slowly drag the young doctor into tragic circumstances that affect him deeply, finally turning him into the object of someone else's gaze in a painful inversion: the observer becomes the observed. This retelling of "A causa secreta" is true to a certain extent, but paraphrases of Machado de Assis tend to fall short because, as a classic quote by Alceu Amoroso Lima warns us, Machado "writes more between the lines than on the lines,…suggests more than he says,…evokes more than manifests,…and…never writes without an ulterior motive" (quoted in Assis 1963, viii).

Taking the cautionary advice of Tristão de Ataide (Alceu Amoroso Lima's famous pseudonym) to heart, I thought of deploying a subtle analytical tool in my reading of "A causa secreta." In his "Tesis sobre el cuento" (2014, 103–37), Ricardo Piglia suggests that every short story is actually composed of two distinct but intimately connected accounts. These two accounts differ, among other ways, in that one is visible while the other is a secret account that is elliptic and fragmentary. The two accounts share the short story's essential chain of events, but those take on different meanings when placed in each account.

In "A causa secreta," these two narrative strains are the account of Garcia's professional rise and sentimental fall and the account of Fortunato's true life, his "secret heart" or "hidden cause." Following Piglia's lead, we must understand the two accounts and then pursue the links between them to unveil the foundations of the story's structure.

To understand Fortunato a little better, it might help to look at the significance of placing the main events of "A causa secreta" between 1860 and 1862. Machado almost always gives us specific years and names of streets and neighborhoods in Rio de Janeiro without further explanation, trusting a shared knowledge he had with his first readers—a contextual knowledge that we are wise to recover. 1862 is the year that large European banks (mostly British) began operating in Rio de Janeiro. According to Luiz Carlos Soares (2007, 32), this was a time of sudden expansion of investment in the city, with the dislocation of capital caused by the pro- hibition of the slave trade in 1850. This expansion would culminate in a crash in 1864 that led to dozens of bankruptcies and weakened the posi- tion of domestic financiers, consolidating the dominance of foreign banks.

In congruence with the etymology of his name and with his situation as a well-off capitalist comfortably placed in the upscale neighborhood of Catumbi[4] in a fast-growing Rio de Janeiro, Fortunato is one of those characters for whom the asymmetry between the inner and the outer life that plagues so many of Machado's characters is resolved in what is (for him) a felicitous arrangement. There is simply no discrepancy between what Fortunato wants to do and what he can do: he manages to indulge his sadistic voyeurism more or less freely, from beginning to end in the story, making him a precursor of Rubem Fonseca's monstrous capitalists who haunt readers with their sadistic desires for revenge in the absence of any perceived need for compensation and with complete impunity in sto- ries such as "Night Drive" (2008, 7–9) and "Placebo" (1995, 95–105).

We can now attempt another retelling of "A causa secreta," also bound to fall short if taken in isolation, but effective in adding another layer to the story. *In medias res*, we suddenly see a theatrical tableau in which the main characters of the story appear in awkward silence. The clock rolls back a couple of years, so we can understand the reasons for this awkward silence. We follow Garcia's eyes as he meets Fortunato and his wife, Maria Luisa. We move forward until we revisit the tableau of the opening scene, when we watch Garcia watch Fortunato slowly torture a rat—arguably, the story's first climax. Then, with the mystery of Fortunato figured out, the second account of "A causa secreta," which had flowed underground until this point, comes to the surface with full force. Now the narrator swiftly turns the denouement into rising action and brings us to a second climax at the very end of the story, when the point of view is finally reversed and the second account comes to full fruition.

Antonio Candido singles out "A causa secreta" as part of "the most frightening and most lucid Machado de Assis" (1995, 37) because the story unveils the sadism in relationships in which "man turned into an object of other men practically falls to the level of a violated animal."[5] But it is important to add that, in this case, the subjection carried out by the capitalist is not only in the name of pure selfish calculated interest. What Alfredo Bosi writes with regard to the female protagonists in Machado's novels is pertinent for the male protagonists of "A causa secreta": Garcia and Fortunato "would fall into the one-sided condition of calculating types" (1999, 21) were they not driven by the passions that provide their pursuits "impetus and gusto." Their passions—Paul Dixon calls them obsessions (1992, 58)—drive the two completing and complementary accounts that structure "A causa secreta." Machado is most frightfully lucid in this story because in the imbrication of Garcia's and Fortunato's accounts (in the overlapping of their passions), he eventually implicates the narrator and his readers in the perverse game of sadistic voyeurism that derives pleasure from the objectification of the Other.

Garcia and Fortunato are obsessed with looking. Accordingly, looking and being looked at are ubiquitous in "A causa secreta." There are 50 instances in the story in which mostly verbs (*ver, olhar, observar, assistir, vigiar, mirar, velar*,and so on), but also nouns (*olho, olhos, vista*) refer to the act of looking or being looked at. The centrality and ubiquityof the protagonists is only natural since, at first, we have a series of encounters in which Garcia dissects and deciphers Fortunato's every movement; since what Fortunato does is to look intently at others. Garcia subsequently finds himself no longer as looking subject, but as dissected, deciphered object by an eerily blissful Fortunato at Maria Luisa's funeral at the end of the story. The fact remains that Garcia and Fortunato are consummate voyeurs, although we can differentiate between their modes of *scopophilia* (Freud's favored term, from the Greek *skopeo*, meaning to watch, to see). They are voyeurs motivated by different fundamental driving instincts, their obsessions triggered by different longings to see different things. Garcia wants to analyze human nature to its core; Fortunato wants to marvel at the aesthetic beauty of sheer suffering. The doctor is driven by the knowledge instinct (*libido sciendi*) and obsesses over the mysterious Fortunato; the capitalist is driven by a particular perversion of the mastery and pleasure instincts and takes pleasure (*libido sentienti*) in watching other beings in pain.

Garcia oscillates between contradictory affects (relish and disgust) as he stalks Fortunato, the object of his libido. The disgust comes from an ominous intuition of what Fortunato's cold, indifferent demeanor signifies, but it is supplanted by the doctor's "love of analysis" and the supreme pleasure of moral vivisection, signified in an array of verbs indicating invasive, destructive investigation that appear, respectively, in Machado, Caldwell, and Gledson: *decifrar*/decipher/decipher, *decompor*/unravel/examine, and *penetrar*/penetrate/cut through in order to *apalpar*/touch/feel.[6]

At first, Fortunato's fundamental difference from Garcia is his sadism. Citing Greimas's semiotic study "Del Cólera" (1989), Pietroforte introduces his anthology of Brazilian sadomasochist fiction (which includes "A causa secreta"), defining the self-sufficient character of sadistic punishment: "Although punishment originates from revenge and retribution against other people's faults, it does not require these relations, since the sadistic act is an end in itself." (2008, 17)[7] No cholera, no need for reparation, no revenge: Fortunato's acts lack what Greimas, in his peculiar wording, calls "power of anaphorization" (1989, 278). In Fortunato's pursuits of scopophiliac pleasure, moral layers are replaced by living tissue, and the focus shifts from the hidden secrets of someone's secret heart to the visible surface of physical pain. The appreciation of suffering as pure form is an experience of unalloyed aesthetic pleasure devoid of empathy. Fortunato watches people and animals in physical pain with "a vast pleasure, quiet and profound" (Assis 2008, 176) and his experience is defined as "something like a pure aesthetic sensation." He is, thus, a sadistic voyeur, described by Machado's narrator as "uma redução de Calígula," (Assis 2008, 176) a curious phrase that is worth examining carefully.

Both Caldwell and Gledson render "uma redução de Calígula" similarly, as "miniature Caligula" (Caldwell) and "Caligula in miniature" (Gledson), indicating that Fortunato is a small-scale replica of the notorious Roman emperor. But the original term has possible additional meanings. It is not a matter of a mistranslation but of an untranslatable, irreducible difference in the transit between different languages.[8] There remains the fact that Machado chose specifically "redução de Calígula" and not "miniatura de

Calígula" in the original Portuguese. Thus I felt compelled to explore "the networks to which the word belongs" (2014. xvii).

"Redução de Calígula" was indeed a careful choice on Machado's part that marks one of the most significant changes in "A causa secreta" from 1885 to 1896. In 1885, the narrator calls Fortunato a "Calígula abortado" (aborted Caligula): someone who stopped short of the grandiloquent and spectacular sadism of the Roman emperor whose four-year reign was turned by Suetonius into an epitome of cruelty. It is as if Fortunato's monstrous desires had positively been restrained by civilization in Rio de Janeiro in the 1860s. Anyone familiar with Machado's view of the power of any civilization (much less the slave-based civilization of Imperial Rio de Janeiro) to quickly and positively restrain human desires understands why the phrase "aborted Caligula" ends up replaced. In 1892 Machado echoes instead one of his most famous characters, Quincas Borba, in his brief appearance in *Memórias Póstumas de Brás Cubas* (first published in the*Revista Brasileira* before "A causa secreta," in 1880). The philosopher explains his *humanitas* to Brás Cubas using two phrasal variations of *redução* in the same paragraph: "Nota que eu não faço do homem um simples veículo de Humanitas; não, ele é ao mesmo tempo veículo, cocheiro e passageiro; ele é o *Humanitas reduzido*; daí a necessidade de adorar-se a si próprio. (…) Sendo cada homem uma *redução de Humanitas*, é claro que nenhum homem é fundamentalmente oposto a outro homem, quaisquer que sejam as aparências contrárias" ["Note that I do not posit man as a simple vehicle of *Humanitas*; rather, he is simultaneously vehicle, driver, and passenger; he is *Humanitas reduced*; hence the need to adore 'himself'…Being that every man is a *reduction of Humanitas*, it is clear that no man is the fundamental opposition of another, regardless of their possible differences in appearance."] (2015, 237; italics added, my translation).

Here, the term "reduced" seems to approximate its use in the culinary arts: making a thickened, intensified version of a concoction by boiling it to evaporate the liquid. In concentrated form, Fortunato is vehicle, coachman, and passenger of what Caligula symbolizes; Fortunato drives and is driven by the cruelty principle he embodies in intimate, intensified form. Instead of the universal every man and the abstract humanitas, "A causa secreta" makes use of the noun *redução* to describe one very particular man (Fortunato) and the concept of cruelty embodied in the figure of Caligula. Indeed, *redução* means miniature, but it also carries a more restricted meaning related to the study of the evolution of word forms from Latin to Portuguese. This meaning, with which Machado was probably familiar, refers to a series of shortenings occurring over time, for instance, by elision or haplology (the elimination of redundant syllables).[9] These are metaplasms, traces of old word forms in the language as it nowadays presents itself to us phonologically as well as orthographically, the inescapable accumulation of minute differences over time, which changes language because of usage in spite of grammar and other prescriptive attempts to congeal it into stable sameness.

It is time to contrast Garcia's and Fortunato's obsessions to integrate everything we have examined so far. There should be a distinction between sadism, in general, and sadistic voyeurism, in particular. Since the beginning, when Garcia watches Fortunato watching violent scenes in the theater, it is clear that Fortunato derives pleasure from looking at either actual or imaginary pain, inflicted on human beings as well as animals. When Fortunato personally inflicts pain on animals (stray dogs on the way home, cats and dogs he vivisects, and finally, the rat he mangles and burns), he does it primarily in order to watch them suffer. This becomes clear in the climax of the story, when we watch Garcia watching Fortunato following the rat's pain with a gaze of frightening intensity.[10] In Fortunato's case as well as Garcia's, affects take precedence over effects and passive observation takes precedence over action.

Fortunato's strain of sadistic voyeurism is particularly disturbing because it remains, at all times, firmly within strict boundaries of acceptability. Fortunato's delight in cruelty does not require action on his part because of its passive, voyeuristic bent. It is a disinterested aesthetic pleasure in the pain of others, rather than a direct engagement in the infliction of pain. Furthermore, there is an important distinction between Fortunato's role in the suffering inflicted on animals and in the suffering inflicted on humans. Direct violence against animals occurs at least twice, in addition to the slow dismemberment and cauterization of the rat in Fortunato's study: he gratuitously beats stray dogs with his cane and make experiments on cats and dogs. In his dealings with human beings, however, Fortunato remains in the role of passive observer rather than active participant in the infliction of pain. That is why Fortunato is particularly disturbing: unlike the series of frightening serial killers paraded tirelessly on television and in cinemas, Machado's sadist never crosses the line that would turn him into a criminal, and thus, he acts with complete impunity. Everything stays within strict limits: he watches the bloody staging of a theatrical play and assists with the treatment of various sick people, and although he may watch in delight the deathly sickness of his own wife, he makes sure she gets the best possible treatment. Here, the power of Fortunato's obsession is notable: not even the indignation of a proud man who realizes he may have been cuckolded trumps his pleasure in watching pain. Whatever the object of his single-minded gaze, the Machadian masks effortlessly cover the sadistic voyeur's face: he becomes a fan of bloody theatrical melodramas, the devoted selfless caretaker of strangers, the dilettante in the art of experimental surgical therapies, the businessman outraged at the damage done by a rat nibbling on his papers, and even the doting husband zealously guarding his wife suffering from tuberculosis.

Garcia's and Fortunato's voyeuristic manifestations may be different, but they are both voyeurs nonetheless, with two forms of libido: Fortunato seeks sentient pleasure derived from concrete form in physical pain while Garcia seeks cognitive pleasure derived from subjective content in spiritual complexity. We more readily accept Garcia's voyeurism when he stalks Fortunato because it is very close to our own as readers, but we are particularly disturbed when the narrator surreptitiously leads us to see the connection between the two forms of voyeurism espoused by the partners in business and in love. Taking Piglia's terms, when the secret account, which is elliptic and fragmentary, bursts into the surface of the more visible account of events, the stories of these two voyeurs approximate them (the voyeurs) to the narrator, and especially, to the reader. Silviano Santiago locates the connection between literary, sadistic, and analytic voyeurisms: "Garcia's sensation— one Other—before the killing of the rat and Fortunato's sensation—another Other—before the kiss the doctor steals from the dead wife are tied to the sensations of each and every reader of the short story or spectator of the two scenes. They are all related by the textual verb of Machado de Assis...to savor" (2008, 202).[11]

Although most instances in which verbs and phrases referring to looking are related to the two protagonists, three of them—*vemos, vimos, note-se*[we see, we saw, notice]—significantly are addressed to the narrator and readers. The pleasure of reading is as Garcia's "pleasure, than which he knew no greater" and Fortunato's "inward savoring of the most exquisite sensation." In all these voyeurisms, the other is *reduced* to an object, which becomes the source of egotistic pleasure. In this reduction lies the link between the desire to see (scopophilia) and the desire to subjugate (sadism). As long as the objectification remains firmly in place of the Other, the voyeur subject, immersed in aesthetic or cognitive libido, feels comfortably insulated from emotional involvement. Lacking the cold objectivity of the savvy capitalist, Garcia bursts his own protective bubble of voyeurism and exposes himself to heartbreaking pain. Thus, the watching subject that dominates the point of view in most of "A causa secreta" becomes, in the end, the observed, reduced object of Fortunato's pleasure. And why should we stop there? Fortunato is himself reduced to a miniature of Caligula by the narrator, who has waited 23 years to tell the story in order to serve his readers voyeuristic pleasure.

Following in the footsteps of Augusto Meyer, who compared Machado's corrosive sarcasm to Dostoyevsky's and even called Machado's mature fiction "his exercise of literary sadism" (1958, 23), Alfredo Bosi singles out "A causa secreta" as exemplary of a strain of cruelty that traverses the smooth and cool surface of Machado's prose: "The gentle Machado can be cruel in extremely abrasive short stories such as 'A causa secreta,' 'The Nurse,' 'Pilades and Orestes,' 'The Cane,' and 'Father versus Mother' I find in these stories extremes of human nature and society stitched together with the threads of evil. In 'A causa secreta' this evil is congenital: Fortunato possesses, as the fortune his name brings within, a malignant character; and we must accept unreservedly that here Machado de Assis openly gazes at the Death Drive" (1982, 454–55). When Machado, his characters, and his readers find pleasure in these "extremely abrasive" stories, are we not entranced by the same Death Drive? Are we not cruel as well?

Machado's approach to what Bosi calls "congenital evil" is the result of his peculiar artistic temperament. Once again, Bosi is its most eloquent critic: for Machado, there is neither utopia, nor conformity; he proposes nothing, expects nothing, and believes in nothing. But he also refuses to hide, obscure, or gloss over the evils of his world. Instead of the loud accents of the gothic or the grotesque or the pornographic, Machado creates in characters such as Fortunato subdued, discreet, almost undetectable monsters and becomes a master manipulator of his readers, imbued with a relentless critical temperament that refuses to let us remain comfortably uninvolved voyeurs. Machado's readers end up like Garcia: they find themselves intimately touched, no longer invulnerable to the dangers described in the stories, turned into the objects of an eerie narrative voice that regards them with "the same tin plates, hard and cold" as Fortunato.

We have yet to deploy one more sophisticated tool to grasp Machado's reach in "A causa secreta." Avoiding moralism as well as mere iconoclastic indifference to moral matters with remarkable critical acumen, Susan Sontag approaches what she calls the "pornographic imagination" as the literary use of the "most extreme forms of consciousness that transcend social personality or psychological individuality" (2013, 44), in which what matters is the "originality, thoroughness, authenticity and power of that 'deranged consciousness' itself, as it is incarnated in a work" (2013, 46). Unless we are willing to reduce the arts to moral or political pedagogy, there is no reason to think such forms of extreme consciousness should not find artistic expression. Beyond that recognition, the power of "A causa secreta" lies in the subtle way the story implicates everyone, including the reader, in its web of quiet, perverted savoring. Besides the discomfort of eventually being placed in the position of the observed subject as Garcia was, at the end of a complex labyrinth of voyeuristic mirrors, we readers find our own faces and feel we have also become brothers of the monster, our eyes also glued on the page, our eyes also "the same tin plates, hard and cold."

Active and passive roles in the same game set the exhibitionist apart from the scopophiliac as well as the sadist from the masochist. Sontag mentions the frequent existence of a "still center in the midst of outrage" (2013, 51), which is Fortunato in "A causa secreta." He is calmly following his single-minded pursuit of aesthetic pleasure in the observation of pain while serving himself as a spectacle for Garcia the stalker. Thus Garcia is slowly dragged into Fortunato's family and business life in the doctor's pursuit of cutting through the moral layers to unveil Fortunato's secret heart. Garcia's analytical voyeurism places him in a role similar to the detective, a popular literary figure since the nineteenth century. By the time Garcia finally detects Fortunato's secret cause (heart), he has been ensnared in a triangular relationship with Fortunato and his wife. Troubled as he is by the increasingly complicated ethical circumstances of his relationship with them, Garcia seems to control the action but is, in fact, fundamentally inactive, observing Fortunato and Maria Luísa and doing nothing until she dies. He is emphatically summoned into Fortunato's house and almost forced into a business partnership with the capitalist, under the disapproving eyes of the wife. Garcia's feelings of tenderness are somehow sadistic, aroused by Maria Luisa's helplessness: "her life of spiritual loneliness...somehow...increased her loveliness" (72), but predictably, Garcia, the voyeur, decides that "it was necessary to observe her." Only at the end does Garcia act: he cannot help kissing Maria Luisa's dead body. A paranoid reading of "A causa secreta" could certainly propose that Fortunato plotted Garcia's life since their first encounter, exploiting the young man's perhaps homoerotic curiosity about him since their first encounter in a less than reputable section of Rio de Janeiro's downtown.[12]

Sontag writes persuasively about the way Sade and his fellow literary pornographers upset the romantic tradition that attributes to our natural instincts a congenital or original goodness:

> Now, what's decisive in the complex of views held by most educated members of the community is the assumption that human sexual appetite is, if untampered with, a natural pleasant function; and that "the obscene" is a convention, the fiction imposed upon nature by a society convinced that there is something vile about the sexual functions, and by extension, about sexual pleasure. It's just these assumptions that are challenged by the French tradition represented by Sade, Lautréamont, Bataille and the authors of *Story of O* and *The Image*. Their assumption seems to be that "the obscene" is a primal notion of human consciousness, something much more profound than the backwash of a sick society's aversion to the body. (221)

In "A causa secreta," Machado brings forth a safe, pedestrian version of watching and an obsession for observation as an expression of human curiosity and cruelty toward the other. Cruelty in observing as well as in representing is an important component of the literary trade. Writers exercise such cruelty both when observing life around them and looking for material for their fiction as well as when writing and subjecting characters to all sorts of atrocities and pain. In an interview, William Faulkner jokingly explained, "If a writer has to rob his mother, he will not hesitate; the 'Ode on a Grecian Urn' is worth any number of old ladies." Machado is a writer particularly capable of great cruelty, both in observing as well as in representing. It may be true that Machado, a daft ironist who avoided hypocrisy, usually cloaked his implacable cruelty in a smooth and very subtle English sense of humor. Nevertheless, the cruelty, which he may have seen in the world around him, is also a dominant presence in many of his works.

At the end of the story, Garcia becomes the object of pleasurable observation, pleasure derived from observing the young doctor in pain, pleasure that supersedes even the wounded pride of the widower who realizes that his business partner was in love with his dead wife. More than business and sentimental partners, Garcia and Fortunato are complementary voyeurs. They seek pleasure from looking at others. Together, these pleasures—the purely analytic one in the case of Garcia and purely aesthetic one in the case of Fortunato—reflect the pleasures of a literary author who cleverly submits his all-too-human characters to all sorts of physical and psychological literary pains. These pleasures also echo the pleasures of Machado's readers, who relish following his pen as it cuts through moral layers and exposes the living heart of his characters.

The carefully described scenes of torture and pain in "A causa secreta" associate this short story with the morbid darkness of Edgar Allan Poe.[13] The emphatic representation of cruelty has become only too familiar in our contemporary culture, marked by subgenres such as splatter, gore, or even torture porn, but Machado points to something that most of these forms carefully avoid facing: the role of the author and of the reader in the sadistic relationships engendered in literary texts. In his remarkable analysis of "A causa secreta," Paul Dixon may have been the first to point out the insufficiency of dealing with this short story as a psychological study, and he writes that the story "refers not only to Fortunato's sadism, but also to an even more obscure secret—to the idea that Fortunato has accomplices, and that those exist within and beyond the fictional world of the short story" (1992, 67, my translation).[14]

Teresa Cristófani Barreto draws an interesting parallel between the sadism with which the Cuban writer Virgilio Piñera submits his narrators to torture and dismemberment and the scenes of Fortunato's sadism, which "Machado describes with millimetric precision and intense style" (2005, 33). In this comparison, it becomes evident that every ritual of literary sadomasochism includes author, narrator, and readers as partners in the pleasurable enjoyment of the moral or physical dismemberment of narrators and characters. We follow Machado's sinuous and deceptive narrative choreography until we discover the disturbing link between the instinct of knowledge and the instinct of mastery, which is also the disturbing link between any form of literary representation and cruelty. This is the hidden cause of Machado's short story, its "secret heart," which comes to the surface when we look at the two accounts contained in it. Machado and his readers take pleasure in dissecting characters to the core. Garcia stands for Machado as well as for his readers: we are all analytic voyeurs, driven by the knowledge instinct in performing and watching our own literary vivisections. Fortunato stands for what none of us would like to accept: that we are also sadistic voyeurs and that there is thirst for cruelty in our hunger for knowledge.

Antonio Candido notes that the "long and terrible" description of torture in "A causa secreta" "escapes Machado's usual discreet, synthetic habits" (1995, 36). More than noting the deviance, we should ask ourselves about its implications. In "A causa secreta," Machado briefly adopts blunter instruments while flashing the sharp teeth of his narratives.

Machado had little interest in extraordinary or abnormal phenomena that could be comfortably looked at from a convenient distance. His sharp critical focus centered on the human miseries that could be fallany of us. Heroes and villains are occasional or even accidental, simply average people in ordinary situations faced with difficult decisions that betray the fragilities of human nature. The reader, whom Machado's narrators so often addressed, was his primary target.

NOTES

1. According to the Mauro Rosso's research published in 2008, only 76 of the 226 short stories published by Machado de Assis in magazines and newspapers were selected for publication in book form by the author.
2. William L. Grossman translated half of the short stories and wrote the introduction to that volume.
3. The expression "causa secreta" appears in *Memorial de Aires*, where it is translated by Caldwell as "the secret motive": "The secret motive of an action many a times escapes the sharpest eyes, not to mention mine, which with age have lost their natural sharpness" (Assis 1972, 133–34). [A causa secreta de um ato escapa muita vez a olhos agudos, e muito mais aos meus que perderam com a idade a natural agudeza (Assis 1908, 185)]. In the above passage, the narrator wonders about the reason for Fidélia's sudden change, quietly concentrating on her painting rather than joining the conversation, as she had done before Tristão arrived.
4. Catumbi was one of the neighborhoods to the west of Rio de Janeiro's city center that received the upper classes fleeing from downtown after independence (Soares 2007, 25–31). The neighborhood appears in several of Machado's works, generally connoting the suburb where the upper middle class lives in *chácaras* (suburban houses surrounded by land). Most famously, in *Memorias póstumas de Brás Cubas,* in 1869, Brás Cubas dies in Catumbi at two o'clock in the afternoon on a Friday in August, "na minha bela chácara" (in my beautiful chácara). Viana and his sister Lívia from *Ressureição*, Luis da Cunha Vilela (Soares's uncle) in "Luis Soares," and the bacharel Duarte in "A chinela turca" also live in Catumbi. In 1860, Andrade buys a house in Catumbi for Marocas in "Singular ocorrência," and in 1874, Joaninha and Cândida meet there in "A inglesinha Barcelos." This is one of the many instances in which I could not help but feel a certain affinity between Machado's Rio de Janeiro and Balzac's Paris.
5. In the original in Portuguese, "O Machado de Assis mais terrível e mais lúcido" and "o homem transformado em objeto do homem cai praticamente no nível do animal violentado."

6. This important passage reads in the original in Portuguese, "o regalo, que dizia ser supremo, de penetrar muitas camadas morais até apalpar o segredo de um organismo" (124–25). Caldwell translates "segredo de un organismo" as "the secret heart of an organism" (70), which gives her the title for her translation. In this passage, Caldwell also strays a bit from the original—within reasonable boundaries—when she renders "camadas morais" as "spiritual strata."

7. In the original in Portuguese, "enquanto os castigos são oriundos de vinganças e reparações de faltas, o sadismo não depende dessas relações, uma vez que o ato sádico se completa em si mesmo."

8. Emily Apter develops a very interesting analysis of comparativism around the term "untranslatable" in her *Against World Literature: On the Politics of Untranslatability* (2013, 32–33). The untranslatable appears as a working concept in *Dictionary of Untranslatables: A Philosophical Lexicon*, a monumental project organized by Barbara Cassin. Cassin's book is an attempt to bring a new perspective on the history of European philosophy by creating "a latter-day version of the humanist *translation studii* and 'a cartography of philosophical differences'" (32). As a rather ironic aside, it should be noted that the French title of Cassin's book was *Vocabulaire européen des philosophies: Dictionnaire des intraduisibles* and that Apter renames Cassin's book in order to de-emphasize its overt Eurocentric focus.

9. A derived meaning of reduction in the linguistic sense has also been used in translation studies. See "Explicitation and implicitation" in Ralph Krüger's *The Interface between Scientific and Technical Translation Studies and Cognitive Linguistics: With Particular Emphasis on Explicitation and Implicitation as Indicators of Translational Text-Context Interaction* (221–74).

10. Alfredo Bosi (1982, 455) points to how a similar scene inspires the sonnet "Suavi Mari Magno," published in Machado de Assis's last poetry volume, *Ocidentais*, in 1901. In the sonnet, every passerby stops to watch a poisoned dog in its agony "as if watching the suffering/gave them joy" [como se lhe desse gozo/Ver padecer"] (my translation). Paul Dixon also notes that in *Dom Casmurro*, there is a similar scene, in which a mouse agonizes in a cat's mouth while Ezequiel watches in fascination (1992, 59).

11. In the original in Portuguese, "A sensação de Garcia—um outro—diante do sacrifício do rato e a sensação de Fortunato—um outro—diante do beijo roubado pelo médico à esposa morta se atam as sensações de todo e qualquer leitor do conto ou espectador das duas cenas. Estão irmanados todos pelo verbo textual de Machado de Assis...saborear."

12. In "solidariedade do aborrecimento humano," Silviano Santiago plays with the possible homoerotic connotations of the relationship between Garcia

and Fortunato by subtly suggesting a parallel between the many encounters of the two men in the streets of Rio de Janeiro and the rituals of homosexual cruising.

13. Fortunato is the name of the antagonist who gets buried alive behind a brick basement wall in Edgar Allan Poe's "The Cask of Amontillado." Machado was the first in Brazil to translate "The Raven" from the English and singled out Poe among his favorite short story writers in his small preface called "Advertência" to his collection *Várias Histórias* in 1896. "A causa secreta" shows Machadoand Poe's shared common interests and similar approach, even though they are writers of very different temperament. Renata Philippov (2011) has studied the relation between the two authors.

14. In the original in Portuguese, "se refere não somente ao sadismo de Fortunato, como também a um segredo ainda mais obscuro—à idéia de que Fortunato tem cúmplices, e que estes existem dentro e fora do mundo fictício do conto."

References

Apter, Emily. 2013. *Against world literature: On the politics of untranslatability.* New York: Verso.

Assis, Joaquim Maria Machado de. 1885. A causa secreta. *Gazeta de Notícias*, August 1. http://memoria.bn.br/DocReader/DocReader.aspx?bib=103730_02&PagFis=8993&Pesq=

Assis, Joaquim Maria Machado de. 1896. *Várias Histórias.* Rio de Janeiro: Laemmert.

Assis, Joaquim Maria Machado de. 1908. *Memorial de Ayres.* Rio de Janeiro: Garnier.

Assis, Joaquim Maria Machado de. 1963. *The Psychiatrist and Other Stories.* Trans. Helen Caldwell and William L. Grossman. Berkeley: University of California Press

Assis, Joaquim Maria Machado de. 1972.*Counselor Ayres' Memorial.* Trans. Helen Caldwell. Berkeley: University of California Press.

Assis, Joaquim Maria Machado de. 2008. *A Chapter of Hats.* Trans. John Gledson. London: Bloomsbury.

Assis, Joaquim Maria Machado de. 2015. *Memórias Póstumas de Brás Cubas.* São Paulo: Editora FTD S.A.

Barreto, Teresa Cristófani. 2005. *A libélula, a pitonisa: Revolução, homossexualismo e literatura em Virgilio Piñera.* São Paulo: Iluminuras/FAPESP.

Bosi, Alfredo. 1982. A máscara e a fenda. In *Machado de Assis: antologia e estudos*, ed. Alfredo Bosi et al., 437–457. São Paulo: Ática.

Bosi, Alfredo. 1999. *O enigma do olhar.* São Paulo: Editora Ática.

Candido, Antonio. 1995. Esquema Machado de Assis. In *Vários Escritos*, 17–39. São Paulo: Duas Cidades.

Cassin, Barbara (ed.). 2014. *Dictionary of untranslatables: A philosophical lexicon.* Princeton: Princeton University Press.

Dixon, Paul. 1992. A lei do escravo. In *Os contos de Machado de Assis: Mais do que sonha a filosofia*, 58–86. Brasil: Movimento.

Fonseca, Rubem. 1995. *Buraco na parede.* São Paulo: Companhia das Letras.

Fonseca, Rubem. 2008. *The Taker and Other Stories.* Trans. Clifford Landers. London: Open Letter.

Greimas, A.J. 1989. De la cólera: Estudio de semántica léxica. In *Del sentido II: Ensayos Semióticos.* Madrid: Gredos.

Jackson, K. David (ed.). 2006. *Oxford anthology of the Brazilian short story.* New York: Oxford University Press.

Meyer, Augusto. 1958. *Machado de Assis, 1935–1958.* Rio de Janeiro: Livraria São José.

Philippov, Renata. 2011. Edgar Allan Poe and Machado de Assis: How did Machado Read Poe? *The Comparatist* 35: 221–226.

Pietroforte, Antonio Vicente Seraphim, and Glauso Mattoso. 2008. *Antologia m(ai)s sado masoquista da literatura brasileira.* São Paulo: Dix.

Piglia, Ricardo. 2014. *Formas breves.* Buenos Aires: Debolsillo.

Rosso, Mauro. 2008. *Contos de Machado de Assis: Relicários e raisonnés.* Rio de Janeiro: Editora PUC-Rio/Edições Loyola.

Santiago, Silviano. 2008. Solidariedade do aborrecimento humano. In *Machado de Assis: Cinco contos comentados*, ed. Marta de Senna, 171–205. Rio de Janeiro: Edições Casa de Rui Barbosa.

Soares, Luiz Carlos. 2007. *O "povo de cam" na capital do Brasil: A escravidão urbana no Rio de Janeiro do Século XIX.* Rio de Janeiro: FAPERJ/7 Letras.

Sontag, Susan. 2013. *Styles of Radical Will.* New York: Picador.

"William Faulkner: The Art of Fiction No. 12." N.d. Interview with Jean Stein in 1956. *Paris Review.* http://www.theparisreview.org/interviews/4954/the-art-of-fiction-no-12-william-faulkner

CHAPTER 16

Framing Violence: Narrator and Reader in "Pai contra mãe"

Giulia Ricco

Although "Pai contra mãe" (Father versus Mother) was published in 1906, in the short-story collection *Relíquias da casa velha* (Relics of the Old House), only 18 years after the formal abolition of slavery in 1888, Machado de Assis purposefully decided to write about slavery as if it were in the distant past, a forgotten tale. The tale narrates a duel to the death between two outcasts, Cândido, a slave catcher (*capitão do mato*), and Arminda, a runaway slave. While Cândido needs to catch Arminda in order to provide for his newborn son, she ran away, precisely to save her own unborn child. Both are products of a society plagued by the classism and racism that still haunt present-day Brazilian society. Machado depicts the violence of slavery—especially its systemic violence structuring social relations as a whole—in a game of "show and not tell": never gruesome or excessive, but, in a way, exceptional in the sense that it is often hidden in what he chooses to leave out of the narration. "Pai contra mãe," one of the few stories in Machado's repertoire that has slavery as its central focus, offers a rich case study for analyzing how this technique of writing violence works and for reflecting on how the reader collaborates with the narrator.

I start this chapter with a close reading of the opening preamble, where Machado offers readers an entrée into the frame of the story. From there,

G. Ricco (✉)
Duke University, Durham, North Carolina, USA

© The Editor(s) (if applicable) and The Author(s) 2016
L. Aidoo, D.F. Silva (eds.), *Emerging Dialogues on Machado de Assis*, DOI 10.1057/978-1-137-54174-1_16

Machado weaves a frame for Cândido and Arminda's story, a frame that the readers will eventually need to close. He offers readers an entrée into the frame of the story and he sustains the story's frame through irony and careful wording throughout the plot. He leaves the conclusion to the reader, without whom the representation, or the framing, of violence cannot be completed. There is a three-dimensionality to Machado's short stories that can be paralleled to that of photography, not only because of the common characteristics that these two media share, but also because of the complicit relationship between author, frame, and audience. As a matter of fact, Machado's contemporaneity lies precisely in the dialogues that his short stories spark between the narrator and the modern reader when representing a violence that still resides and shapes Brazilian society.

Before starting the real narration, Machado opens the story with a pre-amble (*vestíbulo*; Baptista 2005, 284), defining the frame that situates the plot and its finality. In other words, through this *vestíbulo*, Machado not only situates the main plot, but also the finality of the plot, already framing the short story in a specific way. The narrator chooses a precise moment, among infinite possible ones, as Calvino (1991, 225) reminds us, to begin the story. The frame of the story, its delimitation, must be present, because the story is nothing more than a snapshot: without a frame, we are not able to perceive the singularity/exceptionality of that moment nor completely extrapolate it from all other moments. The frame presents to our eyes a specific way of representing that moment and guides us toward understanding it. The frame is visible in the words the narrator chooses, in the ways he interrupts the narrative flow, and what he chooses to tell or not. In the opening of "Pai contra mãe," Machado offers an elaborate description of the instruments used for torturing slaves, followed by an ambiguous comparison between the institution of slavery embodied in an iron mask that slaves were forced to wear as a form of punishment and the current social order: "The mask was grotesque, but order in the human and social realm is not always achieved without grotesquery—cruelty even, sometimes" (Assis 2008, 255).[1] Here, Machado hides his critique of slavery in an obscure irony. He denounces slavery as an institution, but does not offer a clear position regarding the mask. The mask and its potential meaning are left in the reader's hands.

Abruptly steering the conversation away from the mask, as the adversative conjunction indicates, "but let's not think about masks" (Assis 2008, 255), the narrator goes on to discuss the slave catcher, a profession commonly filled by former slaves and poor whites. This abrupt move in the narration can be seen as emblematic of post-emancipation Brazil's erasure of the memory of slavery: the mask still has relevance in the present and its violence is still residual. Telling the story as if it were a distant past, akin to a dream that we would rather forget, now makes more sense as the narration does nothing more than reflect the attitudes of the time regarding slavery. Moreover, the exhortative "let's not think about the mask" implies that the narrator is aware of the reader, hinting at the presence of a "we," highlighting, from the beginning, the narrator's authority by forcing us to be a part of the story, whether we like it or not. But we are also important to the narrator, sharing his memory of this bad dream.

The narrator explains that slaves often ran away because "not all of them liked to be slaves" (Assis 2008, 256)—an ironic affirmation that cannot but make the contemporary reader smirk as it sounds like the explanation you would give to a curious child asking questions whose answers the child cannot comprehend. And in a sense, Machado's audience was so oblivious and indifferent to the violence of slavery to the point of actually believing that being a slave was a matter of taste, almost of choice, further fostering the myth of Brazil's harmonious slavery. Machado's sarcasm in the previous affirmation veils a profound anger and indignation toward an audience who did not care to remember slavery or to think about it. It seems that Machado was already writing for a future audience, aware of the cultural and moral limitations of his contemporaries. There is no explicit description of what those instruments of torture might do to a body. As Antonio Candido (1970) writes, Machado's "technique essentially consists of suggesting the most terrible things in the most candid way" (23).[2] This technique is also visible when Machado closes the preamble in which he directly comments on the profession of the slave catcher: "Maybe it wasn't a noble one, but since it was the forcible instrument whereby law and property were safeguarded, it had that other implicit kind of nobility we owe to the law and its demands" (Assis 2008, 257). Thought of in these terms, it seems that such violence could, to some degree, be justifiable, presenting an instrumental characteristic, intrinsic to rational violence: "Violence is by nature instrumental; like all means it always stands in need of guidance and justification through the end it pursues" (Arendt 1970, 51). After all, slaves were nothing more than property; thus, the slave catcher was simply bringing back this property to its rightful owner, as part of a larger structure of paternalistic power that governed, and still governs, Brazilian society.

Once the preamble is over, we meet the protagonist of the story, Cândido Neves, and his family. Cândido, his wife Clara, and her aunt

Monica are brilliant examples of social stereotypes: he is an indolent loiterer, his wife is a girl without ambitions, and the aunt is an old-school realist and a pragmatist. In nineteenth-century fashion, the names of the characters function as an allegory of the events that will soon unfold; but Cândido Neves (Portuguese "pure snow") is not pure; he is extremely selfish and a parody of Voltaire's Candide and his optimism. Cândido, who still has not found a stable job, is fascinated by the idea of earning a living by capturing runaway slaves: he does not need to learn much and it offers a good reward for easy and quick work. He never stops to reflect whether this job is any way constructive or noble. It is a profession devoid of humanity and thought. Cândido's lack of any trace of interest in the moral implications of his job echoes the philosophy of humanitism (*humanitismo*) theorized by Machado and conceptualized in the figure of the philosopher Quincas Borba. Using this theory, which ridicules the positivistic theories of the late nineteenth century, and in particular, Darwin's evolutionist scheme of the survival of the fittest, Machado explains how the world and society develop through a "general and abrasive devouring that tends to transform the man into the instrument of man" (Candido 1970, 115). In Machado's view, all social relations are nothing more than a struggle for power, for achieving a status quo in which money seems to resolve any tension. According to critic and translator John Gledson (1984), humanitism "leads us to the central philosophical question on which…Machado does meditate in his fiction: the problem of evil" (168), a problem that never appears clear and visible, but is represented in what the narrator does not reveal to the reader. The short story is then the perfect medium for highlighting the importance of what is left out—an exclusion that nonetheless draws attention to its very content. In a way, the short story is a narrative form that is intrinsically violent: in a short amount of time, it must elicit the participation of readers, who are urged to understand and to reflect, who, somehow, also suffer violence in their reading experience. It is as if violence is transversal, spreading from the content to the form of the writing itself. Indeed, the violence that Machado depicts, that evil that ultimately governs human actions, becomes exceptional precisely because it is evident but hidden in that ambiguous irony and in what is purposefully left out of the narration. Moreover, Machado does not offer an alternative to the evil of society. For example, there seems to be no other job that Cândido can take on to support his family.

Things are going well for Cândido's family until slave catching becomes popular, mostly among those who live in poverty. With the increased competition among slave catchers, the number of runaway slaves to be caught is drastically reduced and Cândido's livelihood is in peril. The family is obliged to leave their house because they cannot afford the rent anymore. Meanwhile, Clara and Cândido have a child. The aunt, implacable, insists repeatedly that they must abandon the child. Finally, Clara and Cândido give in to her and decide to abandon the baby—once again, confirming Machado's overall pessimistic view of society. But Cândido is reluctant to leave his son and decides to search among the advertisements for runaway slaves to find the one that offers the highest reward. He hunts intently, but unsuccessfully, for the slave Arminda. Finally, on the night that Cândido brings his child to the orphanage, he sees the slave in the street, and the narrator slowly creeps into the text in the first person: "I won't depict Cândido Neves's commotion here, because I can't convey it with enough intensity. One adjective is enough; let's say it was enormous" (Assis 2008, 267). Machado, in choosing not to describe the scene, wants the reader to imagine this commotion. His aim is to make the reader uncomfortable with what is going on. This sudden change to the first person calls for the reader's attention not only to the narration itself, as we are at a crucial point and Machado wants us to be completely present to the actions following this interruption, but also to the fact that he is still narrating the story. Ultimately, inasmuch as we are free to interpret it, the narrator chooses what to tell us and points us toward a definite idea, his idea.

The short story form, so powerful and exceptional in its formal exiguity, could also be thought of as sovereign since the narrator exercises a power of inclusion and exclusion (Finazzi-Agró and Vecchi 2007, 81–82). The narrator cannot exercise authority if there is no reader to validate the story, the narrator's fragment of reality, and attempt to interpret it. This works just like Arendt's (1970, 56) concept of power, which needs to be recognized collectively and cannot be forcefully instituted. Machado was very much aware of the importance of the act of reading—that is, the effect of his work on his readers. This is evident in the presence of the foyer, in the need for constructing a clear frame for contextualizing the violence, through which he introduces readers to the story. Moreover, sudden interruptions in the narration remind us that he is aware of not telling the story in a vacuum, but to someone. Dixon (2005) notices that the importance that Machado gives to the reader is parallel to the cruciality of social relations in the formation of Machado's characters, who often do not have individual traits per se, but develop out of interaction with and opposition to others: "Just as the character only comes alive when interacting with another character, Machado's theory of character development does not restrict itself to the character solely relating to the author. Machado's characters are fully developed when the author engages the reader" (Dixon 2005, 206). Cândido and Arminda are both outcasts, both victims to different degrees of a classist and racist power structure, troubling the reader's decision about the right way out of their dilemma: is there any solution that will bring no harm to either of them?

When Cândido sees Arminda in the street, he captures her immediately. Meanwhile, he leaves his child at the pharmacy where he stopped to inquire about the fugitive slave. It is interesting that this second time at the pharmacy, Cândido seems to find a cure to his problem, a cure brought about only by chance as he recognizes Arminda almost by accident. Accidents, fragments of bigger events, seem to be the backbone of Machado's fiction, what Candido (1970) calls "fictional situations" (32). Along those lines stands Arminda's revelation to Cândido: she is pregnant and begs him to let her go in the name of his love for his own child. What the slave does not understand is that mostly because of that love, Cândido cannot let her go: in order to avoid abandoning his child, he needs the reward money for Arminda's capture. This reasoning conforms to the theory of humanitism: in order to safeguard his own interests, Cândido does not think twice about his actions, not even when Arminda confesses to him that she is pregnant. Once again, this callousness confirms that slaves were not considered humans but inanimate things, and thus, Cândido cannot make any comparison between himself and Arminda. Machado describes the scene around them: "Passers-by and people in shop doorways understood what was going on and naturally didn't get involved" (Assis 2008, 268). The adverb *naturally* points to a wider problem of social misconduct, and more importantly, to the invisibility of slaves in Brazilian society: it is remarkable that in a story that is supposedly about slavery, we encounter a slave only at the end. We first become familiar with the instruments of oppression and the oppressor, although, in this case, the oppressor is also the product of a larger system based on exploitation and violence. This invisibility is, however, contradictory: the slave is invisible in the bourgeois public sphere but, at the same time, is central to the creation of that space of privilege. The violence in Machado's short stories also lies in those moments of contemplation, where people do not act when faced with an injustice.[3] No hero emerges from the crowd to shield Arminda from such violence and to eventually guide Cândido on a righteous path. Machado is not only pointing his finger at the perpetrator of the violence—in this case, Cândido—but at that same society and institution that nurture and necessitate these forms of violence. It is as if the narrator wants the reader to make that intervention, to be the hero who shields Arminda from Cândido's blows.

Once Cândido and Arminda arrive at the master's house, the slave is pushed back and forth, falls down, and tragically loses her unborn baby: "On the floor, where she was lying, carried away by fear and pain, and after a short struggle, the slave had a miscarriage" (Assis 2008, 269). In these few lines, although the scene is not described in excessive terms or with excess violence inflicted on the woman, the violence reaches its climax. This violence acts on the slave on two levels, as a woman and as a mother: the physical violence of the miscarriage caused by the beating and the psychological violence of not being able to protect her baby, the guilt for not having been able to save her child. In this scene, the three properties of violence described by Arendt—unpredictability, arbitrariness, and instrumentality—are all present. Cândido, who observes the scene, stays at a distance; he does not react to the violence but only watches, reinforcing again the contemplative aspect of Machado's violence. Ultimately, the inflictor of the violence becomes the spectator, and he walks away, just like the passers-by in the scene before, turning his back to the scene, "with no wish to know what the consequences of the disaster were" (Assis 2008, 269). Machado leaves us with no hope for the possibility of an alternative solution, as the narrator himself does not give us enough clues to help us fully comprehend what he thinks or believes, forcing us to form our own opinion about what has been narrated. Should we condone Cândido's actions because he acted to save his own child? Is sacrificing the life of a stranger to save the life of a loved one admissible in this world? Machado does not say, although his choice of the word *disaster* implies a recognition of that violence, and, again, a veiled anger on the narrator's part. It is through very specific and charged vocabulary choices that Machado highlights in his stories the wrongness of violence, playing with what language can offer and showing how irony can be a very powerful tool when representing violence.

In the final scene, language makes room for the irony of Cândido's "genuine tears" and the oblivious justification of the miscarriage: "Cândido Neves, kissing his son amid genuine tears, blessed the escape and was unconcerned about the miscarriage. 'Not all children make it,' said his beating heart" (Assis 2008, 270). In the original Portuguese, those tears are said to be *verdadeiras* (real), suggesting that Cândido might grasp the reality of what has just happened, crying not only because he was able to avoid abandoning his son, but also, for the consequences of his actions. However, after this glimpse of a possibility of acknowledgment, Cândido finds a justification for the disaster—one that absolves him of any responsibility, and that it is indisputable: not all children are destined to be born. This statement allows him to turn his back on Arminda and carry on with his life without thinking further about the implications of what he has done. Suddenly, his violence seems legitimate and justifiable, just as it is for the profession of slave catcher the moment that we accept the idea that slaves are property that needs to be returned. When reading this conclusion, we can see that "what fascinated [Machado] more and more was his observation that people can live with such a doctrine of despair [*humanitismo*] without going mad or considering suicide" (Gledson 1984, 170). Furthermore, the statement closes the short story as if this were the lesson to be learned through its reading, as in a sort of fable intended to supply a moral to readers: when you do something wrong, find an indisputable fact that can justify your actions; make your own, individual right. Irony then, one of Machado's most characteristic stylistic traits, is present also in the final statement. Once again, he counts on readers' understanding of his irony, leaving to them the final framing of the violence laid out in the story. If Machado has supplied a foyer to the frame of the story, it is readers who should close that frame.

Serrano (2008) and Schwarz (2001) discuss Machado's fiction as three-dimensional, precisely because of the important part played by the readers. While Serrano talks about this presence as "torsion," an operation of "coding and decoding, similar to the topologic operations of twisting and cutting…and to the work of writing and reading" (108), Schwarz sees it as a game of alternation: "Machado's narrative formula consists of a certain systemic alternation of perspectives in which several points of view are raised as to how Brazilian society actually functions" (11). Another possible way of interpreting the reader's role is as that of a spectator, thinking about the short story as if it were a snapshot. Photography and the short story have much in common, including brevity, conciseness, and singularity. Both capture one image, one episode among infinite possible ones. In both, there is always active and subjective participation by both the creator of the image or event and the audience that attempts to extract meaning from the representation. In photography, there is a silent agreement between photographer and spectator similar to the one between writer and readers: they do not discuss the creator's authority, but instead, trust the creator's portrayed reality.

The concepts of *studium* and *punctum* developed by Roland Barthes in his text *Camera Lucida* (1980) can help to understand how Machado's readers get involved in defining the frame of the story. Barthes wants to understand what it is that, in certain photographs, attracts him so much. The *studium* is the rational aspect of the photograph; it reveals the cultural meaning of photography: its historical context, its geographical location, hence, the material content. The *punctum* is, instead, the irrational aspect of the photograph, a particular that hits the spectator subjectively. The name *punctum* precisely refers to the idea of a wound that points, or that stings. It is, in a way, the exceptional aspect of the photograph. In Machado's writing, there is a persistent duality, an ambiguous situation where the narrator condemns, but simultaneously joins the crowd in mere observation. An example of this duplicity is the passiveness of society that indifferently watches the brutal scene of the slave's capture in "Pai contra mãe." The *punctum* lies exactly in Machado's ambiguity of not engaging in an open, less veiled, critique of society, in the absence of a lucid discussion regarding the violence intrinsic to a slave-based society. What stings is the perplexity in which we find ourselves after reading a story like "Pai contra mãe," whose ending is open to many interpretations, depending on the reader's singular perspective and experiences. The *punctum* that we see in Machado addresses an extra-representative perception of violence, in the attempt to give concrete meaning, or framing, to the violence of the short story.

In conclusion, the three-dimensionality of Machado's narrative should have a repercussion in the reader's world. The exceptionality of Machado's text is that violence hides in what it is left unsaid, what cannot fit in the frame laid down by the narrator, but can only be added by the reader. Susan Sontag (2003) writes that a representation of violence must provoke a whatever, but necessary, reaction in spectators (or readers). She explains that the representation of violence, photographic or literary, is oriented toward a specific typology of public and, including herself among the spectators, asks, "Who are the 'we' at whom such shock pictures are aimed?" (7). In Machado's case, the "we" can be many different audiences, from the fin de siècle society who erased the memory of slavery and is oblivious to its legacy to the present-day reader discussed here. Sontag's use of the verb *to regard* "implies both a physical activity (to look at, to observe) and an intellectual and emotional evaluation (to take notice, to show consideration, to look upon with some feeling)" (Parra 2003, 5). Sontag focuses on the importance of making the audience stop and reflect when engaging with a representation of violence of any sort, without horrifying or scaring them away, which is what Machado accomplishes through his irony. Regarding Machado's story, the narrator observes and the reader must take notice. After reading a short story like "Pai contra mãe," readers feel lost, confused, because they are not able to find a clear and definite answer or opinion. They have been, according to Barthes, morally *stung*. By writing violence, the author implicitly performs a violent act: readers cannot and should not remain passive; they should somehow be wounded in order to gain the experience required to complete the framing of the violence, to give meaning to the short story and mold it to function in the present.

NOTES

1. All quotations from "Father Against Mother" are taken from the 2008 Bloomsbury edition of *A Chapter of Hats: Selected Stories,* translated and edited by John Gledson.
2. All translations from non-English sources are my own.
3. Jaime Ginzburg, in his anthology *Crítica em tempo de violência* (2012), analyzes the ways in which violence is represented through contemplative action in Machado's fiction, discussing the short story "A causa secreta."

REFERENCES

Arendt, Hannah. 1970. *On violence.* New York: Harcourt.

Assis, Machado de. 2008. Father against mother. In *A chapter of hats: Selected stories,* trans. and ed. John Gledson, 255–270. London: Bloomsbury.

Baptista, Abel Barros. 2005. A emenda de Séneca: Machado de e a forma do conto. *Teresa: Revista de literatura brasileira* 6(7): 207–231.

Barthes, Roland. 1980. *Camera Lucida.* Trans. Richard Howard. New York: Hill and Wang.

Calvino, Italo. 1991. "Cominciare e finire." In *Saggi,* ed. Mario Barenghi, 743–754. Milano: Arnoldo Mondadori Editore.

Candido, Antônio. 1970. Esquema de Machado de Assis. In *Vários Escritos,* 13–32. São Paulo: Livraria Duas Cidades.

Dixon, Paul. 2005. Modelos em movimento: Os contos de Machado de Assis. *Teresa: Revista de literatura brasileira* 6(7): 185–206.

Finazzi-Agrò, Ettore, and Roberto Vecchi. 2007. Pior do que ser assassino.... *Estudos de literatura brasileira contemporânea* 29: 67–86.

Ginzburg, Jaime. 2012. A violência na literatura brasileira: Notas sobre Machado de Assis, Graciliano Ramos e Guimarães Rosa. In *Crítica em tempos de Violência,* 239–254. São Paulo: Edusp.

Gledson, John. 1984. *The deceptive realism of Machado de Assis*. Trowbridge: Redwood Burnt.

Parra, Mauricio. 2003. Regarding violence. *Discourse* 25(3): 3–8.

Schwarz, Roberto. 2001. *Um mestre na periferia do capitalismo*. São Paulo: Livraria Duas Cidades/Editora 34.

Serrano, Lucia Pereira. 2008. *O conto Machadiano: Uma experiência de vertigem*. Rio de Janeiro: Companhia de Freud.

Sontag, Susan. 2003. *Regarding the pain of others*. New York: Picador.

INDEX

Note: Locators followed by 'n' refer to notes.